OFFICE SHOCK

OFFICE SHOCK

SHOCK

CREATING BETTER FUTURES
FOR WORKING AND LIVING

BOB JOHANSEN
JOSEPH PRESS
CHRISTINE BULLEN

INSTITUTE FOR THE FUTURE

BK

Berrett–Koehler Publishers, Inc.

Berrett-Koehler Publishers, Inc.
1333 Broadway, Suite 1000
Oakland, CA 94612-1921
Tel: (510) 817-2277 / Fax: (510) 817-2278
www.bkconnection.com

ORDERING INFORMATION

QUANTITY SALES. Special discounts are available on quantity purchases by corporations, associations, and others. For details, contact the "Special Sales Department" at the Berrett-Koehler address above.

INDIVIDUAL SALES. Berrett-Koehler publications are available through most bookstores. They can also be ordered directly from Berrett-Koehler: Tel: (800) 929-2929; Fax: (802) 864-7626; www.bkconnection.com.

ORDERS FOR COLLEGE TEXTBOOK / COURSE ADOPTION USE. Please contact Berrett-Koehler: Tel: (800) 929-2929; Fax: (802) 864-7626.

Distributed to the U.S. trade and internationally by Penguin Random House Publisher Services.

Berrett-Koehler and the BK logo are registered trademarks of Berrett-Koehler Publishers, Inc.

PRINTED IN CANADA

Berrett-Koehler books are printed on long-lasting acid-free paper. When it is available, we choose paper that has been manufactured by environmentally responsible processes. These may include using trees grown in sustainable forests, incorporating recycled paper, minimizing chlorine in bleaching, or recycling the energy produced at the paper mill.

Library of Congress Cataloging-in-Publication Data
    Names: Johansen, Robert, author. | Press, Joseph, author. | Bullen, Christine V., author.
    Title: Office shock : creating better futures for working and living / Bob Johansen, Joseph Press, Christine Bullen.
    Description: First edition. | Oakland, CA : Berrett-Koehler Publishers, [2023] | Includes bibliographical references and index.
    Identifiers: LCCN 2022025710 (print) | LCCN 2022025711 (ebook) | ISBN 9781523003679 (paperback) | ISBN 9781523003686 (pdf) | ISBN 9781523003693 (epub) | ISBN 9781523003709 (audio)
    Subjects: LCSH: Office management—Social aspects. | COVID-19 Pandemic, 2020—Social aspects. | COVID-19 Pandemic, 2020—Psychological aspects. | Behavior modification.
    Classification: LCC HF5547.5 J637 2023 (print) | LCC HF5547.5 (ebook) | DDC 651.02/46162414—dc23/eng/20220803
    LC record available at https://lccn.loc.gov/2022025710
    LC ebook record available at https://lccn.loc.gov/2022025711

USM Special Edition ISBN: 9781523004973

FIRST EDITION

30 29 28 27 26 25 24 23 22 || 10 9 8 7 6 5 4 3 2 1

Book production: BookMatters; Cover design: Archie Ferguson; Cover illustration: Andy Gilmore

To you, our readers . . .

May this book
help you create
better futures
for working and living.

CONTENTS

Preface   ix

Introduction: The Great Opportunity   I

PART I   WHAT FUTURE?   15
           Better Futures for Working and Living

     1   Futureback Thinking: About Office Shock   17

     2   Looking Back to Look Forward: The Technology Didn't
           Happen Overnight   30

     3   Impossible Futures: Imagining Better Offices and Officing   49

           Office Shock Quick Start Guide appears after page 60.

PART II WHAT NEXT?   61
           Spectrums of Choice for Better Working and Living

     4   In Good Company: The Spectrum of Purpose   65

     5   Pursuing Prosperity: The Spectrum of Outcomes   79

     6   Beyond Sustainability: The Spectrum of Climate Impacts   93

7 Cultivating Community: The Spectrum of Belonging   107

8 Everyone Amplified: The Spectrum of Augmentation   121

9 Better Than Being There: The Spectrum of Place and Time 135

10 Coordinating with Clarity: The Spectrum of Agility   149

PART III WHAT NOW?   161
          Making Smart Choices for Individuals, Organizations,
          and Communities

11 Thinking Futureback about Office Shock: Introducing Our
    Quick Start Guide   163

12 Personal Choices: How You Can Navigate Office Shock   173

13 Organizational Choices: How Your Organization Can
    Navigate Office Shock   180

14 Community Choices: How Your Community Can Navigate
    Office Shock   188

    Conclusion: What We Can Do Now to Create Better Futures 197

    Navigational Stars   207
    Discussion Guide   210
    Notes   221
    Bibliography   242
    Acknowledgments   250
    Index   256
    About the Research   270
    About the Authors   273
    About the Artists and Artwork   277
    About Institute for the Future   281

PREFACE

Office shock is abrupt, unsettling change in *where*, *when*, *how*, and even *why* we work. Office shock and aftershocks will continue with no end in sight. *Why* we work will be at the epicenter of office shock.

Office shock is happening in a time of global turmoil. The world of work is at an inflection point that was triggered by the COVID-19 pandemic, but it will be about much more. Urgent futures like racial injustices, the staggering rich-poor gap, epic climate emergencies, and severely degraded trust in institutions are gnawing away at everyone in varied ways. Such unsettling change can create opportunities though—despite all the threats, challenges, and fears around us. This book will help you make smart choices about the future of your work.

This is no time to lock yourself into any fixed strategy for what was naively called "Return to the Office" or "Hybrid Offices." To make a better future, you must first imagine a better future and then prototype your way to that future. Office futures that used to be impossible are now possible because of office shock.

During the COVID-19 crisis, what was called The Great Resignation began— but most of those people didn't stop working, they just switched to better opportunities. The World Economic Forum called it The Great Reshuffle and

The Great Reset.[1] We call it The Great Opportunity. This is a positive book for negative times.

We aim to help people who want to take the lead on creating better futures for work, including:

- Leaders: Use this book to encourage more human, humane, productive, and sustainable office practices.

- Individuals: Use this book to clarify where and how you want to work—and how you want your work to support how you live.

- Organizations: Shareholders, board members, and stakeholders can use this book to identify the most important functions for offices—given your own purpose, culture, work processes, goals, and priorities.

- Communities: Use this book to guide elected officials, policy makers, and citizen groups to design more equitable and sustainable workplaces.

- Society: Use this book to develop collective clarity about how office work can and should contribute to better futures.

"Office" is both a place and a process, offices and officing. Many traditional offices that were shuttered during the COVID-19 crisis had inherent problems even before the crisis. It took a global pandemic to shake open executive minds to the possibility of better ways of doing office work. Traditional offices were often unfair, uncomfortable, uncreative, and unproductive.

Now fortunately, the traditional office is dead.

COVID-19 forced millions of people to work and live in ways they had never attempted before. Fixed became fluid. Unexamined assumptions about offices and office work opened into probing questions that demanded careful thought. Office work during COVID-19 was freeing for many, but imprisoning for others. Our goal in this book is to empower people, organizations, and society to create better ways of working and living for more people.

This book was written by three humble futurists who see office shock as a great opportunity—as well as a threat. Bob is a sociologist now focused on top leadership for shape-shifting organizations. Joseph is a workplace architect by training and experienced transformation advisor, now focused on designing better futures. Christine is an information systems professor, now focused on critical success factors for climate positive organizations. All our experiences, with lots of outside input, were needed to write this book.

Office Shock will teach you how to move beyond a present-forward view to start thinking futureback from at least ten years ahead. Futureback thinking will help you develop clarity and improve your agility. We call it flexive intent: be very clear about direction but very flexible about execution. By thinking futureback—forecasting futures, provoking insights, and aligning actions—you can reimagine where, when, and how office work can and should be done.

At Institute for the Future, we are trained to spot signals of emerging futures that are just starting to appear but have not yet scaled. We have learned from over fifty years of forecasting that the best way to develop clarity is by looking futureback. Our mission is to reduce uncertainty, so you develop your own clarity—but resist the dangers of certainty.

As futurists, we create stories from the future that provoke insights and actions in the present. This book tells new stories about how to improve offices and officing in a climate of chaos. We will show you how to create future/next/now stories. We include in this book our Office Shock Mixing Board, a guide to making better choices for how you will office. Our choices will help us all hone in on a future that is aspirational yet achievable, neither utopian nor dystopian, with better ways of working and living.

The Great Opportunity

Why do we work in offices at all?

Office shock is abrupt, unsettling change in where, how, when, and even why we work. Office shock and echoing aftershocks will continue indefinitely in unpredictable patterns.

COVID-19 was one of many jaggedly ugly shocks such as chronic climate emergencies, systemic racism, and gender inequality. The mules of war are still with us, but future wars will be weirdly different. Cyber warfare and cyber terrorism will be possible in forms never imagined. Ugly still, but in different ways.

We are facing a rolling risk of further pandemics and further shocks. Office workers, corporations, and policy makers will be shocked, again and again, into making hard choices about where, when, and how we work. Many office workers will refuse to go back to offices the way they were. Unsettling change, however, includes great opportunities—despite all the threats, challenges, and fears around us. Our goal is to help you find your own clarity about offices while avoiding the dangers of certainty. Even with ugliness, there will be unprecedented opportunity.

Hybrid work and flexibility are now normalized, but the future of work is up for grabs. Office shock will continue for many years to come. And that can be an opportunity.

Offices, Officing, Officeverse

Work is about how we come together to make things happen. In the past, most knowledge work was organized in and around office buildings. Gathering in person in buildings was assumed necessary for orientation, trust building, early-stage creativity, and renewal.

Many leaders still assume that organizational culture must be created and sustained through in-person interaction in office buildings. But will those beliefs continue to hold true? Will there be alternatives?

Office shock has revealed hidden assumptions about what might be done without office buildings. There are no proven answers yet, but alternatives are budding everywhere.

The office is a place, but it is also a process.

- *Office* is a noun. Office places are mostly in buildings, but that's changing.
- *Officing* is a verb that describes work processes and social interaction to get work done.
- *Officeverse* is the future anytime/anyplace world of where you will work, when you will work, and how you will work.

Office Work without Offices

Office shock has already created work/life challenges that many people flipped into positives. The experience of working from home during the pandemic, however, was often deeply unfair. Many privileged people loved the flexibility and thrived, but for people with small workspaces at home or little kids and no childcare, the experience was often stressful and sometimes traumatizing. For many the new flexibility was liberating; for others it was awful. But the future of office work doesn't have to be that unfair.

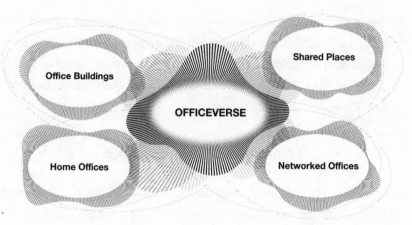

FIGURE 1: Officeverse Emerging. The ever-evolving mix of work, place, and time options will shape new models, with new choices for working and living.

During COVID-19 office shutdowns, many companies reported that they were more productive virtually than in their old office buildings—despite all the pandemic fear and confusion. Shockingly, everyday people with no special training did office work without offices.

In the face of unprecedented office shock, you can be future-ready. We call the range of options from which you will be able to choose for offices and officing the *officeverse*. As conceived in figure 1, the officeverse is an archipelago of anytime/anyplace mixes of media—including office buildings—that you will be able to choose among to determine where, when, and how you work.

The officeverse is still emerging, building on ubiquitous connectivity. The officeverse will defy any corporate control. The global pandemic office shutdowns demanded abrupt radical changes in behavior. Fortunately, fifty years of technology testing and limited-scale use was up to the task, so virtual working worked surprisingly well.

COVID-19 plus the internet meant impossible officing futures became possible with little forewarning.

As Satya Nadella, the CEO of Microsoft, said during the COVID-19 crisis: "As we are coming out of this pandemic and its various stages . . . not only are people talking about when, where, and how they work but also why they work."[1] Indeed, why we work is now at the epicenter of office shock.

Evolution in technology use that would have taken years happened almost overnight during COVID-19, but wild cards—we call them mules—were unleashed. Office shock has only just begun.

Mules Are Loose in the Office

It is difficult to even talk about the future of offices and officing without relying on language that doesn't capture what we are trying to imagine. As futurists, we often turn to fiction for inspiration in situations like this. Science fiction and fantasy help us to stretch how we think and explore the future through the power of stories. Fiction gives us new language and agency. Stories help us imagine and engage with futures we have trouble imagining.

In Isaac Asimov's enduring *Foundation* trilogy,[2] mathematician Hari Seldon invents a new academic discipline he calls psychohistory, an algorithmic science that accurately predicts the future. Then shockingly, a mutant creature named the Mule kicks through their algorithms and suddenly the predictable future becomes unpredictable.

The Mule was impossible—until it wasn't. Office shock will be filled with unpredictable wild cards. In this book, with a tip of the hat to Isaac Asimov, we call them mules.

COVID-19 was a mule, and it will not be the last pandemic mule. In the future, we will confront the rolling risk of pandemics and other global emergencies that arise at the intersection of human health, animal health, insect health, and land use. Public health officials use the eerie label *interpandemic* to describe the uncertain state of life going forward herky-jerky between pandemics. Think interpandemic, not end of pandemics.

COVID-19 plus the internet was the catalyst for office shock and the impossible futures for offices and officing that are now possible. But how can we imagine what's next? What futures can we imagine in this time of great fear and great opportunity?

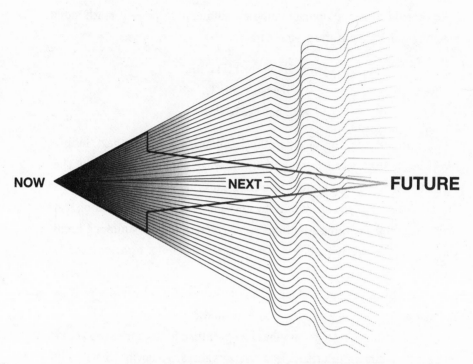

FIGURE 2: Futureback Thinking. Thinking backward from the future rather than from the present-forward.

Think Futureback

The present is so noisy, so painfully and violently noisy.

Many people are stuck in a cage called *now* while occasionally thinking about what's *next* and only rarely thinking about the *future*.

We need to release ourselves from thinking only present-forward. Being here now and mindful can be virtuous, but not if we are trapped in the now. Are you stuck in the present? Do you feel owned by the present? If so, you need futureback thinking to explore where the mules will be heading.

Looking long will help you find your clarity so you can be very clear about your direction but very flexible about how you will get there. You can be clear; you cannot be certain.

In times like these, thinking futureback—future, next, now—is much more revealing than thinking present-forward.

Think about the FUTURE,
then what's NEXT,
and then the NOW.

Most people today, however, are stuck in linear time: Now, next, future. Most people are locked unconsciously in what neuroscientists call "The Eternal Now." Thinking present-forward means that you can see only incremental change, but you are blinded by unexamined categorical thinking that makes the unprecedented seem impossible. Present-forward thinking keeps you in cautious lockstep and hides any future you cannot bring yourself to imagine.

We need to move from thinking present-forward to thinking future-back. As summarized in figure 2, we require a shift in mindset.

Surprisingly, looking ten years ahead is easier than just a year or two ahead. For example, thinking futureback from ten years ahead, it is obvious that sensors will be everywhere, they will be very cheap, many of them will be connected, and some of them will be in our bodies—and the bodies of our pets. Already, many people wear body sensors like smart watches that track biometrics. Ten years from now, most people who want one and can afford it will be wearing a body sensor, and many people will have embedded body sensors. Looking futureback, it is obvious that sensors will be everywhere in the office and the officeverse. The direction of change regarding sensors is clear when you think futureback, even though the implications are not.

If we learn to think futureback, we can see the mules before they arrive in a cloud of dust.

Many More Mules Are Coming

Like the Mule in *Foundation*, the internet, the connective tissue for offices and distributed work around the world, is a mule. The extension of the internet called the *metaverse* will be yet another species of mule. Coined originally as a science-fiction concept in 1992, the metaverse has become an umbrella term for the next generation of the internet.[3] It will be a nested network of networks that won't be owned or controlled by anyone—though many will try.[4] In this book, we use the term *officeverse* to describe the metaverse for offices. A continuing herd of mules will shape the officeverse, including virtual reality, deepfakes, cryptocurrencies, blockchain, ultra-wideband media, machine intelligence, Web3, and quantum computing. The early internet was a mule disguised as computer-to-computer data exchange, the metaverse is a mule disguised as an immersive social media platform, while the officeverse will be a mule disguised as networked offices.

Like the Mule in *Foundation*, future office shocks will be unpredictable and unprecedented. The next shocks could be good or evil—or good *and* evil. Office shocks will open new opportunities and new choices for individuals, organizations, and for policy makers. Our choices will tip the balance for good or evil. People and organizations will be either more or less future-ready. This book will help you prepare to benefit from the opportunities and protect yourself from the threats. The mules will stampede.

Impossible Futures Are Now Possible

People with desk jobs scrambled in the wake of office evacuations. They were disoriented and confused—but shockingly productive. While COVID-19 was a global public health tragedy, it opened an unprecedented opportunity to challenge our assumptions and expectations about office work. It became possible to create hitherto impossible futures for living and working.

What used to be perceived as impossible is now—suddenly because of office shock—possible. Imagining the office of the future will require us to prepare for and embrace surprise. Office shock invites us to envision a world where impossible futures are possible, where you can harness the mules.

We wrote this book to help individuals, organizations, and communities to create stories that inspire us all to create better futures for working and living. Imagine future offices...

- where purpose-driven people work for purpose-driven organizations.

- that contribute to prosperity for stakeholders as well as shareholders.

- with climate positive activities that regenerate the planet.

- that thrive on diversity and equity by providing an authentic sense of belonging for purposely different people.

- where people and computers work together as "superminds" to do things that have never been done before.[5]

- that operate anywhere, are available anytime, with people empowered to decide what options are best to achieve which objectives.

- designed for agility and resilience, where hierarchies shift based on who is in the best position to make which decisions at what times.

The world of work will never be the same again. The mules are here, and they aren't leaving. Office shock will rush in with too much change in too short a time, but it is packed with positive potential. We cannot go back to the office the way it was, but we can make better choices to improve working and living.

The Office Shock Mixing Board

Offices do not need to remain places stuck in the past. Offices can be exciting places with purpose, enabled by new ways of working and empowered by new technologies to achieve real impact. Office shock opens new opportunities to reimagine how, when, and where "office work" can and should be done in the future.

Mules are tearing up the traditional office, so we've created Seven Spectrums of Choice that will help you break out and start thinking futureback about offices and officing.

Office shock is not just about when to go back to the office. It's about opening possibilities for human connection in more meaningful ways. Office shock and its aftershocks will demand that people transform their organizations and themselves.

To prepare for the opportunities of office shock, every individual office worker, organization, and policy maker should ask, in this order:

1. What is the **purpose** of your office and officing? First, consider the personal benefits to the people who work in offices—especially young people. Then ask about collective purpose for organizations and communities. This is not an either/or choice; it is a spectrum between the polarities of individual and collective. Purpose should be your first spectrum of choice. Why do you want an office at all?

2. What are the desired **outcomes** you aim to achieve with your office and by your office activities? What results is your office seeking? What consequences are you seeking for your shareholders and stakeholders? While purpose is about intentions, outcomes are about results—and target results will depend on you and your organization's value systems.

3. What will be the **climate impact** of your office buildings and the ways you are working? We believe that the most important outcome over the next ten years will be the climate impact. To date, office buildings have been more harmful to the environment than helpful. Net-zero impacts, where your office and its activities do not contribute to greenhouse gas emissions in the environment, should be the minimum. We're already at a point now where offices must be climate positive and regenerative.

4. **With whom** do you want to office? This is the spectrum of belonging. In most traditional offices, people look alike, dress alike, and talk alike. Familiarity breeds comfort, cooperation, and understanding. Thinking futureback, however, diversity will be everywhere so offices will need to learn how to rethink inclusion and belonging. In the future, diversity will be a given and purposely different will be a goal.

5. How will you amplify the **intelligence** of your office? This is the spectrum of augmentation. Thinking futureback, we will all be cyborgs—part human

part computer. Which activities do we want to keep for ourselves and which do we want to augment?

6. **Where** and **when** will you office? The question many companies are asking is when to return to the office, but that is not the first question you should ask, it is number six out of the Seven Spectrums of Choice. It is an important question, but it should not be the starting point.

7. How will you design an **agile resilient** office? Finally, how do you put it all together and act with resilience to make smart choices in an increasingly complicated future?

These questions demonstrate the need for clarity and nimbleness in these times of great uncertainty. You must harmonize your choices within each and then across the roles you play. These are not either/or choices, they are both/and.

To assist you, we have framed these spectrums of choice into a metaphorical mixing board.[6] As illustrated in figure 3 and included in the Quick Start Guide just before the beginning of part II of this book, the mixing board has sliding scales representing the range of options office shock has revealed. Also in part II of this book, we have a full chapter on each spectrum of choice to explore the range of options between each polarity.

The choices along this journey are neither binary nor easy. For example, a single individual can get a thrill out of creating a new product. The dopamine rush motivating that person's brain to innovate is real and exciting. If that same innovator also works for a large corporation where their product idea is linked to the corporate purpose, it is possible to be an *intrapreneur* who is rewarded personally and collectively. If that same innovation improves the daily lives of children in the outside world, then there is a larger purpose being served beyond the organization with positive outcomes. If the innovation is a success on all fronts, it can benefit users as well as corporate shareholders and stakeholders.[7]

The mixing board invites you to consider both ends of the spectrums. You should not go to either extreme because there is value in reflecting on both ends

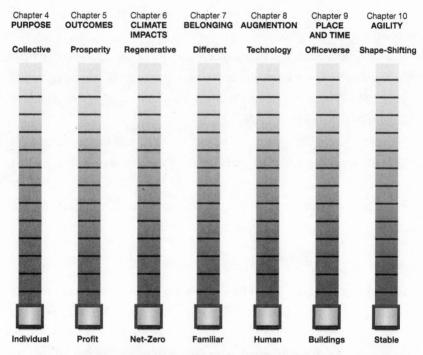

FIGURE 3: Office Shock Mixing Board. A visual metaphor illustrating the Seven Spectrums of Choice.

of each spectrum. You must harmonize the polarities, and the best way to do that is to think futureback to figure out your clarity of direction.

Harmonizing Within and Across the Seven Spectrums

In part III, we move into a format designed to help you write your own stories about the future of offices and officing. This is where we provide coaching for individuals, organizations, and communities.

Chapter 11 introduces our Quick Start Guide for how to use the mixing board to make your own choices as an individual worker, an organization with offices, or a policy maker. For each spectrum of choice, we ask you to "move the slider" between the two polarities to reflect your choices. Thinking futureback will help to first harmonize within each polarity, and then to harmonize across the seven spectrums. This will be about finding the best possible mix; it is about finding the best mix, the one that will set your course toward a better future of working and living.

Thinking futureback will help you develop clarity of direction about where, when, and why you work, but you must stay very agile about how we get to that future. We will have to prototype our way out of the noisy present. Thinking futureback will help bridge divides.

To think futureback, you must leap out ten years and imagine impossible offices. Then you can work backward from the future and make better decisions in the present. We must harmonize within and across the Seven Spectrums of Choice. By harmonize, we mean that you must move the slider in search of combinations that work well (as in sound good) together.

Office Shock Is a Futureback Story

In this book, we apply futureback thinking to help make sense out of office shock, as illustrated in figure 4. We start the book by focusing on the FUTURE (part I), to anticipate directions of change and increase your clarity. NEXT (part II), we introduce the Seven Spectrums of Choice about offices and officing. Finally, we end on the NOW (part III) for individuals, organizations, and communities.

In this book, we will guide you through the application of futureback thinking to imagine impossible futures, harness the mules, and create better futures for working. We will apply full-spectrum thinking and storymaking to rise above the noise of the present.[8] We will give you the tools, perspective, and choices that you can use to create your own story for yourself, your organization, and your community. The best way to harmonize is to think futureback to avoid getting caught up in the polarities of the present.

Synchronizing Individual, Organizational, and Community Choices

After you harmonize your choices across the Seven Spectrums of Choice, you must synchronize your choices so that they benefit individuals, organizations, and society. In part III, we offer our Quick Start Guide (pull out the book insert after page 60) with 4 steps to co-create your own future story for offices and officing:

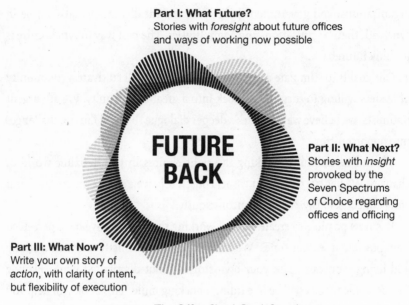

Part I: What Future?
Stories with *foresight* about future offices
and ways of working now possible

FUTURE
BACK

Part II: What Next?
Stories with *insight*
provoked by the
Seven Spectrums
of Choice regarding
offices and officing

Part III: What Now?
Write your own story of
action, with clarity of intent,
but flexibility of execution

FIGURE 4: The Office Shock Book Storyline.

1. **Find Your Future Self,** as an individual, as part of an organization, and as part of a community. How do these three aspects of your Future Self mesh together?

2. **What Future?** Set your intent, your navigational star, with flexibility as to how you might get there. Seek clarity but resist certainty. We call it flexive intent.

3. **What Next?** Make your choices on the Seven Spectrums of Choice for offices and officing. Harmonize within each spectrum and across the seven spectrums.

4. **What Now?** Lead futureback with flexive intent that is expressed in a compelling story. Synchronize with your individual, organizational, and community critical success factors to move forward together.

In chapters 12, 13, and 14, we provide guides for creating your own synchronized stories about the future of offices and officing, for individuals, organizations, and government policy makers. Ideally, individuals will be in sync with their organizations and communities. The best way to synchronize is to think futureback.

Our goal is to stimulate a new conversation that will cultivate a community of leaders willing to turn office shock into a great opportunity. We are urgent optimists: we believe we can spark a deeper dialogue that will flip the challenges into opportunities.

We can be helpful in making the right choices in this dynamic world of changes. We believe that "... if we act consciously we evolve consciously, but if we act unconsciously, we *evolve* unconsciously."[9]

It is now possible to create ways of working that would have been perceived as impossible in earlier times. We can choose to create better ways of working and living. You can write your own stories about distributed work. Playing through office shock will be like riding a bucking mule. This book will help you have a great ride.

PART I

WHAT FUTURE?

Better Futures for Working and Living

By putting ourselves into different possible futures, by becoming open and willing to embrace the uncertainty and discomfort that such an act can bring, we can imagine new possibilities. We can find optimistic futures; we can find paths forward; we can move beyond hope into action.[1]

ANAB JAIN

Even futures that used to be impossible will become possible due to office shock. As futurists we focus ten years ahead and think futureback to what's next and only then to the noisy now. All kinds of possibilities will be available for those who are future-ready. Office shock is an unprecedented opportunity.

Office shock—abrupt, unsettling change in where, when, how, and why we work—will get more intense, both worse and better.

The purpose of part I is to answer the question, "What future?" Our scenarios for offices and officing are aspirational but achievable.

Chapter 1 introduces the futureback method and the full-spectrum mindset to help you create better futures for working and living. With these tools, you will be able to envision what offices and officing could become in the future. The big lesson is that office shock will demand clarity to thrive in an increasingly chaotic future devoid of certainty. Futureback will help you avoid being stuck thinking only present-forward in today's chaotic times. You must prepare to be surprised. You must develop what we call flexive intent.

Full-spectrum thinking is about recognizing patterns across gradients of possibility. Thinking full-spectrum has the potential to reveal things we have in common that are hidden in plain view. A full-spectrum mindset encourages nuance. It provides a mindset for bridging the narrowness of categorical thinking that plagues communication in these polarizing times. A full-spectrum mindset will empower you to make the choices necessary to bring about a better future.

Chapter 2 provides historical context and our take on the evolution of workplace and technology. This history is what will make distributed office work possible in ways that would have been difficult to imagine even a few years ago. History yields patterns, while thinking futureback yields clarity.

In chapter 3, we will use futureback to imagine futures of working and living before they happen. We will enable you to look back with clarity on the spectrums of choice for offices and officing that individuals, organizations, and society will need to create a better future for working and living.

ONE

Futureback Thinking

About Office Shock

Future Shock, Alvin Toffler's landmark book,[1] made the case that if one major change is happening in your life, you should avoid making any other major changes at the same time—or risk experiencing "future shock." Toffler argued that individuals, and even societies, could be future shocked if they experienced "too much change in too short a time."

Toffler was concerned about the dehumanizing effects of the Industrial Age, including technology and office work. Orson Welles, in the movie version of *Future Shock* that he directed, said:

> Our modern technologies have achieved a degree of sophistication beyond our wildest dreams, but this technology has exacted a pretty heavy price. We live in an age of anxiety and a time of stress and with all our sophistication, we are in fact the victims of our own technological strength. We are victims of shock, of future shock.[2]

Remarkably, Welles said this in 1970 when "modern technologies" were unimpressive compared to what we have now—and crude compared to what we will have ten years from now.

The Shocks Keep Coming

The future shock Toffler was describing grew out of the explosive stresses of the 1960s, including the Vietnam War, the Cold War, the building of the Berlin Wall, May 1968 protests in Paris, the civil rights movement, and the deaths of inspirational figures such as John F. Kennedy, Robert F. Kennedy, and Martin Luther King Jr.

The shocks still keep coming, reverberating across working and living. The aftershocks of COVID-19 were amplified by global movements seeking social justice, economic equality, and slowing of climate change, including: Black Lives Matter,[3] #MeToo,[4] Anti-work,[5] PeopleNotProfit,[6] FridaysForFuture,[7] and Scientist Rebellion.[8] The groundswell of underrepresented and suppressed people reveals the depth of the social, economic, and health faults the pandemic exposed. Culture wars fume.

Naomi Klein's *The Shock Doctrine*[9] looked at governmental actions that negatively affected people in war or natural disasters. In 2021, science fiction writer Neal Stephenson published *Termination Shock*,[10] which explored a world so endangered by climate change and governmental inaction that unorthodox solutions were carried out by wealthy private individuals.

During the COVID-19 shutdowns, many people working in offices were shocked by too much change in too short a time regarding where and how they worked. People were stunned by orders to evacuate their office buildings and work from wherever. A cascade of jagged future shocks followed, with second- and third-order consequences. Office work and private life are now intensely entangled, with emotionally mixed consequences. Office shocks were deeply unfair: for some the sudden flexibility was liberating; for others it was awful.

Local governments around the world (with little consistency or coordination) inched at varied rates toward what public health experts call an "inter-pandemic" or an "endemic" period. As incidence of the virus decreased and impatience increased, there were growing top-down executive orders for workers to return to their office buildings. Many workers, however, refused to go back. Many began searches for new jobs and hybrid ways of working with a new sense of mobility and flexibility.

During the COVID-19 crisis, many organizations were surprisingly productive when people were working from home. Owners of office buildings struggled to make their offices safe and adaptable for new hybrid work arrangements, but the sanitized adaptations were often unsettling and rarely welcoming for a warm-and-friendly reunion. Some returned to ghost offices and quickly went back to work-from-home if they could. Nobody understood what permanent hybrid work at scale could become. Many people did want to return to in-person offices.

Some of the old-fashioned offices that were shuttered during the COVID-19 crisis were the epitome of what is wrong with corporate life. The traditional office itself has many inherent problems, even though it took a global pandemic to shock open executive's minds to the possibility of better ways of working. Many of the old offices were unfair, uncomfortable, uncreative, and unproductive. Office workers, corporations, and policy makers were shocked into imagining new realities and new options. In some cities, commercial office real estate is a wobbling house of cards.

The old-fashioned office is dead. Office shock is an opportunity to make offices better than they were—and most offices need to be better.

Early Futureback Thinking

In 1901, science fiction writer H. G. Wells sought to forecast "the way things will probably go in this new century." His aim in writing this nonfiction work was reflected in the title itself: *Anticipations of the Reaction of Mechanical and Scientific Progress upon Human Life*. Later he used the term *foresight* to describe the systemic study of the future.[11] A domain of expertise and practices followed suit, called a variety of names ranging from *futures studies* to *futurology*. Accelerated by World War II and enhanced by the emergence of systems science, futures studies became an academic discipline in the mid-1960s. Sociologists like Fred L. Polak,[12] philosophers like Marshall McLuhan,[13] and environmentalists like Rachel Carson[14] anticipated possible futures across social, technological, economic, environmental, and political spheres of human activity.

In 1968, a group of former RAND Corporation researchers with a grant from the Ford Foundation and Arthur Vining Davis Foundation founded the Institute for the Future (IFTF) to take leading-edge research methodologies into the public and business sectors. Since then, IFTF has been committed to building the future by understanding it deeply. IFTF's mission is to help communities across the globe create stories from the future that provoke insights and actions in the present. For over fifty years, IFTF has applied strategic foresight to help communities develop clarity while avoiding certainty. Many other global communities have contributed to the rise of foresight as a practice, including Singapore,[15] the European Union,[16] the United Arab Emirates,[17] and the Organization for Economic Co-operation and Development.[18]

Strategic foresight is a powerful way to face the VUCA world: Volatile, Uncertain, Complex, and Ambiguous. The VUCA acronym came into being in 1987 at the US Army War College in Carlisle, Pennsylvania.[19] The leadership theories of Warren Bennis and Burt Nanus were influential in helping the military to face the uncertainty of what they often called the fog of war. Today's VUCA world includes the rolling risk of new pandemics, the ongoing challenges of systemic racism, the rich-poor gap (many people cannot afford a decent home office), workers' increasing concerns about work-life navigation, chronic climate emergencies, and severely degraded trust in institutions.

Foresight enables us to think systemically about VUCA and avoid the techno-optimisim plaguing many people who think technology will solve all our *wicked problems*.[20] As IFTF has argued in its research, foresight enables people and organizations to flip VUCA dilemmas into positive opportunities:

- Vision counters Volatility

- Understanding counters Uncertainty

- Clarity counters Complexity

- Agility counters Ambiguity[21]

This approach helps people understand that VUCA is not insurmountable and can be navigated to envision paths to a better future.

VUCA will demand breakthrough ways to "office" for a better future. In the VUCA world, office shock will be an inevitable part of work life, and it won't be just about the office as a place. It will become increasingly obvious that "office" is both place (an office building or workplace) and a process (officing)—both a noun and a verb. Office shock will be about a lot more than office buildings. Returning to offices won't be simple, but office shock is a critical opportunity to reimagine where, when, and how "office work" can and should be done in the future.

Think Futureback

Office Shock profoundly blends two concepts: future and back.

Bob Johansen and Mark Johnson, the cofounder with Clayton Christensen of Innosight, have been engaged with each other's work and started using the term futureback (or future-back) at about the same time.[22] Bob and IFTF focus on the long-term future, thinking at least ten years ahead. Mark Johnson and Innosight are strategy consultants, drawing from foresight but emphasizing the present-value of futures thinking.

Thinking futureback—in contrast to present-forward—transforms our thinking and helps us explore alternative futures. This book shows you how to tell futureback stories. Thinking futureback will help you prepare for and navigate future shocks, including office shock.

Surprisingly, it is easier to anticipate directions of change thinking ten years ahead than it is to look out just one or two years. Thinking futureback allows you to sense directions of change—even when the specifics are yet to be determined. Signals that are very specific innovations or events that stretch our thinking about the future can spark thinking futureback. Institute for the Future scans signals globally and studies the emerging patterns of signals that are emerging.

Think Futureback to Reduce Your Cone of Uncertainty

Even though the future is unpredictable, we can do a lot better than just waiting for the future to happen to us. In the introduction we used the example of sensors. Thinking futureback from ten years ahead, it is obvious that sensors will be everywhere, they will be very cheap, many of them will be connected, and some of them will be in our bodies.

To take that example further many people already wear body sensors like smart watches that track biometrics. Ten years from now, most people who want one and can afford it will be wearing a body sensor and many people will have embedded body sensors. Health data from body sensors will be constant and confusing. We're at the start of a health data gold rush. Like the original California Gold Rush, many people will benefit as this new territory develops, many people will get hurt, and a very few people will discover gold. Looking futureback, the issues—such as privacy, data sensemaking, and equal access to health services for everyone, rich and poor alike—are obvious. The implication of using sensors in other applications, for example, in enhancing knowledge work, is less obvious. The direction of change regarding sensors is clear when you think futureback.

A practical example of the value of futureback is retirement planning. If you are young, it is very difficult to think of yourself as old. People do not tend to be very good at imagining their future selves. If you can think futureback, you can estimate your lifespan and the approximate income you will need as you age. Then, it will be important to consider your sources of income and your strategy for employment and retirement. If you have a traditional job and are planning to retire at age sixty-five, for example, modeling your income needs will be more straightforward than if you are a gig worker or creative artist. As part of a retirement plan, your needs will include mandatory expenses like health care, housing, and food—but your lifestyle choices will make a big differ-ence. Scenario planning can help you play out different lifestyle options under different assumptions. Thinking futureback allows you to see where you need to be and want to be at different stages of your life. Risk tolerance will make a big difference in your choices. The impact of compound interest will be much more visible thinking futureback, even though interest rates are not precisely predictable. Futureback thinking will help prepare you for a better future with financial independence.

An important aspect of retirement planning is deciding where you would like to live as you age. Given the risks of climate change, according to Climate Central,[23] flooding is a very likely phenomenon in many parts of the world.

Since flooding will influence prices and value of homes, you could check out a futureback map for 2050.[24] What will be the flooding risks in areas where you think you might like to retire?[25]

Even when we look at the forecasts, however, it is very difficult to imagine areas of major cities under water. It is even harder to imagine your own home being flooded. People do not tend to be very good at imagining their future selves. Our colleague Jane McGonigal, in her book *Imaginable*, describes the difference between thinking futureback based on available forecast data and your personal feelings about places. A data-based forecast of a future with climate change might be: "By 2050, sea levels may rise by as much as 9 feet (2.75 meters) and 750 million people may be displaced." Your personal forecast of a future with climate change might be something like this: "I'll be seventy-five years old in 2050. The two airports I use now will both be at risk of flooding. Flying will be less reliable due to extreme weather, so I'll live near my kids." You may even want to imagine an innovative solution, such as designing a home with a mechanism to move like a crab to higher ground. Danish architect Bjarke Ingels[26] imagined that Manhattan could have a protective green cushion, called the Dryline,[27] to protect its coastline from flooding.

Thinking futureback can help you explore different housing options under different assumptions. Risk tolerance will make a big difference in your choices. The possible impacts of climate change will be much more visible thinking futureback. Futureback thinking will help you prepare and be more future-ready.

Futureback is an uncommon common sense today. Ten years from now, thinking futureback will be a survival skill that all successful people will practice. This book will help readers get a head start by teaching your brain new tricks. Thinking futureback is liberating.

In times of great uncertainty, thinking futureback—*FUTURE, next, now*—is much more revealing than thinking present-forward.

FUTURE, then NEXT, then NOW

Most people today, however, are stuck in linear time: *NOW, next, future*. Most people are constrained by what some neuroscientists call "The Eternal Now."

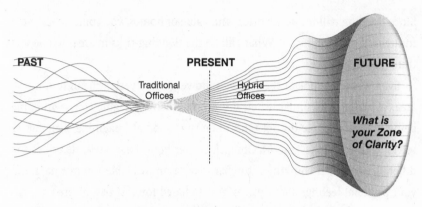

FIGURE 5: The Cone of Uncertainty for Offices.
A wide range of choices for offices and officing.

Futureback is not the way most people think today. The prefrontal cortex resists thinking futureback, it is focused on protecting you in the present.

Present-forward thinking is fraught with the urgent details of everyday life— as well as blinders and burdens from the past. Futureback is counterintuitive. Thinking futureback is a challenge of imagination, not of intelligence.

For most adults, especially successful young adults, thinking present-forward is so much of an unexamined assumption that they would never even consider thinking futureback. Thinking back from the future feels off-kilter if you are trapped in the present worrying about pressures like making money, career advancement, paying off mortgages, and child-rearing. The present is so very noisy, so demanding, and so mind-numbing—particularly in chaotic times.

Thinking futureback will help you develop your clarity and moderate your certainty. It is easier to develop clarity when you think futureback—especially in times of crisis. To thrive in the increasingly VUCA world of the future, we will all need to be very clear where we want to go, but very flexible about how we get there. We call this flexive intent, and this is a theme that will continue through the rest of this book.

Our goal is to reduce the cone of uncertainty, help people develop their own zones of clarity while resisting certainty. We can develop clarity by looking futureback, even though we can't have certainty.

At the present time, the cone of uncertainty, as shown in figure 5, is very wide regarding the future of office buildings and distributed office work. "Return to Office" is a term often used with certainty, but not clarity. The past is known and certain. The present is all-consuming. The future is unknown and filled with uncertainties. Futureback thinking can help narrow the range of uncertainty and help bring clarity. Nobody yet knows what hybrid work will look like in the future. Each worker and each organization will need to develop their own zone of clarity regarding where, when, how, and why they work.

Think Futureback with Stories

Thinking futureback is like a good story—magical, mythic, and fun. Like the outback, the futureback is the mysterious back of the beyond. Like the diamondback rattlesnake, the futureback is dangerous. Like a setback, there will be pathways forward that fail, but provide learning experiences. If you aren't at least a little frightened by the future, you're not paying attention. Thinking futureback allows you to sense directions of change and prepare—even when the specifics are impossible to predict.

Our brains look into the future automatically to protect us from what might be coming next.[28] The hippocampus contributes to creating visions by using past information to construct the scene of a possible future event. The power of stories lies in breaking free of our prefrontal cortex (the locus of logical thinking), to refocus our attention on what is beyond.[29] Recent research on the neuroscience of storytelling has concluded that our brains are wired for stories and, if we do not hear stories, we make them up.[30]

Stories help us make some sense out of what's going on around us. They help us to connect with others, either reconstructing the past or imagining a future, using verbal and visual language capabilities. We fill these mental-made worlds with the fictional narratives we call identities. Games are enacted stories. We play games of aspiration, decision, action, and learning that expand our connections with new stories.

A good story is unforgettable when it provokes the brain's neurotransmitters. Storyteller David Philips[31] describes a good story as offering listeners a neurochemical cocktail: endorphins are secreted when people laugh, characters that create empathy and trust release oxytocin, and a dopamine rush is experienced by piquing curiosity with problems and suspense, rather than the exhilaration of resolution.[32]

Consider this brief story: Go is perhaps the most complex game ever designed by humans, the oldest continuously played board game, and the biggest challenge for AI competitions with humans. In 2016, the DeepMind program AlphaGo defeated legendary human Go player Lee Sodel, who said afterward that "this experience made me grow. . . . I found my reason to play Go."[33] When a computer program defeated a human Go player, it wasn't the end of the Go game (in fact, global sales went up), it was the beginning of new ways to play Go. Augmented humans now play Go, and they play it differently than before. This story animates the facts, brings them to life, and makes them more memorable.

Stories can take many forms, including visual. For example, as more data are available about us, about what we eat, who we interact with, what we say, how we feel, our stories of self will take on new significance. In the future, cheap sensors will be everywhere, including inside our bodies, and they will generate lots of data. As this health data gold rush increases,[34] we will be able to make stories about ourselves come true by manipulating how we eat, work, and play.

Will Storr believes "we are all story makers."[35] A 2020 *MIT Technology Review* cover story introduces readers to the next generation's stories of multiple selves. By using technology to describe, reveal, expand, and sometimes mask identities, a new generation is expressing itself in ways not part of the traditional office.[36] Future projections of the self, based on data from the present, open new paths to explore identity in more meaningful ways.[37] Cross-generational communication is so important right now, since the officeverse will be created largely by young people—some of whom are not even in the workforce yet.

Stories and their accompanying neural networks correspond loosely to the ways we absorb, manipulate, and socialize information. This helps us step away from focusing on an individual's intelligence to an individual's interactions with others.[38]

Anthropologists believe storytelling to be one of the primary reasons *Homo sapiens* survived over other species.[39] Sharing stories is powerful because it synchronizes the brain activity of the teller and the listener.[40] The stronger the synchronization, the better the understanding between people.[41] Storymaking—the co-creation of a shared story—amplifies synchronization and mobilizes people for change.[42]

Our practice of worldbuilding extends the boundaries of experience with characteristics such as history, geography, and even ecology.[43] Worldbuilding establishes boundaries with characteristics such as history, geography, and ecology. These worlds enable listeners to fill in the details, making the story a shared experience.

Futureback Thinking Requires a Full-Spectrum Mindset

This is no time to lock yourself into any fixed way of thinking, or any fixed strategy about offices.

The office shock provoked by the COVID-19 pandemic was just the first of many related shocks to come. This is the beginning of a major cycle of change in the ways we organize work and labor, and ultimately our lives. The traditional office is a social and physical technology that no longer works for many people. We cannot go back to the office the way it was, and the path forward is not at all clear.

Thinking futureback requires a full-spectrum mindset:[44] the ability to seek patterns and clarity across gradients of possibility, outside, across, beyond traditional boxed categories, or maybe even without any boxes or categories, while resisting false certainty. It helps us find the multidimensional ways in which things are connected—not just the ways in which they are distinct from each other. To think and act across gradients of possibility is to avoid simplistic categorizations or false certainty. We need to look beyond binary choices. In this book, we apply full-spectrum thinking to the future of offices and officing by identifying spectrums of choices that must be made in the present to start chart-ing the paths to the future.

At the core of a full-spectrum mindset are both the ancient traditions and lat-est neuroscience findings that encourage humans to find balance and navigate life's ambiguities. In a real sense, human life has always been a VUCA world, beginning with the fact that we all must die. This universal message is central to the teachings of the Tao, concepts of heaven and earth, and even "The Force" in the *Star Wars* movies. It is also reinforced by scientific understanding of homeo-stasis for any biological system. Humans maintain optimal stability for survival by adjusting our internal chemistry according to external conditions. Full-spectrum thinking seeks a balance between the dichotomies of life: alone and together, giving and taking, surviving and providing. A full-spectrum mindset aims to empower us to find the balance necessary for creating better futures for working and living.

In these times of great uncertainty, thinking futureback and with a full-spectrum mindset is much more revealing about the future than staying stuck in present-forward mode. African American writer and activist James Baldwin added a cautionary note:

> Not everything that is faced can be changed, but nothing can be changed until it is faced.[45]

Your Choices about Futureback Thinking

Strategic foresight using futureback thinking with a full-spectrum mindset will help you write your own stories of offices and officing:

1. How can you break out of thinking present-forward, reduce your own cone of uncertainty, and move toward the futureback thinking of Future-Next-Now?

2. Full-spectrum thinking requires breaking out of the ingrained patterns of categorizing things into familiar boxes. How might you grow your full-spectrum mindset?

3. How can you develop and practice your storymaking skills?

TWO

Looking Back to Look Forward

The Technology Didn't Happen Overnight

Thinking futureback includes looking back from the present. Almost nothing happens that is truly new: almost everything was tried and failed years before it succeeded. When thinking about the future, there is limited utility in asking "What's new?" because if it is truly new it is almost certainly not going to happen anytime soon. It is much more useful to ask "What's ready to take off?" When COVID-19 hit, many technologies were ready to take off and most of them were not new.

Zoom wasn't just invented out of nowhere when the COVID-19 shutdown hit.[1] "Let's do a zoom call" became the term that many people used to describe the entire medium of video conferencing. Zoom, FaceTime, Microsoft Teams, WebEx, Skype, GoToMeeting, BlueJeans, and an array of other 2020 brands built on the graves of many failed video conferencing services over a period of more than fifty years. Luckily, desktop video conferencing was well tested and in modest use, so it was ready when it was needed urgently at scale.

At Institute for the Future, we typically think in sixty-year swaths of time: at least ten years ahead and at least fifty years back. While we look to the future for clarity, we look to the past for patterns. A futureback view provides context—the conditions that might allow something to take off.

It is important to take stock of how we got to where we are now regarding offices and officing. This chapter provides our take on the history of offices and officing before the COVID-19 office shutdowns. It provides context for understanding how we got here. Having this context provides a foundation for launching into futureback thinking about offices and officing.

Hierarchical Organizations Want Hierarchical Offices

In 1943, Sir Winston Churchill requested that the House of Commons be rebuilt after the war bombing exactly as it was before its destruction in October 1941. In his speech to the House of Lords, Churchill said, "We shape our buildings; thereafter they shape us."[2] It is important that we are conscious of how our buildings shape us and that we make smart choices. Churchill chose to rebuild buildings like before the war, but now is a time to do something different so our buildings shape us in better ways.

In 1909, Frederick Winslow Taylor published *The Principles of Scientific Management*.[3] In response to the Industrial Revolution, Taylor's system that he called "scientific management" broke down jobs into basic tasks. Job specialization distributed tasks among workers, each of whom performed one set of actions. Job planning was given to management, along with training and monitoring of employees to be sure they were performing.

In 1920, German sociologist Max Weber built on Taylor's principles in his seminal work, *The Theory of Social and Economic Organizations*, which described bureaucracy as the most efficient way of running large organizations.[4] Weber agreed with the need for job specialization where jobs were broken down into simple, routine, and well-defined tasks.

Taylorism and bureaucracy are arguably the most significant influences on workplace architecture—in the design of physical offices, in the management of physical offices, and in how work was carried out in physical offices.[5]

IMAGE I: Atrium of the Larkin Administration Building.
Collection of the Buffalo History Museum. Larkin
Company photograph collection, Picture .L37, # I-35.

Early office building designs such as Frank Lloyd Wright's Larkin Building[6] (see images 1 and 2) reflected this focus on efficiency, a design trend that continued for decades.

Interior windowless spaces for lower-level employees were surrounded by private offices for managers, often sized and furnished according to the rank of each executive. In addition to displaying a perceived need for supervision of lower-level workers, the space was organized for task specialization. The workflow logically grouped responsibilities to facilitate smooth production, as if the office were a factory.

IMAGE 2: Typing Department in the Larkin Administration
Building. Collection of the Buffalo History Museum. Larkin
Company photograph collection, Picture .L37, #2-51.

Spurred by the elevator, new construction methods in concrete, and new ways
to cool offices, high-rise buildings began to grow. Despite these innovations, the
workplace continued to be organized using Taylor's principles. Hierarchies and
ways of working were poured into those concrete office buildings and furniture
arrangements.

Unpleasant Offices

Twentieth-century offices evolved little in the period between 1945 and 1970.
Most improvements in the 1950s focused on making traditional tasks more efficient using improved manipulation, storage, and retrieval of information stored
on paper. The Rolodex, for example, was introduced in 1958 and allowed contact
details to be readily at hand on a wheel that twirled through cards that were
handwritten or typed individually. It was considered a marvel at the time.

The offices of the past were often awful, at least for lower-level employees. In
the 1950s and '60s, life in the office was characterized in popular media as men
and women in formal business attire smoking cigarettes. Women were in the

lower-level positions (secretaries and typists), while mostly white men were in managerial positions. There was a significant lack of diversity in all positions except the lowest. The Dolly Parton movie *9 to 5*, a comedy grounded in a dreary sexist office, told a realistically creepy story of office life. The popular TV series *Mad Men* told disturbing stories of office behavior. In a classic film farce of modernity, *Playtime*, director Jacques Tati brought the unpleasant office to life in a very possible future.

While *Playtime*, *Mad Men*, and *9 to 5* were stereotypes, there was a lot of accuracy in how offices of old were portrayed in these films. Office work was organized for command-and-control efficiency. Old-fashioned offices and the executives who ran them were both stodgy and slow to change.

In the 1960s, for example, the IBM Selectric typewriter was viewed as a major innovation, something that was hard to imagine given the long history of the typewriter. Prior to this technology, office communications were typed on a traditional typewriter, which had an unchangeable font and moveable arms for each letter. Fast typists easily jammed the typewriter. The Selectric had a revolving ball with the letters on it, which did not jam and, most importantly, could be switched out to provide a variety of fonts. The people who used to be called "secretaries" were delighted by the variety, but what they were typing and how they worked didn't change.

Turmoil in the World around Offices

Outside the office, countercultural shocks were everywhere. Major events in the 1960s and '70s included the Stonewall riots, which many credit with the beginning of the gay rights movement; the first moonwalk on July 20, 1969; a popular music revolution characterized by the Beatles and Woodstock; the resignation of US president Richard Nixon; and the cultural revolution in China. The civil rights movement dates back even further but also had major milestones in the 1960s.

In San Francisco, the first Earth Day was proclaimed in 1970, but little was done to ameliorate the negative effects of human activity on the planet, and no office policies or procedures were changed to lessen its impact. *Future Shock* became an international bestseller in 1970, an early indication that people recognized that there is volatility in their lives and that it may be harmful.

In 1971, the singer, songwriter, and activist Marvin Gaye asked in song, "What's Going On?" as a plea for change in the social, economic, environmental, and political turbulence of the times.[7] Although these events were shocking to most people, the owners and executives who ran offices were deeply committed to business as usual.

Traditional office buildings were organized for orderliness. They exuded command-and-control efficiency. They were designed so workers could be observed, to ensure they were working hard. Most offices were not designed to encourage trust or develop community. The traditional office was often unproductive and unfair. Many were boxed-in rooms crammed with cubicles and unhappy people.

Technologies for Remote Work Came Slowly

As most offices were focused on efficiency, technological breakthroughs were laying a foundation for potential changes in how work got done. Specifically, the introduction of microcomputers and networks in the 1960s laid the technological foundation for new ways of working and living that didn't happen until decades later.

Our story of office shock starts in 1945, when Vannevar Bush, the former head of the US Office of Scientific Research and Development, published his vision of the global brain he called "Memex."[8] We think of the Memex as an early vision of the officeverse. Influenced by Bush's vision, the US Department of Defense began work on the ARPANET, the first distributed network of computers. During the Cold War, the central computers of the day were vulnerable to attack, where distributed processing promised to be more resistant and robust. The ARPANET was the predecessor of the internet.

It is important to note that the ARPANET was a government-seeded innovation that involved many public-private institutions. We will come back to this in chapter 13 on choices for policy makers regarding offices and officing. The distributed ways of working that are common today would have taken much longer to develop if not for government seed money.

While it was initially developed in secret, the ARPANET was introduced to the public in 1972. Bob presented his first professional paper at that conference, which was called the International Conference on Computer Communications. By "communications," they meant machines communicating with machines. The ARPANET was intended to be a major incremental improvement for data communications for enhanced military security. When people started using that early and very crude internet to communicate with other people, they were chastised for wasting scarce computing power. Using that early internet as a marketplace for buying and selling was unthinkable, until that's what it became suddenly years afterward. Once those early computers were connected, the mules came to life and started kicking.

In 1972, the National Science Foundation and the Defense Advanced Research Projects Agency funded Institute for the Future to think futureback about this unprecedented technology that was unfolding in staggering ways. This first-of-its-kind network had no center, it grew from the edges, and it could not be controlled—though many tried to control it.

Later in Europe, CERN, a high-energy physics research facility, became a major wide-area network hub and is considered the birthplace of the World Wide Web.[9]

The internet is still evolving in unpredictable ways. The internet and its descendants will always be mules that appear in wildly varied incarnations.

A Mule Disguised as a Mouse

Inventor Douglas C. Engelbart created the first mouse, which looked more like a rat. It provided a new way for ordinary humans—not just computer programmers—to interact with computers easily. The mouse turned out to be a mule.

Engelbart also invented the first windows interface, the first hypermedia capability, the first split-screen video conferencing, and a range of other innovative digital tools that are only now becoming practical. Try searching the web for

"The Mother of all Demos" to see the best demo we have ever seen and remember as you watch it that it was done in 1968.

Inspired by Bush's Memex, Engelbart created the first prototype of a comprehensive integrated office system in Silicon Valley before it was called that. Engelbart's bold vision was to augment the human intellect, to boost human abilities to collectively deal with complex societal problems. His team at Stanford Research Institute (now SRI International) built and ran the Network Information Center (NIC), the first library on the ARPANET. Engelbart's integrated office system, initially called NLS (for oNLine System) was marketed unsuccessfully for a short period of time by Tymshare as "Augment." A quiet, kind, and humble man, Engelbart turned out to be a mule. The world was not ready for him.

When Bob came to the Institute for the Future in 1973, he was the first PhD level social scientist on a team of technologists that was building and testing the new idea of group communication through computer networks. The leader of the team was computer scientist Jacques Vallee, who had just joined IFTF from Engelbart's lab. Nobody knew what to call the medium they were prototyping on the ARPANET (awkwardly, they called it "computer conferencing"), but today most people would call it social media or collaborative media. The vision and tools for distributed office work were gradually coming to life. For example, since participants in IFTF's prototype trials were from around the world, the team had wildly varied work hours. When the ARPANET "crashed" (that is, abruptly stopped working—which happened frequently), the ghostly message broadcast to all participants was this: "HOST DEAD," with no guess about when it might arise from the dead. These early systems were very interesting when they worked, but not ready to scale.

In the early 1970s, the first general purpose microprocessors made their way to offices, without a mouse yet. By the 1980s, the presence of personal computers in the workplace grew rapidly, the global internet was prominent in academic communities, and, in 1989, the World Wide Web was established as the platform for global communication for anyone who wanted to join in. In 1989, Tim

Berners-Lee created the World Wide Web, built on the ARPANET infrastructure, which by then had evolved into the internet.

New Tools for Working

Gradually, a series of specialized business tools was introduced into the office. Wang Laboratories invented a word processor in the 1970s that incorporated many of the attributes of today and included a screen (CRT—cathode ray tube—like a television) for viewing and editing the input. Next came specialized software that could be used on a general-purpose microcomputer—essentially a personal computer—like spreadsheet software such as VisiCalc (1979) and Lotus 1-2-3 (1983). This was an important transition in showing that the microcomputer could be used for many different purposes in the office. But the substantial change was in understanding that these general-purpose computers could be linked together through communications software and provide a way for work to be shared and distributed among knowledge workers. A computer on every desk took a long time, followed by a computer in every pocket or purse.

Initially, the communication took place within separate organizations, but with the ARPANET as a model, the opportunity for connecting organizations and people became the goal. People communicating through computers with other people anywhere in the world became possible.

For networks like the internet to expand, there needed to be computers to connect. As with the introduction of the telephone, initially there were very few people who had one and therefore very few people to call. Each computer (or telephone) is a node on a network, and for the network to succeed there must be active nodes. Personal computing emerged as a major innovation when active nodes included computers in organizations and when people took them into their homes. At first, home computers were stand-alone toys for hobbyists, but the communications opportunities and the growth of many kinds of software applications that people enjoyed using catapulted the growth in personal computing.

Although computers could now be personal, and span the globe, understanding how interacting with these new technologies could enhance officing and the workplace was the essential ingredient to change the world of working and living. This was a painfully slow process of fitting new distributed tools into old hierarchal offices.

Telecommuting Was Possible Long before COVID-19

Jack Nilles,[10] who coined the term "telecommuting" in the 1970s, was a professor at the University of Southern California studying urban transportation. Recall that the Los Angeles metropolitan area had chosen by this time to de-emphasize its innovative public transportation system in favor of a network of automobile freeways.

Nilles had the vision to see that working remotely was much more possible and desirable than most people thought at the time.[11] He was an inspirational part of a global movement, most active in Western Europe, that promoted several novel concepts, including:

- Travel/telecommunications Substitution

- Travel/telecommunications Trade-offs

- Remote Work

In his experiments and research, Jack Nilles proved that telecommuting was viable and desirable, but most companies still weren't interested. In these early days, many managers expressed their concern that, if they could not see people at their desks, they couldn't tell if they were really working. Many individual workers liked the idea of telecommuting, but the owners and executives who ran offices were not yet ready to change.

In 1988, Bob wrote a book called *Groupware: Computer Support for Business Teams* that included seventeen scenarios, only three of which required that people be in person in offices.[12] Scenario 17 was focused on nonhuman participants in location-flexible team meetings. Computers were evolving from large central rooms to personal desktops, to distributed networks. *Groupware* was dedicated to Doug Engelbart and Jacques Vallee.

The notion of augmented group intelligence has been a long time in the making. For example, the Institute for the Future designed and prototyped a collaborative system in 1982 that included nonhuman participants that were computer models.[13] *Groupware* included a scenario called "Nonhuman Participants (Support for Electronic Meetings)" in which the nonhuman advisor on risks associated with various possible investment options was called Coach:

> The team meeting for new brokers is just convening. Each trainee has spent the
> better part of the preceding day working with the Coach, an expert system that has
> specialized expertise about investment options that the new brokers will be selling
> in another three weeks. There are many opinions about investment options; even
> the Coach is only expressing an opinion. The new team discusses the options, con-
> sulting again with the Coach at several points during the meeting. The Coach has
> specialized knowledge that nobody on the team has, but it does not have definitive
> answers. It is a collaborative process, with all the team members (including the
> Coach) contributing.[14]

The Coach was an early prototype for intelligent agents who could augment both individuals and groups. Now, decades later, such things are becoming practical. Once the stuff of science fiction, AI coaches, and companions, are now available.[15] In chapter 8, for example, we used a current generation text genera-tor to create a futureback story.

In *Groupware*, Bob highlighted the innovative work going on at Xerox PARC (Palo Alto Research Center). An innovation hub in the hills of Palo Alto overlooking Stanford University, Xerox PARC led the way with technologies like WYSIWIG (What You See Is What You Get) and GUI (Graphical User Interfaces), which began to make using microprocessor-based computers much easier for any knowledge worker. In addition, Danny Bobrow and Mark Stefik created COLAB to prototype computer support for collaborative work—either in a single location or for distributed teams. Mark Weiser, who later joined IFTF's board of trustees, invented the term *ubiquitous computing*: computer sup-port "wherever you go and however you move." Adele Goldberg and Alan Kay used computers in amazing ways in their work with children and storytelling.

There has always been a strong culture of idea exchange in Silicon Valley. The first time Bob did a presentation at PARC, he was the only social scientist in a room filled with a large group of engineers and computer scientists. Bob was discussing the work of people communicating with people through the ARPANET, and they weren't buying it since the original purpose of the network was computers communicating with computers. Bob was standing in the room while all of them were slouching on bean bag chairs. Just a few years later, under John Seely Brown, PARC became about half social scientists and half computer scientists. Bill English joined PARC from Engelbart's lab and PARC brought Engelbart's core ideas closer to real life. Important PARC innovations made their way into commercial use.

These new insights about how people interacted with computers, and the software to assist knowledge work (for example, word processing and spreadsheets), accelerated the use of personal computing into the 1990s, and by the 2000s social networking (such as Facebook in 2004). This growth continues as more software applications are created that augment knowledge work, provide leisure-time entertainment, and fuel distributed offices and office work of every kind.

Architects Envisioned the Networked Office

As technologies for distributed work were improving gradually, Frank Duffy, workplace architect pioneer and researcher, was among the first to imagine a very different kind of office. Duffy thought that the open and unplanned spaces of office landscaping (inspired by the bürolandschaft from West Germany[16]) failed to live up to expectations due to noise levels and the excessive interruptions it encouraged. It offended individual concerns for privacy, comfort, environmental control, and personal identity.[17]

The unresolvable tension between corporate and individual aspirations was a significant problem for bürolandschaft and other open office designs. In the United States, Herman Miller's "Action Office" provided an alternative: a kit of parts matched to the varied tasks for office work. It addressed the conflicts between privacy and communication inherent to the bürolandschaft schemes.

In Europe, the response was quite different. The "Combi" office sought to balance the relationship between individual aspirations and corporate identity by providing space for both. Herman Hertzberger's the Centraal Beheer Office,

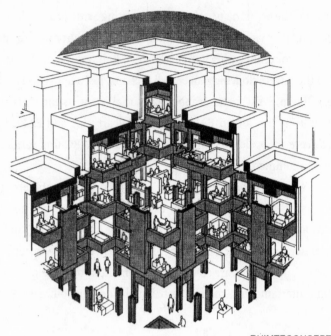

RUIMTECONCEPT

IMAGE 3: Centraal Beheer Office, Axonometric Sketch of Interior Space Plan. Office building Centraal Beheer, Apeldoorn, The Netherlands (1986–1972). Architect Herman Hertzberger.

illustrated in images 3 and 4, sought to mitigate these tensions by encouraging separate "hives" for varied activities.[18]

Flat screens had a major impact on creating hives, according to architect Colin Macgadie:

> The widespread introduction of flat screen technology in the late 90s enabled desks to be grouped together in "benches" and freed up valuable space that could now be used to create the café's, lounge areas, and breakout spaces that helped co-workers and teams feel connected, and began to challenge the thought processes around office design. The Centraal Beheer's whole concept and architecture encouraged early versions of "Breakout Areas," but this process was given real impetus and democratized with the physical flexibility the flat screen offered organizations.[19]

IMAGE 4: Centraal Beheer Office, Interior Photo. Office building
Centraal Beheer, Apeldoorn, The Netherlands (1986–1972).
Architect Herman Hertzberger. © Willem Diepraam

Spurred on by the revolutionary potential of information technology, Philip Stone and Robert Luchetti claimed that "Your Office Is Where You Are."[20] For the first time the assumption of "one seat per person" in offices was questioned. Reconfiguring the space and time of officing sparked a fundamental rethinking of office design itself.[21]

Drawing inspiration and insight from the Environmental Behaviorists[22] and new information technologies, Francis Duffy wrote in 1997:

Ways of working are changing radically. Information technology sees to that. Based on very new and very different assumptions about the use of time in space, new ways of working are emerging fast. They are inherently more interactive than old office routines and give people far more control over the timing, the content, the tools, and the place of work.[23]

Resonating with Franklin Becker and Fritz Steel's perspective on workplaces, Duffy's design expressed organizational ecology.[24] DEGW, Duffy's architectural practice in which Joseph was working at the time, promoted four types of spaces in offices:

1. The Den   3. The Hive
2. The Club   4. The Cell

DEGW's four different workspaces offered "organizations the capacity to both add value through ways of working and to minimize costs."[25] Such innovative rethinking, wrote DEGW's director of research at the time: "is the major means by which architectural design can provide buildings and workplaces that better support user's emerging organizational needs."[26]

Duffy's Networked Office allocated space based on work patterns, informed by use. Networked Offices combine the potential of virtuality in the power of in-person experiences. Networked Offices transcend conventional architectural boundaries offering a different kind of relationship between technology and people, and between time and place.

Office shock accelerated Duffy's spatial dreams into reality, with a new name: the hybrid office. Churchill's proclamation that our buildings shape us is still true, but now our options for building and communicating are much richer. We don't have to go back to the way it was.

Impossible Offices Became Mandatory in 2020

The novel coronavirus pandemic of 2020 shoved companies and workers out of their office buildings abruptly. Owners and executives had to open their minds about different ways of working. Alternatives were no longer optional; they were required.

The technology, tools, and visions had been bubbling away in labs and universities for more than half a century, but the concept of "office" was still packed with habits and unexamined assumptions that were not easy to change. Digital tools were gradually coming alive, but there was little demand for change.

At the same time, knowledge workers were more comfortable with using the technology that supported work from anytime/anyplace. Young people or other early users of technology seemed to have an advantage. The rolling risk of pandemics, chronic climate crises, and social injustices shocked everyone. For the first time, many organizations—after being required to work remotely because of COVID-19 shutdowns—began to question the value of traditional offices. Were there other ways to achieve the goals of the organization through creative use of alternative workplaces? Individuals, organizations, and policy makers now can imagine better offices and better ways of officing.

Fortunately, by the time COVID-19 happened, the technology was good enough to use on a large scale. Earlier visionary mules like Engelbart and Nilles had been ignored, but the technology kept improving anyway, and by 2020 when COVID-19 hit, impossible office futures became possible because:

- *There was an obvious and urgent need to change behaviors regarding where, when, and how work got done.* The oil shortage in the late 1970s and the 9/11 terrorist attacks hadn't been enough to create office shocks that were lasting. COVID-19 was the tipping point that demanded a change that was impossible for years before, but now was mandatory. Indefinite office closures shook everyone, including the people who run offices.

- *Robust and functional technology made distributed work possible.* The early technology for remote work has been in small-scale use since 1968, but it was not easy to use, it was expensive, and it was not dependable until recently. By 2020, the technology, the tools, and the media were at least good enough and they were ready to scale. We expect that the next decade, now that the

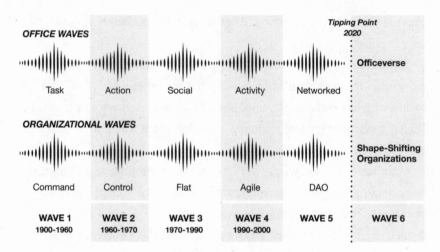

FIGURE 6A: Office and Organizational Waves. Innovations enabling the Great Opportunity of an officeverse and shape-shifting organizations.

need is clear, will see dramatic improvements in technology and media for distributed work.

- *Practical success stories of distributed work spread quickly as the pandemic spread.* Until the crisis, visions of distributed work—and the words used to describe these visions—were either not inspirational enough or not practical enough. By the end of 2020, working remotely was the only way to work for millions of people around the world. And some of these new ways of working were very attractive to workers and companies alike.

Office shock challenged foundational assumptions about where, how, when, and why we work. As office shock becomes a way of life, new fault lines will reveal opportunities for new ways of working and living. Office shock hit hard in 2020, but the aftershocks will roll on into the future for at least a decade or beyond.

Looking futureback, we see a convergence of three drivers of change—technology (internet waves), places (office waves), and people (organizational waves)—that underlie what we're calling the Great Opportunity for deep change

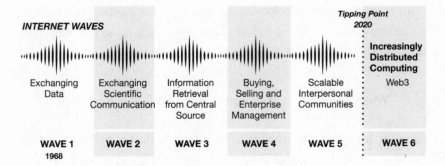

FIGURE 6B: Internet Waves. Innovations enabling the Great
Opportunity of increasingly distributed computing.

in offices and officing. Figure 6a illustrates the timeline of evolution in where we work and the ways we organize ourselves to work.

COVID-19 sparked new ways of using internet connectivity in ways that had never been attempted at massive scale. As illustrated in figure 6b, the internet was already the connective tissue for offices and distributed work, but suddenly the stakes went up dramatically. Both COVID-19 and the internet are mules—unpredictable wild cards that cannot be controlled.

Triggered by COVID-19, the waves of office, organization, and technology changes cascaded into unprecedented tipping points changing where, when, and how we work. The year 2020 was when so many mules converged, sparking office shock and a great opportunity to do offices and officing a lot better than what had been done in the past.

With increasingly distributed computing, shape-shifting organizations, and happier workers, after nearly a decade the officeverse is now a great possibility because the directions of change are clear:

From	Toward
Hierarchical and Centralized	Networked and Distributed
Standalone and Individual	Connected and Cross-Organizational
Fixed Offices	Shape-Shifting Ways of Working
Specialized Jobs	Augmented Generalists

By thinking futureback—forecasting futures, provoking insight, and align-ing actions—individuals, organizations, and policy makers can now reimagine where and how office work can and should be done in the future.

Your Choices as You Look Back to Look Forward

Everyone has a choice of whether to learn from history or risk remaking old mistakes. It took more than fifty years for distributed digital technologies to be an overnight success in 2020. Zooming wasn't just created anew when COVID-19 hit. In this chapter we shared our stories of this evolution and what it implies about what's next as the officeverse emerges.

As you think about your own personal story and reflect on technologies for distributed work over the last fifty years, consider these questions:

1. The networked office broke resistance to change in hierarchical offices. The year 2020 was a tipping point for change. How can you use futureback thinking to imagine better ways of working for yourself and your organization from now going forward?

2. The birth of augmented knowledge work began to grow slowly in the 1970s, and we are still asking the question of how we best combine what humans do with what machines can do. What is your stance regarding augmented intelligence (more on this coming in chapter 8)? What are the aspects of work where you need the most augmentation? What areas do you want to keep to yourself?

3. Technology has evolved dramatically in the past fifty years, making impossible things possible. In this chapter, we've shared our stories about this evolution. What are the lessons you take from this history?

4. The past is riddled with present-forward thinking about technology that limits imagination. How might you encourage more futureback thinking?

THREE

Impossible Futures

Imagining Better Offices and Officing

Office shock invites us all to envision a world in which previously impossible futures are possible, where we can harness the mules.

Mules are extreme surprises, impossible futures that happen despite their perceived impossibility. Sometimes, mules are playful. Always, mules are stubborn. Mules do not fit our frames of understanding. It is difficult to categorize these mules or even talk about them without using terminology that doesn't capture their full potential.

Impossible Futures Are Now Possible

Science fiction brings to life our hopes and fears in visceral ways. Throughout the history of fiction, science fiction has provided a stage for multiple impossible futures. As Yuval Noah Harari writes: "Today science fiction is the most important artistic genre." For example, Cyberpunk[1] imagined impossible futures of technology taking over and bending life as we knew it, while Steampunk[2] portrayed impossible futures where industry and energy dominated daily life. Solarpunk probes climate-positive futures that are also more equitable. In the

Afrofuturism genre, impossible futures of ethnic equality are often explored as achievable aspirations.[3]

The twenty-first century opened with more optimism as Afrofuturism[4] envisioned social equality and Solarpunk[5] a symbiotic relationship between people and planet. Science fiction stretches our thinking and prepares us to be surprised. It also suggests new futures we might want to make.

Continuing this tradition, world building has become the trope in Hollywood for creating compelling stories about the future. Popularized by narrative designer and creative director Alex McDowell in films like *Minority Report* and *Man of Steel*, world building enables everyone to enter an impossible future.[6] Epic fantasy is set in alternative worlds where heroes go on quests and magic abounds. The story arcs are spectacular. Having roots in epic poetry like *The Iliad* and *The Odyssey*, epic fantasy includes the works of J. R. R. Tolkien up through George R. R. Martin, Robert Jordan, and Brandon Sanderson. The worldbuilding in epic fantasy inspires readers to imagine new stories about a range of alternative futures.

The worldbuilding of science fiction and epic fantasy readies us to envision impossible futures,[7] including:

- *Impossible futures that happen too fast to be believable.* Before the COVID-19 shutdowns in 2020, many people thought it was impossible to have low-cost high-quality home video teleconferencing available. Many imagined it was possible, but not so soon.

- *Impossible futures that require convergence of many unlikely scenarios.* A global pandemic on the scale of COVID-19, with global office shutdowns, was viewed as impossible by many people. It was also impossible to imagine that so many businesses could be so productive so quickly without physical offices. These types of impossible futures involve the convergence of so many factors that it is sometimes unclear how they could have occurred, even after they happen.

- *Impossible futures that break the accepted rules of reality.* The rapid development of a vaccine for the new and deadly COVID-19 was viewed by many as impossible because it required so much information sharing among competing companies and such novel approaches to development. The accepted rules of reality for vaccine development suggested that rapid development of an effective vaccine could not happen, but it did.

- *Impossible futures that depend on alien concepts.* Development of an mRNA vaccine (where a copy of a molecule called messenger RNA is used to produce an immune response), was unheard of in most circles. Dr. Katalin Kariko's dedicated and unorthodox research into mRNA laid the groundwork that led to the development of the vaccine.[8] Futures based on alien concepts are the most unpredictable, the true wild cards. They don't fit any of our frames of understanding.

Impossible futures are not easy to categorize, and combinations of the four types are likely, as is apparent in the examples already presented. Consider a few other recent examples of heretofore impossible futures: your personal smartphone now has what used to be called "supercomputer" power. We now have access to fast, low-cost, and complete sequencing of DNA. We have increasingly good and increasingly cheap ways of being there without being there. Office shock has the potential for impossible futures of all types—and others we have yet to imagine.

The Language of Impossible Futures

Talking about impossible futures, however, is difficult. As futurists, we have learned over the years that if you get your terms right to describe a future, the terms draw you toward that future. If you get your terms wrong, you fight that future.

For example, the "horseless carriage" was a bad term used to describe the automobile in its early stages because the automobile was so very different. "Office automation" was a bad term since it implied straightforward mechanizing what was basically human activity in offices. "Groupware" was a bad term because it was more about the group than the ware. "Reengineering" was a bad term because most organizations were never engineered in the first place.

"Telecommuting" was a bad term because it implied that telecommunications would simply replace the office commute. "Artificial Intelligence" is one of the worst terms ever to describe a new technology because it implies that computers will replace humans in some simple manner—which is rarely the case. We believe that negative reactions to the term "artificial intelligence" slowed the acceptance of symbolic computing dramatically. The term "augmented intelligence," would have been much more accurate and would have speeded acceptance.

"World Wide Web" is a great term because it reflects global connectivity. "Internet" is a great term because it emphasizes communications across networks. "Metaverse" is an even better term, since it stretches our imaginations into fully blended realities. Unfortunately, corporations often attempt to own such visionary terms, even though that (fortunately) will be impossible.

The way to prepare for impossible futures is to create stories about them, with accurate and compelling language that stretches our collective imagination.[9]

The UN Global Goals Are a Good Start

Good stories about better futures for living and working also benefit from guideposts along the route toward an achievable future. In looking for stories of better futures, the United Nations Sustainable Development Goals provide a strong framework. The SDGs are a thoughtful and international "blueprint to achieve a better and more sustainable future for all." As defined by the UN Global Compact (UNGC) and adopted by the UN General Assembly in 2015, this collection of seventeen interlinked global goals is accompanied by detailed descriptions, with specific targets to measure progress.[10]

Sustainable Development Goals help to inspire stories of aspirational, not utopian, futures. They are interdependent, not independent, and require pathways for systemic change. For example, Quality Education, Good Health and Well-Being will enable a future with no poverty and zero Hunger. Gender Equality will increase diversity and inclusiveness. Industry, Innovation, and Infrastructure will use Affordable and Clean Energy to fuel Decent Work and Economic Growth. Responsible Consumption and Production will use Clean Water and Sanitation to support Sustainable Cities and Communities. Climate

Actions for the planet will ensure Life on Land and will be sustainable along with the essential Life below Water.

As Ban Ki-Moon, Secretary General of the United Nations from 2007 to 2016 has said, the Sustainable Development Goals form an agenda that is:

> A universal, integrated, and transformative vision for a better world. It is an agenda for people to end poverty in all its forms. An agenda for the planet, our common home. An agenda for shared prosperity, peace, and partnership. It conveys the urgency of climate action. It is rooted in gender equality and respect for the rights of all. Above all, it pledges to leave no one behind.[11]

These heretofore impossible futures could become possible through working in global partnerships to do things that have never been done before. Governments, organizations, and individuals have pledged to work toward the future described by the UN global goals. Despite the shared intentions, these futures still appear impossible. However, as Philip Alston, former UN Rapporteur on Extreme Poverty and Human Rights, writes, "The SDGs should not be abandoned but . . . business as usual should not be an option." We agree that recalibrating, not scrapping, the Sustainable Development Goals will be an important part of co-creating a new story of better futures.

Heretofore Impossible Offices

In part II, we will start each chapter with an aspirational scenario for offices, thinking futureback from about ten years ahead. Some of these scenarios will appear impossible now, but office shock will shake the constraints and open new opportunities. As you stretch your thinking about what might become possible for future offices, consider these questions:

Purpose: Why do you have an office at all?

Imagine a world in which purpose will be expressed in office buildings, workspaces, and how organizations do their work. Money will remain an important part of this spectrum to fulfill personal and family needs (particularly until you reach basic levels of safety and sustenance), but the higher ground will be meaningful work. Creating a sense of individual and shared purpose in work environments will lead to increased meaning for individuals and increased value for organizations. Intentions will be clear.

Outcomes: What results are you seeking from your office?

Imagine a world in which the outcomes of offices and officing generate both personal financial return and social value. Shareholder value will balance better with the larger community of stakeholders who are touched by the actions of an organization. Traditional tensions between individual gain and common good will be organized around social assets and shared value. The mistrust of institutions will be replaced by an expectation of continuous change and achievable futures that were considered impossible in earlier days.

The polarizing categories of economic thought will be replaced by new ways to work together to create prosperity that are yet to be described well. Organizations will provide vital bridges between living and working, generating social assets, and improving prosperity for the community. Individuals, stakeholders, and the community will have a better chance to thrive because opportunities for success will increase.

Impacts: What will be the climate impacts of your office activities?

Imagine a world in which people will respond to the urgent concerns about climate futures by focusing directly on smarter choices. Most consumables will be sustainable, transported with much greater efficiency. In some areas, the banning of all fossil-fuel-powered vehicles will provide the impetus for water and air purification. A state of symbiosis with no degradation of the environment will be achievable.

At a global level, we will balance production and consumption, revolutionizing the throwaway society of the previous generations. Companies will lead the way in circular design on a global scale. Circular design will reduce material use, redesign materials to be less resource intensive, and recapture waste as a resource to manufacture new materials and products. Organizations will develop new technologies to power sustainable solutions. Individuals will lead the way in monitoring and ensuring circularity with access to real-time data related to the life cycle of their products.

Worldwide cooperation will win out, after many struggles, and the planet will be on a path to regeneration. Most people around the world will know their carbon allotment and use AI to keep on track toward their goals. Individuals will be prepared to relinquish some privacy to create a better world for all. Throughout the journey to this new state of symbiosis, the UN Sustainable Development Goals will help to guide countries, companies, and individuals toward sustainable solutions. PPP—People Planet Prosperity—summarizes the overall clarity of direction of change, and it will work.

Belonging: With whom do you want to office?

Imagine a world in which diversity is expected and rewarded as the standard. Credible edgy people with all kinds of backgrounds and aspirations will be valued for their innovation. Trust will be high and expressed in rituals that embody organizational culture and purpose—in person and in virtual worlds.

Where traditional diversity programs sought only to bring outliers into the established order of offices, more advanced programs will create spaces that support all differences—not just people categorized as "other." Those who win in this world will be those who can present their difference as a value-added value to support the organization's purpose. Embracing varied cultures and thinking styles will be an everyday skill for everyone in this liquid world of mixing and matching. The most successful people will celebrate their roots and routes.

Amplified Intelligence: How will humans be augmented in the office?

Imagine a world in which humans and computers work together to extend human intelligence and enhance work. Some dangers will intensify as computing becomes more intelligent, but so will the opportunities. Computers will replace humans for specific kinds of work, but the bigger story will be about humans and computers working together to do things that have never been done before. Offices and officing will be augmented, and futureback thinking will be amplified and enhanced.

All of us will be digitally augmented in some way, with more potential for good than harm. Everyone will be amplified, some people truly enhanced. Most of us will be cyborgs—and that will be a good thing, most of the time. Even as people become increasingly augmented, the opportunities to highlight their distinct talents and contributions will increase.

Place and Time: How might virtual officing be better than being there?

Imagine a world in which you can go somewhere better, be something better, manage time better, and make something better—all without ever leaving your preferred physical location. Realities will be blended and digitally enhanced, making it easy to move between in-person and virtual experiences. In this world, we will always be online and enhanced, unless we choose to be offline in the (original in-person) real world.

By 2033, we will remember the original metaverse by its clunky virtual reality headsets. As our avatars walk alive in the future, graceful digital media interfaces will filter, clarify, and amplify our in-person experiences. We will converse with our AI companions, co-creating augmented identities.

The officeverse will emerge as a nested network of networks, not owned or controlled by anyone or any company. In the officeverse, mules will stampede. There will be a continuous carnival of wildly varied offerings, and there also will be many places focused on work. While many people still go to the officeverse to escape, many more will go there to get things done.

While in the early days, the goal of virtual meetings was to simulate in-person meetings, the new mantra will be *better* than being there. In-person meetings will be even more important than before for deeply human experiences, but the range of officeverse meetings and experiences will make impossible ways of working possible. There are many limitations to office buildings and in-person meetings. The officeverse will be a multisensory alternative virtual world that blends with and extends the physical world. Extending the physical world to anytime/anyplace is a key ingredient to creating the agile and resilient office, allowing the most qualified knowledge worker to be the decision maker regardless of hierarchical authority.

Agility: How can you coordinate with clarity—but not certainty?

Imagine a world in which agility and resilience will be prioritized over efficiency. Command-and-control will yield to clarity of intent, with leaders who are very clear about where they want to go but very flexible about how their teams of teams might get there. Everyone will have license to act freely within the envelope of clarity provided by top leadership and organizational purpose. Distributed authority hierarchies will come and go based on who is in the best position to make which decision at what time. Scenarios, simulation, and gaming will be used constantly to practice in low-risk ways for the highly uncertain future.

Economies of scale (where bigger is almost always better) will yield to economies of organization. You will be what you organize.

The Office Shock Mixing Board

To organize for the future of work, you will need to harmonize a range of choices regarding where, when, and how you work. We use a music mixing board metaphor to provide you with a framework for choice making. The mixing board will help you think futureback about your choices for offices, officing, and the officeverse.[12]

The big mistake here is to focus only on when to go back to the office or how to create hybrid offices.

Choices about where, when, and how we work are very complex. There are no simple solutions.

Based on our forecasts, there are Seven Spectrums of Choice to consider, and they begin with a careful assessment of your purpose and the outcomes you are seeking from offices and officing. Part II will give you a framework for choice making, with one chapter for each of the Seven Spectrums of Choice.

We drew inspiration from the world of music because we need more harmony in the world. Used during a performance or a recording, a mixing board is

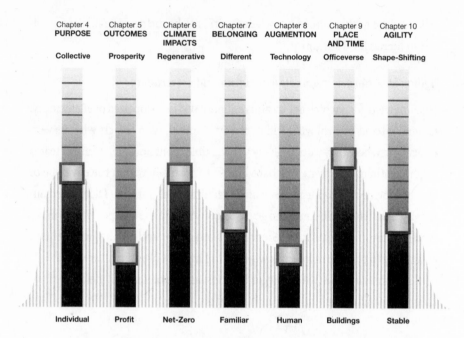

FIGURE 7: The Office Shock Mixing Board. Each chapter in part II illustrates a spectrum of choice for navigating office shock.

a panel for adjusting and combining musical sounds. A mixing board is a mechanism to blend the sounds of various instruments, across the channels for each instrument. The sliders on a mixing board can be moved up and down, allowing musicians and producers to make choices about the sounds of each channel. Most importantly, the mixing board provides a powerful place to combine individual choices to create collective, synchronized sounds.

As illustrated in figure 7, our mixing board aims to help you harmonize your choices of offices and officing, and to synchronize with others. In this way, the mixing board metaphor aims to guide a jazz-like dialogue as you seek to create with others a better future for offices and officing.[13]

The choices across the spectrums are not binary, either/or choices. There is a full spectrum of possibilities between the polarities. The mixing board provides a way to help you see and think through your choices—and the implications of your choices for others.

Your Choices to Navigate Office Shock

As you think about your own personal story across the Seven Spectrums of Choice, consider the following:

1. Imagine a world where you and your organization are empowered to make the future a better place. What might that impossible future look like and feel like to you?

2. Create a story about the kind of future workplace in which you would want to work and live. For example, your story could answer these questions:
   - What is your purpose in working in this office?
   - What outcomes will you aim to accomplish?
   - Do you have any concerns about climate change?
   - Who would be your ideal coworkers?
   - How would you like technology to enhance your abilities?
   - Where, when, and how often do you want to work?
   - How would you increase your ability to be agile and resilient?

3. What could you do now to be ready for this future?

OFFICE SHOCK
QUICK START
GUIDE

FIND YOUR FUTURE SELF
Identify your individual,
organization, or
community persona.

2 WHAT FUTURE?
Think futureback by setting
a better future with a
navigational star, illustrated
with a visual story.

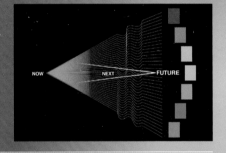

3 WHAT NEXT?
Harmonize your choices for
critical success across the
Seven Spectrums of Choice
using the Mixing Board
(see reverse side).

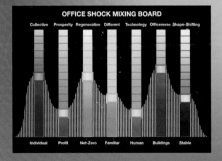

4 WHAT NOW?
Lead futureback by
synchronizing your actions
with flexive intent to create
a better future.

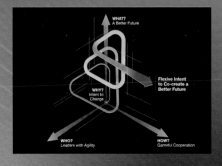

CK MIXING BOARD

across the Seven Spectrums of Choice?

ONGING	AUGMENTION	PLACE AND TIME	AGILITY
ferent	Technology	Officeverse	Shape-Shifting

| liar | Human | Buildings | Stable |

THE OFFICE SHOC

How might you harmonize your choices

	OUTCOMES	CLIMATE IMPACTS	BEL
Collective	**Prosperity**	**Regenerative**	**Di**

| **Individual** | **Profit** | **Net-Zero** | |

HOW MIGHT YOU VISUALIZE YOUR FUTURE?

Inspirational Illustrations of Futureback Stories

iFTF
Institute for the Future

For more inspiration, visit:
www.officeshock.org

PART II

WHAT NEXT?

Spectrums of Choice for Better Working and Living

I don't predict the future. All I do is look around at the problems we are neglecting now and give them about 30 years to grow into full-fledged disasters.[1]

OCTAVIA E. BUTLER

As the initial COVID-19 crisis raged, the What Next? question that preoccupied many organizations was this: When can we go back to the office?

We agree that when to go back is an important question, but it is number six on our list of Seven Spectrums of Choice for offices and officing that we introduce in part II. The first question to ask is the purpose question: *Why do you want to go to an office at all?*

There are good reasons why some organizations want physical offices, but whether or not to have an office should be a question asked, not an assumption made. You must look at a complex range of choices that cross the seven spectrums we explore—and it should not be a simple choice. Each chapter in part II applies futureback thinking to increase your clarity by spotting signals, sensing drivers, and forecasting possible futures.

The purpose of part II is to explore the question: What Next? To inform your choices for a better future, consider that each of the Seven Spectrums of Choice for offices has a sliding scale. Remember, there is a full spectrum of possibilities between each of the polarities. There are no simple binary choices.

To help imagine what's next, we invited artists from across the globe to read our forecasts and create illustrations inspired by the scenarios in each part II chapter.[2] These remarkable people (and one AI art generator called Midjourney) created the art of *Office Shock*.

We invite you to read our scenarios, look at their illustrations, and visualize your own stories.

- Purpose (chapter 4): *Sharing Navigational Stars*, Katia Herrera, Dominican Republic

- Outcomes (chapter 5): *Cascading Outcomes*, Yeti Iglesias, Mexico, and Anaelle Press, Israel

- Climate Impacts (chapter 6): *A Regenerative Office*, Dustin Jacobus, Belgium

- Belonging (chapter 7): *Celebrating Uniqueness*, Analia Iglesias, Argentina

- Augmentation (chapter 8): *Embodied Augmentation*, Proxima Centauri B, Germany

- Place and Time (chapter 9): *Officeverse Emerging*, Joseph Press, augmented by Midjourney

- Agility (chapter 10): *Braided Agility*, Yeti Iglesias, Mexico

FOUR

In Good Company

The Spectrum of Purpose

Imagine a world
in which more office workers are motivated by a sense of
purpose and meaning. Money and personal needs will still
be part of this spectrum (particularly until you reach basic
levels of safety and sustenance), but the higher ground will
be meaningful work. People will understand the wisdom
of purpose—as well as its business value. Leaders especially
will be very mindful about personal and organizational
intentions, sense of purpose, and clarity of direction.

Sharing Navigational Stars *(opposite)*
Illustration by Katia Herrera from the Dominican Republic.
*After reading this chapter, consider how you might illustrate
your story about the Spectrum of Purpose.*

Purpose is all about *intentions*. To be "in good company" is to work with people you like and respect, people who give you a sense of well-being and purpose. When in good company, people from diverse backgrounds all have a sense of belonging. Good companies are those who treat their workers well.

What was initially called The Great Resignation, where many people quit their jobs instead of returning after the COVID-19 shutdown, was a signal that many people do not believe that they are in good company. What looked like an antiwork sentiment, was much deeper. As Beyoncé's hit single of 2022 "Break My Soul" describes, resignation was a rejection of dehumanizing, boring, or destructive work.[1] It was a search for more meaningful work and life.

In 2020 when office workers were asked suddenly to stay home for the safety of themselves and others, many people began rethinking their lives. With no commuting and no activities outside of the home, some people were able to engage in activities that they loved. Some explored new hobbies. Many had extra time and space to reflect on work and life. Some people began asking themselves big questions like, Is my work meaningful to me? What brings me joy? What is my responsibility to others? Who are the people that I value most? Does my work allow me to contribute to something greater than myself?

Of course, asking such questions was a luxury that many could not afford because they didn't have a decent job or a decent place to work at home. Many people had childcare or elder care responsibilities that made the COVID-19 office shutdowns extra difficult.

The spectrum of choices for purpose on the mixing board is visualized as in figure 8. The word *purpose* can be interpreted in many ways. Usually, purpose is the reason for which something is done. On the Spectrum of Purpose, we are asking: what is your intention?

What is the purpose of your office, and officing?

Collective

Individual

FIGURE 8:
Spectrum of Purpose

The Spectrum of Purpose ranges from personal to collective, individual needs to societal needs. Office shock is fueling a shift from work as what we do to make money, to work as something transcendent, something we do that is connected to our larger goals and values. Purpose-driven people have resolve: their intentions are clear.

Hierarchy of Needs Reimagined

In 2020, psychologist Scott Barry Kaufman reconceptualized Abraham Maslow's well-known hierarchy of needs[2] in a new book called *Transcend: The New Science of Self-Actualization*.[3] Kaufman concluded that Maslow never intended his work to be depicted as a rigid pyramid. Instead, Kaufman's interpretation uses the metaphor of a sailboat floating on the choppy seas of life. Kaufman describes the hull of the boat as made up of the security dimensions of safety, connection, and self-esteem. Each of us can sail in our own direction, and the boat protects us from the dangers of the sea swelling around us. Kaufman emphasizes that life is not like climbing a pyramid on solid ground, life is more like opening a sail in the wind, a sail that is made up of the growth dimensions of exploration, love, and purpose.

Kaufman concludes with Maslow's final paper called Theory Z, where he argues that healthy people evolve their priorities from beyond themselves as they age. Kaufman writes:

> Maslow proposed that "transcenders" are [motivated] by higher ideals and values that go beyond the satisfaction of basic needs in the fulfillment of one's unique self. These meta-motivations include a devotion to a calling outside oneself . . . , to go beyond and above self-fulfillment to self-actualization. Seeking purpose is a legitimate and important human aspiration.[4]

Having purpose requires transcendence beyond your isolated self. Maslow suggested thirty-five conceptualizations of the word *transcendence*, while Kaufman offers twenty-four alternate descriptions.[5] The fact that *transcendence* is described by these two thoughtful writers using fifty-nine different words—most of them linked to purpose—suggests that purpose is both very important and very difficult to describe.

Purpose is expressed externally as the reason for doing something and can even have a set of metrics to determine its success. Purpose provides a bond with an office or a community. Purpose is a shared intent, and it can be very motivational. Meaning, on the other hand, is experienced internally and with emotions. People need both purpose and meaning. The best organizations have an explicit purpose and an officing experience that provides a sense of emotional meaning.

The Neuroscience of Purpose

In her work as CEO and chief happiness officer of Delivering Happiness, a company redesigning workplace organization around positive psychology, Jenn Lim found individuals who both do purpose-driven work and operate with a sense of purpose linked to helping others and improving broader society were most likely to be happy with their work.[6]

The brain chemistry underlying these motivations is our catalyst for change. Change starts in the brain, in an essential activity called neuroplasticity. First postulated in the late 1800s, and empirically seen every day in thousands of brain scans across the globe, neuroplasticity is the brain's ability to adapt and learn. The brain grows by creating synapses (connections between neurons) in response to experience.[7] Neuroplasticity describes the changes in nerve pathways to adapt to changes in experience. It is brain chemistry that underlies the brain's ability to adapt and learn from experience. As the neuropsychologist Donald Hebb said: "Neurons that fire together, wire together."[8]

Neuroplasticity powers the search for purpose. Seeking a better future accelerates finding purpose. When the search happens with others, purpose is amplified significantly because it is now firing in what the American psychologist Louis Cozolino refers to as the "social synapse"—neurological clusters we have in common with other people.[9]

Experiences that trigger neuroplasticity for both the individual and the collective have powerful effects. This search for meaning can be so strong that it can enable humans to overcome physical hardships. Our brains must grow.

People tend to be motivated by the hope of future rewards. Columnist David Brooks discussed unrealized hope in describing the new culture wars around the world:

Human beings are powerfully driven by what are known as thymotic desires. These are the needs to be seen, respected, appreciated. If you give people the impression that they are unseen, disrespected and unappreciated, they will become enraged, resentful, and vengeful. They will perceive diminishment as injustice and respond with aggressive indignation.[10]

Having a sense of purpose is motivating but being denied your sense of purpose is deeply threatening. Also, it is one thing to have a strong sense of purpose that makes you feel that you are right. It is quite another thing to have a strong purpose with a belief that others are wrong.

Writing about Elizabeth Holmes, the founder of Theranos, *Wall Street Journal* investigative journalist John Carreyrou said:

> Her father had drilled into her the notion that she should live a purposeful life. . . .
> The message Elizabeth took away from them [her parents] is that if she wanted to truly leave her mark on the world, she would need to accomplish something that furthered the greater good, not just become rich.[11]

Elizabeth Holmes said she had a sense of purpose, but she also lied to investors and patients. She was convicted of fraud. Purpose is a powerful motivator, but not always for good.

Living a purpose-driven life has direct positive effects on your brain. Dopamine is released in your brain to motivate you to do things you need or enjoy, such as painting a picture, reading a good book, or dancing. Praise increases dopamine levels. Knowing a reward is possible stimulates the release of dopamine to achieve the reward, to achieve the sensation of satisfaction (associated with other neurotransmitters). Fulfilling the essentials of life—exercise, food, and sex—all stimulate the release of dopamine.

In her book, *Dopamine Nation: Finding Balance in the Age of Indulgence,*[12] psychiatrist Anna Lembke documents how dopamine levels influence the balance between pleasure and pain in the brain. In the noisy present, addictive behaviors—not just to drugs and alcohol, but also to food, sex, and smartphones—happen because we overindulge, raising the levels of dopamine to beyond what we need, causing the imbalances of addiction.

Aspiration for a better future is a powerful trigger for dopamine, which empowers the brain and body to move toward that better world and adapt along the way. Dopamine drives us to find balance. It encourages us to find the good feelings of serotonin, which regulates mood and other cognitive functions, after doing something that was dopamine driven.

Finding purpose is creating harmony between our individual need for dopamine stimulus and our collective interest in making the world a better place. Meaning-making is a reward-filled world that requires understanding and modulating your own brain chemistry. Finding an equilibrium among the hierarchy of needs (from survival to transcendence) remains one of the biggest challenges of life.

Is Your Job Your Purpose?

James Suzman, in his book called *Work: A Deep History, from the Stone Age to the Age of Robots*,[13] describes how, in the preindustrialized era, people were defined by the communities where they lived. As people took jobs and moved away from those communities, they lost that personal definition and established relationships of belonging to their offices, factories, and companies. Gradually, many of them became defined by their jobs. But many of those jobs provided little sense of meaning or purpose—even if they did provide more economic security.

Now, in many parts of the world—particularly in the United States—people can be defined by their jobs. For some people, their job *is* their purpose in life. For many, work occupies so much of their time and energy that it becomes difficult to fully understand who they are outside of their office. In recent history, there has been little time or motivation for people to reflect on what matters and what they genuinely enjoy.

Being newly able to engage these big questions during the pandemic led to a shift in how people are making decisions about the work that they do as well as the people and companies with which they do it. Many workers want to do work that aligns with their goals, values, and beliefs. Although these things are rooted in an individual's perspective, they have much broader implications for the larger communities within which a person participates.

Understanding the relationship between your purpose and your work re-quires mindfulness and reflection. For example, accountants are sometimes stereotyped as one-dimensional math nerds whose necessary attention to detail prevents them from having a larger vision. But there are certainly accountants who love what they do and derive meaning from it. When asked why they chose accounting as a career path, some might say something like, "I was great at math in high school, and I love working in Excel." However, a purpose-driven ac-countant might say, "I enjoy helping people reduce their fear and stress around financial matters." While the person in each of these examples might love their work, only the accountant who enjoys helping people has understood how their work is linked to their own purpose, how it brings harmony to their life, and how it contributes to the broader society.

Particularly in the United States, people are often conditioned to make deci-sions about work based on status and income earning potential. Because certain positions are more prestigious than others and allow for more affluent living, these considerations take priority over the question of if and how a role embod-ies a person's wants and values. For some, work is not about personal enjoyment or fulfillment but rather about access to a certain lifestyle. But the reality is that work that does not fulfill us in some deeper way may not be sustainable. For this reason, it's worth thinking about the relationship between enjoyment and work. Enjoyment is a way into talking about purpose, not just what you do but why you do it. Many purpose-driven people find their sense of purpose in their work. They have moved beyond having a job to making a living in good com-pany with others.

So, the next time you meet someone for the first time at a party, instead of asking the usual, "What do you do (for a living)?" try asking "What do you *enjoy* doing?" Notice how this adjustment makes a different conversation. Office shock has given us a chance to ask ourselves if we are in good company now—or if we could be in better company.

The world's shifting relationship to work is evident in conversations around the role that work should play in one's life. Many people seem to be moving from a culture where people live to work toward one where people work to live. The pandemic has provided young professionals with the opportunity to reconfigure their relationship to purposeful work. Rather than seeking purpose through their passions outside of work, while finding work that allows financial security, some are increasingly engaged in lucrative freelance work that incorporates their passions, rather than full-time jobs where they were underpaid and overworked.

The Nap Ministry[14] believes rest is a spiritual practice and a racial and social justice issue. It explores the liberating and restorative power of naps and has a catchy rallying cry: "Rest Is Resistance." Tricia Hersey, a performance artist and healer, was inspired to create the Nap Ministry while studying the science of sleep and sleep deprivation. She began experimenting with rest as a portal to connect with her enslaved ancestors, whose "rest and dream space were stolen from them." Rest gives people time to think about basic questions about work and life, and to create new synapses for changing behavior.

In China, young professionals have been rallying under the concept of lying flat. Lying flat,[15] known as "tang ping" in Chinese, is a growing philosophy and movement that challenges competitiveness. As a reaction to being held to such high standards for academic and work excellence, many Chinese millennials are opting to "lay flat" by doing the bare minimum. This means not striving to build their career through attaining high-power and high-pay positions. Some are even choosing not to have children as a form of resistance, saying they don't want to bring more people into a culture that they deem unhealthy.

Purpose-Driven Organizations

Office shock will give everyone a better chance to seek out or create our own good company. Organizations like the B Corp certify companies that seek to benefit all people, communities, and the planet.[16]

New legal models are enabling and encouraging companies to take steps along the Spectrum of Purpose. The Public Benefit LLC, first established in August 2018, is a for-profit limited liability entity to promote a general or specific social public benefit. It has additional statutory requirements to be transparent, accountable, and to uphold its public benefit purpose while maintaining its fiduciary duties.

Taking advantage of this new legal entity, in 2018 Danone North America decided to become the world's largest Public Benefit Corporation. In 2020 the parent company Danone followed suit by incorporating purpose into its articles of association under a new legal entity in France called "enterprise à mission." The board accepted salary reductions to finance the Dan'Cares program of employees' health coverage. The strategic objective of Danone's new CEO is to accelerate the path to becoming a globally certified B Corp.[17]

Another example is the Community Interest Company (CIC), created in the United Kingdom in 2005, which allows for easy to establish organizations with all the flexibility and certainty of the company form, but with some special features to ensure they are working for the benefit of the community. Examples of CICs range widely. Innovative Training Centers such as Striding Out[18] (located in London) focus on helping young social entrepreneurs. Affordable Natural Health Centers, such as The Healing Clinic[19] (located in York, UK), offers an array of alternative therapies and keeps them affordable for the entire community served.

The Purpose Foundation provides another example of a new corporate structure that creates a perpetual-purpose trust for socially conscious business owners to protect their organizations. The foundation works with business owners to use existing trust laws to embody whatever pro-social values are desired by the owner(s) into the legal framework of the organization. Camille Canon, the cofounder and executive director, speaks futureback when she says:

> We often think of the system as unchangeable when, in fact, the rules can be rewritten. The imperative to make money can be transformed into a requirement to do good. "It's not sufficient to just have an idea of what the future could look like—you have to make it actually possible in practice," Canon said. Business owners now have a potent new tool to translate their ideas for a better future into reality.[20]

Being a purpose-driven company is hard, and as Neil Bedwell wrote in *Forbes*, "it's not enough."[21] If a purpose is co-created, it can shift officing from solely transactional to more meaningful engagement for change.

Purpose Imbedded in Place

The Spectrum of Purpose can go even further than good companies by physically building good communities. [freespace][22] is a collaborative initiative that works with community members to co-create spaces by temporarily transforming vacant buildings into community hubs for cultural and civic engagement. Our IFTF colleagues Ilana Lipsett, Mike Zuckerman, and a team of community members in San Francisco created the [freespace] concept during an economic boom. The [freespace] team convinced a landlord to lease them an unused building for $1 and turn it into a place where anyone in the neighborhood could experience art, culture, dialogue, public input, and new opportunities for a period of a few months. [freespace] had only two rules: (1) Everything is free and, (2) Everything was participatory. The result was a shared workplace and community imbued with purpose. It was a physical space in which different social ecosystems could meet, interact, and create together.[23] Now [freespace] communities are happening in other parts of the world, particularly after crises.

Architects over the years have sought to infuse the physical environment with purpose. For example, Frank Gehry's design for the Guggenheim Museum in Bilbao, Spain: Originally designed to reinvigorate the ailing port city of Bilbao, since its inauguration in 1997, it has evolved into a complete rejuvenation of not only the city but the entire region, with a renaissance of local culture. Dubbed the "Guggenheim Effect," not only does the building ask people to reinterpret its purpose, its presence sparks reinvention.[24]

The Guggenheim Museum reflects how co-creating purpose can be at the epicenter of changing the relationship between actors in a community. Economist Mariana Mazzucato argues that we should change organizations and governance structures in the design of the practical levers of economic policy—the tools we need to build a purpose-oriented economy. Mazzucato concludes by stating:

Only by redirecting our economy—with notions of the common good and public value of the center of production, distribution and consumption—can we shape and co-create the economy to produce a more inclusive and sustainable society.[25]

Although many companies are calling themselves purpose driven, Mazzucato argues that "not much is changing."[26] Perhaps it is because the word has so many different definitions that company claims are not authentic (as with "greenwashing" where companies claim environmental standing when not credible) or that the definitions are too abstract. Purpose is often imbedded in work culture and may not be explicit. There is a rising acknowledgment that traditional definitions of purpose will not be enough to make a difference in a VUCA world. Mazzucato emphasizes that co-creating public purpose is critical to economic and political change. This is not an easy task.

Shared Missions

In 1973, economist John Kenneth Galbraith wrote in his landmark book *Economics and the Public Purpose* that the American economy had been captured by business interests and government had lost its way.[27] Forty years later, French economist Thomas Piketty argued that wealth inequality will only continue unless knowledge, skills, and wealth is redistributed.[28]

In 2021, Mariana Mazzucato builds on both to rethink the narrative of innovation in *Mission Economy: A Moonshot Guide to Changing Capitalism*. She describes how social purpose can guide how public and private actors work together to co-create what she calls public value. Expanding on the example of the United States placing the first man on the moon, she proposes the creation of "mission maps" to address wicked problems of education and health regarding climate change. In Mazzucato's view, "public" does not mean the government acting alone, but rather acting with the community, in the public interest.[29]

Increasing consciousness around social injustice and economic inequality are catalysts for change. Since 2017, we have seen an uptick in awareness surrounding social justice issues as reflected through movements such as #MeToo and Black Lives Matter as well as increasing climate activism. Although COVID-19 alone did not begin conversations around gender and race equity or climate change, the pandemic served as a catalyst for individuals and organizations to think more deeply about these issues. Some social movement scholars classify COVID-19 as a "trigger movement," a sudden historical event that shifts the social, political, and economic trajectory:

> Trigger events can create confusion and unease. But they also present tremendous opportunities for people who have a plan and know how to use the moment to push forward their agendas.[30]

The UN Sustainable Development Goals raise the significance of purpose as a motivator for people because they also trigger what neuroscientist Andrew Huberman refers to as *prosocial* activity. The Sustainable Development Goal that explicitly addresses meaningful work (Goal #8) emphasizes the importance of economic security for both the individual and the organization. It is important to harmonize both ends of the spectrum to find the right mix for you and your organization's future.

The Wisdom of Purpose

The Spectrum of Purpose invites more conscious choices along the path of creating a mix between individual and collective purpose. These choices will not be easy, because purpose is often defined narrowly. Such categorical thinking pushes people away from exploring the nuances of purpose, essential in creating better futures for working and living.

Thinking futureback about this spectrum is a potent way to demonstrate the wisdom required to span the complexities of purpose. Kaufman describes this trait as an "openness to experience, the capacity for self-examination and introspection, motivation for personal growth, and the willingness to remain skeptical of oneself, continually questioning assumptions and beliefs, and exploring in evaluating new information that is relevant to one's identity."[31]

Clinical psychologist Deirdre Kramer describes how wisdom enables individuals to span the spectrum toward more collective purpose:

Wise people have learned to view the positive and negative and synthesize them to create a more human, more integrated sense of self, in all its frailty and vulnerability. ... They seem able to first embrace and then transcend self-concerns to integrate their capacity for introspection with a deep and abiding concern for human relationships and generative concern for others.[32]

Thinking futureback, leaders will need to play the wisdom game to attract people who are seeking meaningful work and harmony between themselves and their offices, to provide a chance for them to be in good company with others.

Your Choices on the Spectrum of Purpose

The Spectrum of Purpose invites you to move the mixing board slider between Individual and Collective, in search of harmony. This first pass will set you up to make your choices more specific in part III for you as an individual, your organization, and your community.

As you think about your own personal story across this spectrum, consider these questions:

1. How might you illustrate your story about a future with a more positive experience of purpose?

2. Do you derive a personal sense of meaning from your work today? If not, how would you change your experience of purpose?

3. What social value (beyond your own personal income) are you contributing through your officing?

4. Does your organization enhance your individual purpose by having a corporate purpose that is linked to community, beyond individuals?

5. Does your organization have a focus on stakeholders, in addition to shareholders?

6. How can thinking futureback enhance your ability to seek meaningful work?

FIVE

Pursuing Prosperity

The Spectrum of Outcomes

Imagine a world
in which offices generate both financial return and social value.
Corporations will provide vital bridges between working and
living, increasing prosperity (social assets and shared value) for
more people—both shareholders and stakeholders. New models
of ownership and membership will emerge to empower people
to feel a great stake in the outcomes that their organizations
produce. It will be possible to achieve harmony between
personal and social profit—even in a corporate setting.

Cascading Outcomes *(opposite)*
Illustration by Yeti Iglesias from Mexico and Anaelle Press from Israel.
*After reading this chapter, consider how you might illustrate your story about
the Spectrum of Outcomes.*

Where the Spectrum of Purpose (chapter 4) focused on *intentions*, chapter 5 on the Spectrum of Outcomes focuses on *results*.

What outcomes will you aim to accomplish with your office, and officing?

The results of officing should bring more prosperity to individuals, organizations, workers, and communities. In September 2020, the World Economic Forum published a report calling for a rebalancing of shareholder value with stakeholder value.[1] The WEF proposed metrics for measuring what they called *stakeholder capitalism*, a system in which corporations are oriented to serve the interests of all their stakeholders, including local communities. The report proposed four principles—governance, planet, people, and prosperity—to improve the ways in which companies measure and demonstrate their performance against the UN Sustainable Development Goals.

The Spectrum of Outcomes, illustrated in figure 9, is about the value of office work and the results it produces. Spanning this spectrum between profit and prosperity reveals an opportunity to reflect on how we define value, how we organize ourselves, who makes decisions, the nature of working relationships, and ultimately our economic models.

FIGURE 9:
Spectrum of Outcomes

Futureback thinking can yield clarity on these complex choices so conscientious leaders can walk the path toward a more inclusive and prosperous future reality. Choosing where to participate and how to succeed in office shock raises profound questions for all offices. The choices on the Spectrum of Outcomes are wide and nonbinary.

Value for Whom?

Many business leaders and economists[2] argue for a rethinking of Milton Friedman's conclusion that the only social responsibility of business is to create value for shareholders.[3] In *The Value of Everything: Making and Taking in the Global Economy*, Mariana Mazzucato sees that some players in market economies get rich by extracting value from those who create it and not adding value themselves.[4] She argues that reevaluating the activities that create wealth will trigger a new valuation for the work, and the workers as well. In this manner, rebalancing value-extraction with value-creation, organizational outcomes can become catalysts for cultivating a healthy economy and society.

What kind of value do you want to create? Yanis Varoufakis identifies a critical difference in economic activities that create experiential value versus exchange value. Experiential value is meaningful—a wonderful dinner conversation, a beautiful sunset, fulfilling a favor for a friend. The value of these experiences is essentially intrinsic, they cannot be tangibly shared with others. Exchange value, on the other hand, is when we can receive something in exchange for something we have to offer (i.e., money for services or products). Varoufakis argues that these conceptions of value belie the confusion between goods and commodities in the modern era.[5] He argues that goods need to go back to having goodness—filling our life with good feelings—whereas commodities need to re-focus on being things (products and services) that we can exchange with others.

Defining value is at the heart of choosing where you want to play across the Spectrum of Outcomes. It enables us to choose if we are providing experiences for others or supporting the production of products or services. These are the catalysts needed to reinvigorate an ongoing commitment of organizations to improve the lives of individuals, communities, and the planet. Despite a growing enthusiasm for outcomes with greater social value, determining how to best pursue—or even measure—value can be difficult. Futureback thinking encourages leaders to consider better outcomes for society, beyond just financial performance.

Distributed Value

For many years, organizations were designed for efficiency and control, stemming from Frederick Taylor's seminal work. But this view failed to capture the complexity of social and economic life within organizations.[6] The realities of production and management combined with the prevailing theory resulted in workers (metaphorically and sometimes literally) who became parts of an efficient machine, designed to generate profit for owners and their shareholders—but often not social value for the larger society.

This traditional model of organizations is challenged in a world with pervasive outsourcing of production with armies of gig workers. Professor Jerry Davis, in his book *The Vanishing American Corporation*,[7] points out that the number of corporations today is about half of what it was twenty-five years ago. He sees the digital transformation of economic activity as drastically reducing transaction costs and reshaping the markets for both goods and workers. He argues new models will replace the traditional company, and in response to COVID-19 the trend will only accelerate.[8]

While there are many concerns arising from the digitalization of markets— particularly the unequal distribution of wealth and the transactional relationship with those creating value—these new technologies are sparking a shift away from Taylorism toward new definitions of efficiency and new outcomes.

The decentralized autonomous organization (DAO) will become supercharged when Web3 brings more potential for decentralized governance and regulation.[9] Cabin, for instance, is a DAO started outside Austin, Texas, to manage a set of homes. The group's cofounder, Jonathan Hillis, had previously left a job at Instacart and built a house in the countryside. He brought friends to stay there, and they had the idea to start a residency program for other tech creators.

> "We didn't intend to be a DAO. The DAO tools were the best tools to accomplish what we were trying to accomplish".... Hillis described the organization as a "decentralized city," aiming to build spaces around the world and connect them through digital tools.... With any technology, Hillis said, "eventually the infrastructure becomes invisible." Ultimately, the DAO framework matters less than what an organization actually accomplishes.[10]

Web3-based platforms have the potential to span this spectrum toward prosperity. These platforms enable members to own the means of production, access shared resources within the remit of their expertise, and be eligible for a fair percentage of profits.[11] As Aaron Dignan, author of *Brave New Work* and cohost of the *Brave New Work* podcast, writes: "the full potential of blockchain smart contracts is the basis for new kinds of on-chain organizations that resemble the open, participatory, and adaptive organizations."[12] These technologies will not only digitalize governance but also create new models of ownership. However, Web3 and blockchain are in their infancy and many have already tried to subvert their use, so watchful waiting will be critical in the use of such new technologies.

Coupled with robotics and machine learning, decision-making in these new organizations will be quite different from traditional organizational models. With blockchain-based smart contracts, or the tokens of Web3, human managerial tasks like verifying and monitoring could fundamentally change. In a future where the need for oversight and control will be significantly reduced, leaders of organizations will be freer to choose how to organize themselves.

New Models for Ownership

A growing variety of more equitable enterprise models indicates a shift away from business models based on pure profit for shareholders toward prosperity for everyone who contributes to creating value, that is, stakeholders. The Spectrum of Outcomes provides options for sliding the scale for harmonizing between profit and prosperity.

Most companies are owner-managed, by founders, partners, or shareholders. There are other models, however, such as worker-owned cooperatives. There are many variations, with the key choice being the distribution of economic stake and decision-making power. In traditional organizational models, economic stake usually comes in the form of shares and decision-making in the form of representation. Research indicates that providing both is a powerful way to engage employees for both profit and prosperity.[13] Marina Gorbis sees the emergence of a worldwide digital coordination economy as an opportunity for *Prosperity By Design*.[14]

A traditional corporation is a hierarchical structure owned and managed by people within a legal framework. Given the potential conflict of interest between profit and prosperity, Nick Romeo, in the *New Yorker* in early 2022, asked a critical question: "Can Companies Force Themselves to Do Good?"[15] The answer lies with ownership, and like the nuances of value and organizational models, ownership can come in a variety of forms.

Romeo's article highlighted the work of the Purpose Foundation. Originally launched in Germany in 2015 and in California in 2017, the Purpose Foundation advises companies to transition to a new kind of corporate structure, the perpetual-purpose trust, that can make the values of prosocial companies permanent. The foundation works with companies to either design or transition their legal structure to protect the social values of the founders. In addition, they help find investors who support this concept and are willing to back these new trust structures despite lower expected returns on their investment.[16] Companies like OrganicallyGrown,[17] Wildplastic,[18] and Einhorn[19] are signals of a new potential for steward-ownership. Steward-ownership is an example of futureback thinking in models of ownership: the owners' vision of their company provides a permanent prosocial outcome that involves looking well into the future and then applying the tools to make this future a reality.

In the current version of DAOs, blockchain-based tokens offer members the opportunity to earn and vote, "different than any previous attempts at creating liquid democracies."[20] In 2019, OpenLaw became the first limited liability for-profit DAO, named the LAO. In April 2021, Wyoming governor Mark Gordon signed Bill 38 recognizing DAOs as LLCs. These and other DAO LLCs are moving worker democracy into new models of shared capitalism for the digital age. The DAO mechanism is a signal of what may become a new model; particularly if Web3 fulfills the promise of decentralizing the web. We recommend watching this space closely as these are strong signals of changing how more equitable enterprises might be organized.

In addition, the convergence of innovative ownership models and technologies is happening with platform cooperatives. Although the usefulness of cooperatives has been challenged in the past,[21] Nathan Schneider, in his book *Everything for Everyone*, illustrates that with new technology the model can help realize the important intentions of democratic decision-making and employee ownership.[22] Zebras Unite is taking the platform co-op model into entrepreneurship. This community of entrepreneurs, investors, and allies is dedicated to building companies that balance both profit and purpose. It pools resources and teaches how to build more inclusive and ethical entrepreneurship.[23]

New Models for Membership

Changing offices into communities with active members will require a different kind of organizational structure and technological support. A model of membership that includes how the organization can contribute to a social and secure identity gives meaning and agency to the community members. Membership restores the agency of workers and rejuvenates worker dignity in opportunities for ownership and influence. Membership allows individual workers to actively harmonize their choices on the Spectrum of Outcomes in sync with the organization itself. It combines what may be two steps in other organizations where employees do not have the influence of membership to work in concert with the organization. Membership enables harmony to be found more easily, leading to better futures of working and living.

Considering the ways to be an active member in an organization is an important catalyst of organizing for greater prosperity. It opens choices for individual workers ranging from the transactional contracts of freelancers to workplace democracy practices[24] and financial stakes, proportional to the value of the contributions.[25]

In a hyperconnected world, workers still need to make a living, regardless of what the organization's intended outcomes are. As organizations embrace the transactional model of hiring freelance experts, there is concern that officing can become an endless series of unconnected gigs, where individual workers move on to the next task for hire. But for many office workers the freelance model means they do not have to be stuck in a specific job. They can freelance to do a variety of work that appeals to them. This allows everyone to both be an expert in certain areas and a student in others. It allows lifelong learning and growth. It helps bring creativity and variety to the individual's workplace.

Regardless of the contractual relationship, meaningful employment is based on practices that include fair compensation, good benefits, reasonable work hours and expectations, flexible schedules, and possibly remote working options. Membership benefits like health care, retirement, stocks, and other incentives should be designed to encourage collective behavior in the offices and officing.[26] However, in a world of freelance working, some of these traditional benefits may be provided, not by the hiring organization, but by third parties such as professional organizations. The primary form of payment from an organization to a worker for a specific task may be the only thing that resembles what happens today.

Although these practices are necessary, they are not sufficient for making work more meaningful. Nor can they instill a sense of membership in a community by themselves. These outcomes and the effort to create them will become more meaningful when they are aligned to individual aspirations and collective needs. For the individual, meaningful employment engages neurological stimulation and social cognition in more explicit ways. Although exercising our cognitive functions—like setting goals, completing, or failing at those tasks—is fundamental, both individual and collective learning will become an explicit experience when officing.

When employment choices become meaningful experiences, the way to achieve outcomes will not be about hiring. Outcomes will increase by matching opportunities to interests. Technology will match people with tasks more effectively than anything we have seen previously. This will allow both the hiring entity and the individual to connect in more meaningful ways. The review of qualifications could become more holistic, considering experience more than formal degrees, and in the process, open more resources for professional and personal development.

More clarity on what is needed will enable better aligning with what we aspire to, individually and collectively. Offering more meaningful opportunities will trigger a shift in how work is distributed. This shift can potentially open new opportunities to traditionally marginalized groups who have better knowledge of how to best contribute to the prosperity of their community.

More Equitable Economies

As markets emerged as places for economic activity, some raised a fundamental question: is social good best achieved individually or through coordinated action?[27] One economist, Kate Raworth, proposes a reconceptualization of economics she calls Doughnut Economics.

Doughnut Economics seeks to change our goal from surviving amid supply and demand, to thriving inside interdependent social and ecological spheres. Raworth's image of a doughnut provides an alternative language to help us shift away from the insatiable linear models of growth. Doughnut Economics aims for the far bigger goal of the twenty-first century: "meeting the human rights of every person within the means of our life-giving planet."[28] Her model recognizes that human behavior can be "cooperative and caring, just as it can be competitive and individualistic." Using system thinking, Doughnut Economics acknowledges the complexity and interdependency between economic activity and the social living world. It calls for turning today's degenerative economies into regenerative ones and divisive economies into economies that distribute wealth more broadly and fairly.

These and other signals of more equitable models are all based on the assumption that economies of scale (where bigger is almost always better) will yield to economies of organization (where your ability to thrive is dependent on what you can organize). This new narrative is a catalyst intended to mobilize organizations to leverage office shock to accelerate the transition to more sustainable practices for regenerating the communities that organizations are intended to serve.

As economic models evolve and new ones emerge, signals abound that indicate measurement will look different in a more equitable economy. Many countries[29] are exploring new metrics to rectify the limitations of Gross Domestic Product, or GDP. GDP is the monetary value of all finished goods and services made within a country during a specific time period and includes costs and waste as economic development. It does not include informal or unrecorded economic activity, such as volunteer work, nor the value of education, leisure time, or household production. It emphasizes material output without considering overall well-being.[30]

Equitable Enterprises

The Institute for the Future's research on "Equitable Enterprises" is an ongoing exploration into the accelerated evolution of new models of ownership.[31]

A multitude of institutions are organizing themselves differently to distribute assets and wealth equitably among those who contribute value. The increase in stewardship and employee-owned companies signals significant change. Equitable enterprises aim to reverse decades-long policies and practices based on the idea that the only social responsibility of business is to increase shareholder profits. These enterprises bring alternative models of ownership, such as partnership, stewardship, cooperative, and commons. Their goal is to distribute value more equally, replacing the economic inefficiencies of hierarchy with more flat and transparent models.

For many mature companies, shifting to a more equitable entity will be nearly impossible. The inertia of business and organizational models built primarily for profit will render even the bravest of decision makers docile in the face of executive commitments, shareholders, and board members who are accustomed to the profit paradigms. But their future success may depend on this change.

Thinking full spectrum about facilitating the shift toward more prosperity and community benefit requires imagination to define the new norms emerging in the post-pandemic, inequitable world grappling with climate crises. Using futureback thinking will inspire the creation of new stories with narratives of a shared journey to a more equitable economy, delivering social as well as financial value to the members of the communities we serve. As more young people enter the workforce they will challenge current office practices about racial justice, gender equity, and climate impacts. They will bring their own values into the workplace and create more office shock. Only futureback thinking now will prepare organizational leaders for the impact of these workers.

A key element in considering how to transition to more social value is the focus on what we do when we work. In an increasingly virtual world, what will be meaningful catalysts for bringing people together for collective action? Choices that contribute to creating communities will be critical. Finding harmony among the choices of the spectrum will be key. The higher ground is choice, and the choices on the Spectrum of Outcomes are challenging.

An Economics of Hope

A new narrative is required to accelerate the transition to more equitable economics and enterprises. Mazzucato calls for serious reforms, including focusing the financial sector on long-run investments,[32] changing the governance structures to focus less on the share price, and legally curbing the excesses of executive pay.[33] She argues that such changes can stimulate what is needed in economic models today: An economics of hope.[34]

Just before the outbreak of COVID-19, Thomas L. Friedman wrote a column called "The Answers to Our Problems Aren't as Simple as Left or Right: The Old Binary Choices No Longer Work." Friedman quotes IFTF executive director Marina Gorbis when she says:

> The answer is not socialism or abandoning free markets, but a vibrant state that can use taxes and regulations to reshape markets in ways that divide the pie, grow the pie, and create more public wealth—mass transit, schools, parks, scholarships, libraries, and basic scientific research—so that more individuals, start-ups, and communities have more tools to adapt and thrive.[35]

Friedman ends his analysis by observing that "real solutions require a left-wing wrench, a right-wing hammer, and all sorts of new tools and combinations we never imagined.... Leave your rigid right-left grid on the hook outside the door. That's happening locally. But tackling that nationally (or globally) is very difficult."[36]

Thriving does not necessarily mean growing. Alternatives for more abundance are on the rise.[37] The paradigm shifts of Doughnut Economics and other economic evolutions offer a spectrum of choices for brave organizations and the citizens they serve. They demonstrate that economies of organization will be more important than economies of scale. It is time to choose economic models with more hope.

Your Choices on the Spectrum of Outcomes

As you think about your own personal story across this spectrum, consider these questions:

1. How might you illustrate your story about a future with more positive outcomes?

2. What are the desired results or outcomes—both individual and social—that you are seeking from your office?

3. Who is obtaining value from the outcomes of your work and the work of your organization?

4. How might you organize yourself to increase a sense of membership among your workers? Will this call for a new model of ownership?

5. What path do you want to take in the pursuit of increasing prosperity for all your stakeholders?

SIX

Beyond Sustainablity

The Spectrum of Climate Impacts

Imagine a world
in which people (in a messy and haphazard way) figure
out how to equalize the balance between production and
consumption. Circular design on a global scale will revolutionize
the throwaway society of 2023. Symbiosis and regeneration
will be credible mantras. Offices around the world will know
their carbon allotment and use AI to keep track of their goals.
Giving up some privacy for individuals will be necessary to
create a better climate balance. PPP—People Planet Prosperity—
will express the intention and direction of change.

A Regenerative Office (*opposite*)
Illustration by Dustin Jacobus from Belgium.
*After reading this chapter, consider how you might illustrate
your story about the Spectrum of Climate Impacts.*

This chapter builds on chapter 5 to go deeper on what we feel is the dominant outcome to be concerned about over the next decade, epic climate emergencies. Certainly, there are many urgent futures to be concerned about, but regenerating life on this planet is so very basic. Office buildings in the past have been more the source of climate problems than solutions. Office shock has created new opportunities to do much better.

Epic Climate Emergencies

Around the world, people are already experiencing chronic climate emergencies such as droughts,[1] increasing food insecurity, wildfires, and decreasing biodiversity with entire species disappearing. Infrastructure at risk includes airports, hospitals, police stations, power stations, schools, hazardous waste sites, and military bases. Climate is now a global security issue. These dangers go even beyond the damage to the planet, including conflicts between countries, rising numbers of climate refugees, and state competition over resources.[2] Above us, satellite and debris pollution in space is already a problem affecting the international viability of low earth orbit.

We are at the intersection of major climate-related disruptions in animal and insect populations, human health, and land use. We know that people, organizations, and offices that cause emission of greenhouse gases create costs for everyone on the planet. Although the super-rich may pine for another planet and tech leaders may seek refuge in the metaverse, mother earth is going to be our home for the foreseeable future. The cost will be highest for those who consume the least. Future generations will pay the most.

Spanning the Spectrum of Climate Impacts, as illustrated in figure 10, will not be easy. The UK Design Council offers a systemic design approach to go

What will be the climate impacts of your office, and officing?

Regenerative

Net-Zero

FIGURE 10: Spectrum of Climate Impacts

Beyond Net Zero, but more than methods will be required.[3] Booker Prize nominee Amitav Ghosh frames our challenge well:

> When future generations look back upon the Great Derangement, they will certainly blame the leaders and politicians of this time for their failure to address the climate crisis. . . . But they may well hold artists and writers to be equally culpable—for the imagining of possibilities is not, after all, the job of politicians and bureaucrats.[4]

Climate-Negative Supply Chains

In the corporate real estate industry, architect Frank Duffy argued that the root cause of climate abuse by offices is the office supply chain and its incentives. Facility managers should be rewarded for maintaining highly sustainable environments, not merely reducing costs. Design and construction professionals should be rewarded for making the most imaginative and efficient use of existing spaces, rather than for new building. Finance and development providers should be rewarded for sustainably managing what exists already, rather than new ventures.

There is so much that we can all do to improve the regenerative capabilities of offices. Critical choices must be made to change consumption, produce with circularity, and regenerate the planet. Office shock could be a much-needed spark for the choices about our future that could rein in impending disasters. Office shock is an opportunity to reverse the many unsuccessful attempts at doing the right thing, and the window of opportunity is closing quickly.

As we were writing this book, the UN Secretary-General, António Guterres, reacted to the Intergovernmental Panel on Climate Change (IPCC) Sixth Assessment Report published on April 4, 2022.[5] He said the report reveals "a litany of broken climate promises" by governments and businesses. He even accused many of lying when claiming to be on track to limiting future heating to 1.5°C above preindustrial levels. In a strongly worded rebuke, he said: "It is a file of shame, cataloguing the empty pledges that put us firmly on track towards an unlivable world." It's "now or never" if the world is to stave off climate disaster.[6]

While technical solutions are necessary, they are an insufficient condition to bringing about a change in behavior. To have an effect, we will need to change minds and systems. A climate positive future will need to incorporate social, economic, political, and cultural changes. The Spectrum of Climate Impacts addresses this urgent need and provides a way to examine the span of choices from net-zero, where people and offices do not contribute to the emission of greenhouse gases, to Regenerative, where active steps can be taken to cultivate and renew the resources of our planet. Finding the harmony of choices that will enable you to fight in this battle for survival is critical to a better future.

Offices and officing have an opportunity to be an important catalyst in climate choices. Buildings and their construction are among the largest contributors to global resource use.

In considering the opportunity offices can play in changing the narrative for a better future, Duffy offered a stark indictment of traditional offices:

> The Taylorist office building has been a perfect machine for delivering environmental degradation because it's so completely the product of supply side thinking which overrides user interests, ignores the public good and takes no account of collateral damage.[7]

A sustainable future requires making choices today to make a climate-positive impact. The office can be the place where organizations converge on a shared purpose of sustainability. To take advantage of the opportunity of office shock, we can think futureback to change consumption, produce with circularity, and regenerate the planet.

To Consume or Not to Consume?

The choices each person can make to reduce greenhouse gases are plentiful, but many of those choices are painful. Individuals can try to eliminate all plastic in daily life, for example, but plastic presence is nearly everywhere. Many of today's recycling efforts simply move the problem to another location. Driving or sharing an all-electric vehicle uses a battery containing unsustainably mined materials. Electric usage in homes is only as efficient as the grid it is connected to. Building housing that uses geothermal energy for heating and cooling will still create emissions in the construction process. The choices of what we consume, and how often, are only as effective as the organizations that provide the products.

Organizations also are able to decrease their carbon footprints in their offices through a variety of options. For example, they can allow knowledge workers to work from home to reduce commuting. They can choose building materials that sequester carbon while using HVAC systems with alternative energy sources like geothermal. They can educate and incentivize employees to be regenerators rather than mindless consumers.

Although the consumption choices for organizations have similarities to consumer choices, there is a very important difference. In the office, our business choices are influenced by the drive to prosper, succeed, and win. The question now, in the face of the degradation of our planet, is how organizations can choose sustainable options rather than those based purely on consumption underlying growth.

The climate crisis should encourage us to make more conscious choices about consumption. If individuals begin to see themselves as part of a larger community that shares the bounty of the earth without destroying it for future generations, then organizations that seek to fulfill every desire may consider more consciously their role in the value chain.

A Circular Economy

People will need to choose between unfettered consumption and the more sustainable choices of extending the life of our possessions through repair, reuse, donation, and recycling. Thinking futureback, we will all ask ourselves: Where do our products come from, and how far up the value chain are they truly sustainable? What happens after we purchase and use a product, and can it contribute to a new product or experience for someone else?

According to the World Economic Forum's definition, a circular economy is an industrial system that is restorative or regenerative by intention and design. It replaces the end-of-life concept with restoration, shifts toward the use of renewable energy, eliminates the use of toxic chemicals, which impair reuse and return to the biosphere, and aims for the elimination of waste through the superior design of materials, products, systems, and business models.[8] In the near future, the internet of everything will provide data that will make the circularity of products, from cradle to rebirth, completely and cheaply visible.

Futurist William Gibson made it clear how important it will be for local, regional, and global communities to make major changes in our behavior around the effects of climate change:

> All imagined futures lacking recognition of anthropogenic climate change will increasingly seem absurdly shortsighted. Virtually the entire genre will be seen to have utterly missed the single most important thing we were doing with technology.[9]

Our children—and especially our grandchildren—will ask, "What were they thinking? Why didn't they do something about climate emergencies?" The most basic strategic choice is about the range of circularity. In a hyperconnected world, circular production is not enough. Most global companies have global supply chains, so they have visibility on the raw materials and how they are sourced. Environmental, social, and corporate governance (ESG) will be the baseline in setting priorities for the range of products and services. These criteria are a set of standards for a company's operations that socially conscious investors use to screen potential investments. Environmental criteria consider how a company performs as a steward of nature. Social criteria examine how it manages relationships with employees, suppliers, customers, and the communities where it operates. Governance deals with a company's leadership, executive pay, audits, internal controls, and shareholder rights. These criteria are becoming an increasingly popular way for investors to evaluate companies as well as avoid investing in companies that might pose risks to their own criteria.

In addition, the way a product is handed over to a consumer influences the choices of business models. Ownership of a product versus renting it to the consumer will influence the business models as offices transition to more sustainable practices. Across all industries more strategic choices will need to be made to fight climate change. In the automotive industry, more local transportation, sharing and climate-friendly mobility infrastructure will rebalance ownership with exclusivity to sharing and inclusivity. For example, BedZED[10] in the United Kingdom is a large-scale, mixed-use, zero-carbon community that was built sustainably and includes homes and office space. One of the amenities is a car club where cars are available for the residents to share, thereby reducing vehicle ownership. The notion and need for ownership are choices underlying circularity.

New Ownership Models

Thinking futureback, we will need to view our products like our pets—something you own for its lifetime. Just as any person should carefully consider the act of acquiring a pet and its long-term consequences, we will need to start thinking the same way for every product we acquire. Ownership of goods can remain with the producer, with responsibility to resell, recycle, or even repurpose.

In a sustainable future, new business models will need to make a strategic choice: control the linearity of the value chain or move toward a more circular business model. The latter contains a business model choice: produce only when necessary, and offer to repair, recover, recycle, or even better, reuse the basic materials.[11]

For example, jeans have had a negative impact on the environment due to the large amounts of water and energy used in the manufacturing process. In addition, the way jeans are designed makes it difficult to remake and recycle them. For the fashion industry, redesigning this iconic fashion staple became the perfect starting point on the journey toward more circularity. Together with the Ellen MacArthur Foundation, the Jeans Redesign initiative brought together sixty collaborators and competitors across the jeans value chain to create the standards to transform the way jeans are made.[12] The resulting guidelines for brands, mills, and manufacturers has become "a blueprint for collective action to scale circular practices."[13]

Another example of circular design is Chikatai, a company located in the country of Georgia:

Chikatai launched its Toy Hospital, with the aim to raise awareness about over-consumption and encourage customers to fix rather than discard their soft toys, promoting responsible consumption through reducing post-consumer waste. They also developed a recycled line of baby décor and toys, where pre-consumer waste from the cutting stage and leftover fabrics from other companies are collected and given a new life.[14]

The new business models will trigger another choice, do we continue to compete, or can we cooperate? Thinking futureback, with the shared vision of "People Planet Prosperity" and enabled by technology, we envision new partnerships flourishing across the entire value web, not just supply chains but also customer and consumer relationships.

Needed: More Regenerative Communities

Climate change requires us to imagine how we can work together to create a more sustainable society. Indeed, sustainability is focused on eliminating carbon emissions and is dependent on an economy that is circular. However, sustainability needs to be much broader than this functional focus. Climate change is a systemic problem, and the solution will only emerge when all community members can thrive, not just survive. As architect Bill Reed wrote in 2007:

> Sustainability is a progression towards a functional awareness that all things are connected; that the systems of commerce, building, society, geology, and nature are really one system of integrated relationships; that these systems are co-participants in the evolution of life.[15]

A regenerative economy promotes care rather than carelessness, cooperation rather than competition, creating abundance rather than depleting resources. It necessitates making choices to avoid the tragedy of the commons.[16]

The signals of regeneration are multiplying. More consumers are looking for locally grown, locally produced products and services. The intrinsic value of a product or service is increased when a good or service is exchanged between people—there is a deeper connection in the exchange. A connection with the brand is made, which is in many ways higher than the profit margin. While globalization has had the benefit of increasing choice for many people, it does not always increase value. Localization can often add much greater value, in addition to supporting individual and organizational values.

Communities thrive when living and working complement each other. This is the goal in Tottenville, a community on Staten Island in New York City to re-empower the local community by attracting and building mutually beneficial businesses. Seeds of regeneration are being planted that include a new marine economy and urban farming.[17]

This initiative takes advantage of natural assets such as its seaside location and open space that can be developed into sustainable farming. Tottenville also has a rich history of successful small businesses. The Tottenville plan brings together production and consumption in the local community and provides for investment in a marine economy that can benefit the New York City metropolitan area.

In the wake of office shock, community members can benefit, and policy makers will have more opportunities to converge on a shared path toward collective climate change. Office shock opens an opportunity to swing the pendulum back to give more agency to communities.

An example of where government is taking powerful and creative action to confront climate change is provided by Chile, where the process of mining lithium has had extensive negative effects on the environment in the Atacama Desert in the north. Mining is affecting water levels, salinity, and temperature, which are all affecting the people who live in the area and threatening wildlife, triggering a national reinvention:

> After months of protests over social and environmental grievances, 155 Chileans have been elected to write a new constitution amid what they have declared a "climate and ecological emergency." Their work will not only shape how this country of 19 million is governed. It will also determine the future of a soft, lustrous metal, lithium, lurking in the salt waters beneath this vast ethereal desert beside the Andes Mountains.[18]

Those writing the new constitution will address the negative impacts and the potential economic value, and will most likely redefine "water." Indeed, designing and cultivating a regenerative culture requires a new language to tell a story of co-creating a new balance between the inherent selfishness of individual consumption and the unselfishness of community prosperity. This is futureback thinking at its finest: envisioning a future of economic value in harmony with regenerating the environment and creating the legal structure to enable it all.

Regenerative culture encourages shared stories that increase awareness of one another.[19] Whether through religious rituals or ethnic narratives, members can generate new connections and new levels of trust. As practitioners of regenerative practices, they tackle the challenge of unequal distribution of resources with a shared vision of what a regenerative future looks and feels like.

Regenerative Systems

Spanning the Spectrum of Climate Impacts reveals the importance of learning from ecology, and being inspired by its interworking, to create better futures for working and living.

A Systems View of Offices and Officing

In Capra and Luisi's masterwork *The Systems View of Life*,[20] life is described within a framework with four dimensions: biological, cognitive, social, and ecological.

Building on the work of cognitive biology and sociology, this book posits that life is a system capable of producing and maintaining itself. Like the homeostasis of our bodies, our planetary environment is homeostatic, maintaining temperature and atmospheric composition, despite changing conditions. Our planet's regulatory system is surprisingly like the regulatory system of the human body. A regenerative strategy is self-creating, and the spectrum is not only about what we do in the environment but also about how we can gain inspiration from the environment. Embracing the complexities and dynamics of living organizations should encourage a shift in how we organize ourselves. For example, biomimicry is a growing design movement that "learns from and mimics the strategies found in nature to solve human design challenges—and find hope."[21] Biomimicry applies an empathetic, interconnected understanding of how life works "to not only learn from nature's wisdom, but also heal ourselves—and this planet—in the process."[22]

Another example is the work of Chinese ecological urbanist and architect Kongjian Yu.[23] To deal with the increasing problem of flooding, Yu designed *Sponge Cities* for urban environments.[24] His design allows water to filter through the ground by absorbing rainwater like a sponge, rather than trying to keep it out. The water is then naturally filtered by the soil and allowed to reach urban aquifers, where it can easily be treated and used for the city water supply. All human networks, including offices and officing, have the capacity for regeneration.

Sustainability Will Not Be Enough

Daniel Christian Wahl takes this argument further: "*Sustainability is not enough: we need regenerative cultures.* A regenerative human culture is healthy, resilient, and adaptable; that cares for the planet, and that cares for life in the awareness that this is the most effective way to create a thriving future for all of humanity."[25]

The MIT Sloan Sustainability Initiative routinely polls business leaders about progress in their firms toward embracing sustainability. Despite a plethora of companies with good intentions,[26] the unwelcome news delivered by Jon Sterman, cofounder of the initiative, is:

> companies issue reports through public or government relations departments,
> engage in sustainability activities only when they believe it is profitable, or comply
> with applicable environmental laws and regulations—nothing more.[27]

The transition from today's attitudes to our aspirational scenario of planet regeneration highlights the massive worldwide cooperation required. Urgent choices must be made by individuals, offices, and communities to change consumption, produce with circularity, and regenerate the planet.

Despite the overwhelming evidence, it would seem we are challenged as a society to see a shared vision of a regenerative future. Perhaps we can draw inspiration from those who have found belonging through their relationship to the environment. Perhaps the Spectrum of Climate Impacts can open the conversation, explore the polarities, and help to harmonize solutions for workers and their offices.

No single government, company, or person can achieve the goal alone. Despite the challenges of establishing "ecological diplomacy,"[28] according to the MIT Technology Review, in 2022 many nations and territories are on the path toward a Green Future.[29] With Environmental, Social, and Governance regulations on the horizon in many countries, organizations[30] have to begin the transition to more sustainable business practices.

The United Nations Sustainable Development Goals offer a global opportunity to bridge national differences with flexive intent to adopt planet-friendly practices. Three of the seventeen UN Sustainable Development Goals focus on climate issues. Others connect to climate by advocating good health and well-being, reducing poverty, and creating sustainable communities. They all aim to guide humanity toward a better future (See "Office Shock Navigational Stars" at the back of the book for details of the climate-oriented SDGs #13, #14, and #15).

What will guide our great transition from a world that consumes more than it can sustainably produce to one of worldwide cooperation and symbiosis as in our aspirational scenario at the start of the chapter? The record to date is not promising, and the Spectrum of Climate Impacts is central to creating a just world and a healthy regenerating planet.

As two of the authors of the 2015 Paris Climate Accords said in their book *The Future We Choose: Surviving the Climate Crisis*:

> When you are faced with the hard realities, look at them with clarity, but also know that you are incredibly lucky to be alive at a time when you can make a transformative difference to the future of all life on earth.[31]

Your Choices on the Spectrum of Climate Impacts

As you think about your own personal story across this spectrum, consider these questions:

1. How might you illustrate your story about a future with more positive climate impacts?

2. How has the question of "to consume or not to consume" affected your behavior and that of your organization? How might you change your practices to become more sustainable?

3. How do you see yourself participating in the circular economy?

4. How can offices and officing contribute to restoring the planet and increasing its regenerative capacity?

5. How can we get the world working on a more cooperative basis to prevent planetary destruction?

6. How can we convince organizations—particularly corporations—that they have a huge role to play in climate regeneration and that in the long run it will enhance their business performance?

SEVEN

Cultivating Community

The Spectrum of Belonging

Imagine a world

in which robust diversity is expected and rewarded. Traditional
diversity programs sought to bring "others" into an established
order. Future diversity programs for offices and officing will create
a culture of belonging for all varieties of difference. Those who
win in this world will be those who can present themselves as
having fluid identities that engage positively with differences.
Moving among cultures and styles will be a crucial everyday
skill in this ever-changing world of mixing and matching. The
most successful people will be mindfully aware of their roots
and the routes they have pursued to get to where they are.

Celebrating Uniqueness *(opposite)*
Illustration by Analia Iglesias from Argentina.
*After reading this chapter, consider how you might illustrate your story
about the Spectrum of Belonging.*

In 2018, Greta Thunberg stood outside the Swedish Parliament building to protest the lack of legislation to fight climate change. As the days and months and eventually years passed, her peers around the world organized in support of Greta Thunberg's cause—but now there are many more young people from around the world with similar concerns about climate emergencies. For example, Global Citizen identified "6 Young Activists in Africa Working to Save the World,"[1] and there are many more. Others include Vanessa Nakate of Uganda, Ayakha Melithafa of South Africa, and Makenna Muigai of Kenya.

Hilda Flavia Nakabuye, the founder of Fridays for Future Uganda, is a leader of this "generation of scared people" who are "very good at action."[2] Young people who were on the verge of becoming adults during the 2010 Threshold, when the internet shifted from separate tools to a media ecology, are different. As they matured, they developed with the sense of frustration and urgency that we see today. Young people on the verge of becoming adults during the turbulent crisis of COVID-19 share similar values and a sense of urgency—what we call the 2020 Threshold[3] for digitally amplified change.

For the first time in human history, young people ages twenty-four and under make up the largest portion of the global population. Many of these young people are angry, and they are becoming politically and socially active in meaningful ways. Many young people don't feel like they belong in the world they are inheriting. Hope is fleeting.

Their anger derives from the many social issues we face, such as economic inequality, changing climate impacts, institutional racism, gender inequality, and questionable corporate practices. Oxfam, a respected global relief organization, titled its latest report "Inequality Kills: The Unparalleled Action Needed to Combat Unprecedented Inequality in the Wake of COVID-19":

> Widening economic, gender, and racial inequalities—as well as the inequality that exists between countries—are tearing our world apart.[4]

We are optimistic about young people *if* they have hope.

Most offices we see are not ready for the influx of digitally savvy young people. The concerns they bring will be explosive, and they will not be easy to

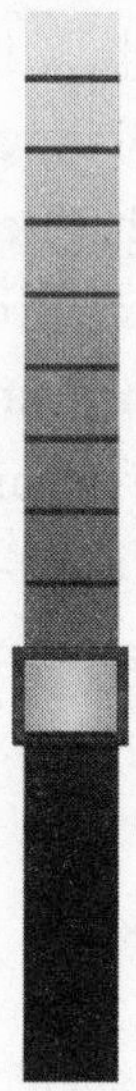

With whom do you
want to office?

Different

Familiar

FIGURE 11: Spectrum
of Belonging

integrate with offices and officing. Their differences are powerful, and they will demand change. They will increasingly expect organizations to be both purposely and usefully different. Thriving offices in the future will need more sense of belonging.

As illustrated in figure 11, the Spectrum of Belonging starts with our natural bias toward people who are familiar. However, as mixed teams of workers flourish, the spectrum encourages reaching out to those who are different. The opportunity of office shock is to move, seek out, accept, and reward full-spectrum diversity—diversity that moves beyond simplistic labels, categories, and buckets—in an outside world dominated by differences.

Our identity—how we define ourselves—is shaped by personal roots, the routes we have taken in our lives, and the aspirations that we have for the future. If we can understand our history, we have the potential to right the wrongs and build on the positives. Office shock can spark a new sense of belonging, with the power and potential of community.

The Diversity Dilemma

As office shock punctures the boundaries of the past, it is becoming clear that there will be no mainstream, no dominant category of people. Today's understanding of diversity is based on integrating the other, those different from the mainstream. Diversity is everywhere already and growing rapidly. Diversity will become more important in the future—and harder to measure, label, or categorize. We will need to embrace what makes others different as well as what we have in common with others. Thinking futureback sheds new light on the diversity dilemma and opens a path to real change.

By expressing and appreciating our differences, without deference, impossible futures will become possible. Thinking futureback will open opportunities based on contribution rather than categories. Thinking futureback will inform how to redress injustice and empower an inclusive future.

In the future, people who can express their differences authentically will have an advantage. Neurologically, this future will require embracing the discomforts of difference. This future will require us to resist the temptation to conform. Stress receptors will fire in our brains from fear of the unknown. But we can grow new synaptic connections to prepare our brains for future offices and officing. We can teach ourselves to celebrate our otherness from each other—as well as our common ground. Knowing your roots and routes is the starting point to navigating the diversity dilemma of the present.

Know Your Roots and Your Routes

Connections between people have always been an essential ingredient in seeding social identities. In an era of identity politics, legacy categories are in a constant state of flux, rendering them meaningless for some.[5] Despite this fluidity, identity is still an important psychological need. When our IFTF colleague Gabe Cervantes, a major contributor to this chapter, was a student at Williams College, he was introduced to the notion of roots and routes as integral to understanding diaspora studies and the nature of identity:

> One of the most important shifts in diaspora studies is to de-emphasize group solidarity and cohesiveness in favor of recognizing internal complexities—including multi-ethnic, multi-faith, multi-lingual, multi-cohort, multi-mobile and hybrid diasporas.[6]

Multihyphenated people, connected via digital media, will create digital diasporas to form what are becoming cohort groups that, while harder to categorize, are increasingly important. These connected networks of people communicate and work together to allow diversity to be a new tool for solving complex problems. This emerging officeverse will introduce new ways to engage with the continuing challenges of diversity and inclusion at work.

Journalist/writer Alex Haley introduced the concept of roots to a very wide audience by telling very personal stories about his own family history. Roots are your lineage. How far back can you trace yourself in terms of race, age, gender, ethnicity, socioeconomic status, and other categories that contribute to your identity? Your roots are all about your ancestors; their legacy and their dreams empower your future. Calling on ancestors reveals generational change. Knowing your roots helps you and the outside world understand what experiences, cultural expressions, stories, and other elements inform who you are in the present.

A deep understanding of roots also helps to illuminate the route, the walk of life, that people have taken.

Poisoned by Collective Trauma

Social injustice has created a sense of collective trauma for so many people in the world today. Roots can be painful. Roots can be political. Roots may be influenced by events and experiences of local, national, and global communities. Knowing your roots gives you historical context. Understanding someone else's roots can give you the basis for empathy, even if full understanding is not possible.

Organizations have roots too. For example, what is the history of your office buildings? How have your offices contributed to—or taken away from—the neighborhoods around the buildings? What management policies defined your purpose and the overall philosophy of your organization? Does your organization provide psychological safety for those who have experienced collective trauma? COVID-19 provided its own kind of collective trauma, but it is often mixed with traumas of racial injustice, climate emergencies, or forced disruptions of family life.

Collective trauma is part of life for many people.[7] In the case of Black Americans, Martin Luther King Jr. said:

White America must see that no other ethnic group has been a slave on American soil. That is one thing that other immigrant groups haven't had to face.[8]

Bob attended the same divinity school as Martin Luther King Jr., and he was there in Upland, Pennsylvania, when Dr. King was killed. Bob got to work with Dr. Kenneth Smith, Martin Luther King Jr.'s professor of Christian Ethics, and he was a student in a course designed to recreate the intellectual influences Dr. King was moved by while at Crozer Theological Seminary. One of Bob's strongest memories of that course was how Martin Luther King Jr.'s clarity was focused on social justice, not just civil rights. Because of his concern about social justice, he was very active in the antipoverty movement, protesting the Vietnam War, and advocating for the environmental movement. In his last years, Dr. King was often criticized for not focusing on civil rights alone, but his response was always that the more profound issue was social justice.

Your route defines your life trajectory, including cognitive ways of thinking, preferences, and future planning for you and possibly your family. Your route is your path forward for the future, although it is influenced by your past roots. Roots, however, don't determine a person's future route. Neither your roots nor routes are static. Roots can become routes.

The dreams and aspirations that arise from your roots and routes will shape your futureback thinking and the kind of futures you are able to imagine. For individuals to rise, organizations must honor roots and routes. What are the paths to the future, for what people? What glass ceilings or constraints must be broken?

In Search of Belonging

Looking futureback from ten years ahead, the world will be more diverse, and that diversity will be harder to categorize. The multitude of diversity programs in many organizations will most likely contribute to better futures for working and living.

However, thinking futureback also reveals that diversity is much deeper than what is revealed by merely measuring it by checking off boxes. Each of us is more than the categories we represent, the boxes we check off. The future will blur demographic diversity labels beyond recognition. Simple diversity filters just won't work well as people who are mixed category "multi's" and "hypenated's" grow in number. Everyone will be an "other" in some sense.

In traditional diversity programs, the marginalized "others" have been given priority status with a goal of diversifying workforces, boardrooms, and the office in general. It has been a just cause to find those missing, prioritize getting them in the door, and including them.

Diversity isn't just about "others" that don't fit the established order. As belonging catalyst and consultant Ibrahim Jackson says, diversity is the easy part. The hard part is inclusion, belonging, and equity. Thinking futureback, it is easy to imagine that the word *diversity* won't be necessary in ten years because it will be so obvious. Everything and everyone will be diverse.

Building communities with belonging will be complex. Diversity is about attracting people with different roots and who have followed different routes to get to where they are. Inclusion and belonging are about giving the space to aspire, rise, and grow—no matter the roots or routes you have followed to be where you are now.

As Ibrahim Jackson says, "Diversity is the person, Inclusion is an invitation to the party, Belonging is being asked to dance, hearing a genre of music that you enjoy and food you love to consume."[9] Equity weaves through all three concepts of diversity, inclusion, and belonging. Jackson proposes a framework that is illustrated by three overlapping circles within an overarching context of equity (figure 12).

- **Diversity** is about understanding that every person brings something unique to an organization. To truly connect with employees at all levels, diversity needs to be a focus. The more you have, the broader your reach in ideas, inventions, and innovation.

- **Inclusion** fosters an environment where everyone has a voice and is a part of a team or community. An inclusive culture is best achieved by celebrating individual diversity and unique contributions in the workplace.

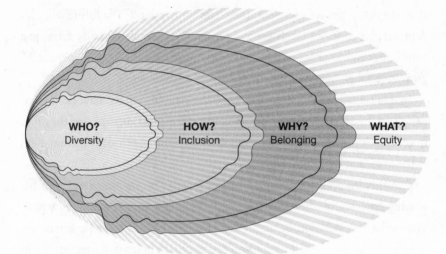

FIGURE 12: The Belonging Organization (adapted from Ibrahim Jackson). A framework to integrate diversity, inclusion, and belonging, built on an underlying foundation of equitable practices.

- **Belonging** sets the stage for people to know they are accepted, valued, and have the freedom to contribute without hesitation.

- **Equity** interweaves among diversity, inclusion, and belonging. Although not the endgame, equity shapes the playing field. Equity is all about fairness and accessibility—not necessarily equality. Not everyone is the same, nor should they be treated in the same manner. Equity allows for differences, while equality alone does not. Equity is very much a part of social justice.

Office shock provides an opportunity for a fresh start, and many diversity programs need a fresh start. Office shock will disrupt identities and puncture diversity categories. Identities will be constantly changing and increasingly difficult to label. The Spectrum of Belonging spans from the comfort of familiar people to the excitement of working with people who are purposely different. Finding harmony for your personal journey within the spectrum will help build better futures.

Dignity is an important aspect of belonging. Marc Bamuthi Joseph is a poet, playwright, musician, and actor, and currently serves as the vice president and artistic director of social impact at the Kennedy Center in Washington, DC. In a passionate spoken-word video, he advocates for the importance of dignity and its role as a moral compass for collective healing.[10]

Understanding the role of dignity is essential in growing diversity and empathy. To thrive, organizations in the future will seek purposely different people whose combined talents and experience will accomplish an organization's purpose. Officing will be about an artful blending of dynamic digital diasporas, not just checking off a box when we have all the categories of others represented in the room. Technology will support the formation of communities of people, regardless of location or organizational affiliation. These digital diasporas in the emerging officeverse will be powerful agents of change and contribute to valuable solutions for organizations.

Impossible futures for belonging will become possible, but this won't be easy. We are all hardwired to reinforce our identity among those who are familiar. The boundaries of belonging can be deep and wide. Full-spectrum thinking will be needed to span this spectrum, because the questions cut across who we are, how we connect with others, and the ways we can come together for collective action. Also, many excluded groups are impatient or angry.

Purposely Different

Office shock is an opportunity to look at those we office with and provide a spectrum of choices. On the one hand, we maintain the ability to keep our office connections with those who are familiar to us in their routes—their journey to the future aligns with our values, our contributions, and our experiences. On the other hand, looking at officing with those who are purposefully different from us allows us to bring in individuals with diverse roots so that we may leverage their communities' experiences in innovative ways.

There is value in working with people who know each other well: they have shared context, they know language shortcuts, and they have shared experiences. New digital diasporas popularized by office shock are increasing and providing access to raw, unfiltered talent from varied roots and routes. This will not only help us value and embrace those who are different, it will reveal who we are by highlighting who we are not.

Beyond Labels

Instead of merely presenting ourselves as a list of categorical designations around age, race, gender, ethnicity, and more, we will first ask, "What experiences, information, and perspectives are missing?" The relationships we form in future offices will be centered on finding those who represent diasporas unique to our own. This will happen in both physical office spaces and through networked workplaces.

Thinking futureback, anything that can be distributed will be distributed. The in-person office will still be important for activities like orientation, onboarding, trust building, and renewal. But digitally enhanced diasporas will be a critical part of your office of the future.

The role of policy makers in responding to office shock encourages us to consider the spectrum of choices of whom we work with, and it is varied and complex. At the policy level, choices about zoning, public transportation, equitable access, availability of free networking, the rights of individuals, health benefits, and child-care options are just a few of the areas where policies can influence with whom we work.

Office diversity in the future will look and feel very different from the present. Instead of offering advantages, special privileges, or unique spaces for those who are in the minority, everyone's difference can be recognized and valued. In a future where differences are made visible and distinguished, people will be valued by the skills and experience they contribute.

But what is often called code-switching behavior (adapting your language, appearance, or behavior so you can interact successfully with people who come from different roots or routes) will still be a factor. A recent *Harvard Business Review* issue contributed to by five diverse researchers reached this conclusion:

Based on our research and the work of others, we argue that code-switching is one of the key dilemmas that black employees face around race at work. While it is frequently seen as crucial for professional advancement, code-switching often comes at a great psychological cost. If leaders are truly seeking to promote inclusion and address social inequality, they must begin by understanding why a segment of their workforce believes that they cannot truly be themselves in the office. Then they should address what everyone at the company needs to do to change this.[11]

This article was written just before the COVID-19 office closures. If someone feels that they "cannot truly be themselves in the office," how do they feel when their office colleagues are present in their homes via Zoom? Their lifestyle and personal preferences become visible to all. Some describe how they rearrange the backgrounds for their calls, a version of code-switching with furniture.

Stories of Work in the Future

The best offices have been places where people gathered, worked toward a common purpose, found connections, built relationships, and thrived. The office and office work of the future will seek the same purpose, but in different ways. Where office work of the past tended to help you find people like you and your background, the office and office work of the future will allow you to work with those who are purposefully different. Meeting the challenges of an increasingly complex world and unlocking innovation will require a thoughtful mixing and matching of roots and routes. The most successful teams will be those that are diverse and distinct.

Belonging communities bring together identities, aspirations, and rituals. Science fiction and epic fantasy spark our imaginations about many things and, in some instances, about more belonging. For example, authors in the genre of Afrofuturism are adding to and updating the mule-like concepts of stubbornly breaking from the past and the constraints of history:

"Afrofuturism, like post blackness, destabilizes previous analyses of blackness," says Reynaldo Anderson, assistant professor of humanities at Harris-Stowe State University and a writer of Afrofuturist critical theory. "What I like about

Afrofuturism is it helps us create our own space in the future; it allows us to control our imagination. An Afrofuturist is not ignorant of history, but they don't let history restrain their creative impulses either."[12]

In addition to Afrofuturism, futures genres can be found everywhere, and for everyone, including Latinfuturism,[13] Chicanafuturism,[14] Sinofuturism,[15] Arab Futurism,[16] and Gulf Futurism.[17] This mixing and matching will accelerate creating better futures for working and living, for all.

Fantasy came to life on the subtropical island of Madeira, called "Zoom Island" by residents of the Digital Nomad Villages who moved there to live and work during the COVID-19 pandemic. Many cities and countries are trying to lure digital nomads to come work and live, but Digital Nomads Madeira is focused on providing a sense of belonging and community. "Community is the key. It's why everybody else is completely failing at attracting digital nomads. They miss the most important thing, which is that nomads travel between communities, not between places."[18] As the tourists come back to Madeira, what will happen to these communities of digital nomads? Zoom Island is a fascinating prototype, but will concepts like this be sustainable over time?

Throughout this book we have related the concepts of each spectrum of choice to the UN Sustainable Development Goals. In this area of diversity, inclusion, and belonging, three of the goals apply:

- Goal #3: "Ensure healthy lives and promote well-being for all at all ages." This goal focuses on all, but also on age diversity.

- Goal #8: "Promote sustained, inclusive and sustainable economic growth, full and productive employment and decent work for all." The key words here are *productive*, *inclusive*, and *sustainable*.

- Goal #16: "Promote peaceful and inclusive societies for sustainable development, provide access to justice for all and build effective, accountable and inclusive institutions at all levels." The application of diversity and inclusion is ramped up to society as a whole and ties into justice, which is also a key issue in diversity.

Your Choices on the Spectrum of Belonging

In the VUCA world, who we office with may be in constant flux. Although we may belong to and work for the same company, organization, or goal, the teams that help us accomplish our work may change. Although we lose some comfortable familiarity, purposefully mixing and matching will provoke new approaches to the challenges of the future.

As you think about your own personal story across this spectrum, consider these questions:

1. How might you illustrate your story about a future with more belonging?

2. What makes you different, and how can you celebrate your otherness authentically while still engaging with others?

3. In your present moment, in your present community, what are the aspects of every member that can contribute to a vibrant organization?

4. How can you use the concepts of roots and routes to bring a purposely different mix of talent into your organization?

5. How will you address the diversity dilemma in your office?

6. The digital natives will likely have very different expectations for offices and officing. They are likely to be less loyal and more critical of current ways of working. How are you preparing for their arrival? How will you benefit from cross-generational communication now?

EIGHT

Everyone Amplified

The Spectrum of Augmentation

Imagine a world

in which people, offices, and officing will be augmented, amplified, and enhanced. Humans and computers will work together to extend human intelligence and enhance work. Computers will replace humans for certain limited functions, but the bigger stories will be about humans and computers working together to do things that have never been done before. Everyone will be augmented in some way, while a growing number of people will be truly enhanced. Risk will intensify as computing becomes more intelligent and criminals more augmented, but opportunity will increase more than risk. Many of us will be cyborgs—and that will be a good thing, most of the time.

Embodied Augmentation *(opposite)*
Illustration by Proxima Centauri B from Germany.
After reading this chapter, consider how you might illustrate your story about the Spectrum of Augmentation.

Amber Case may be the world's first cyborg anthropologist.[1] She defines "cyborg" as an extension of an organism for the purpose of surviving and thriving in new, uncertain, or changing environments. A cyborg anthropologist studies and thinks systematically about relations among people, technology, and society. In simple ways, we are all cyborgs already in the sense that we all use tools of some kind. A spacesuit is a great example of a tool that helps humans survive in the hostile environment of space. Astronauts are cyborgs. Over the next decade, digital media and tools will extend and enhance our human capabilities to survive and thrive on Earth. The data they capture, consider, and communicate will be essential for creating better futures for working and living.

By 2033, the workforce will be amplified by exoskeletons, software, and processes that work with humans to prevent repetitive injuries, increase strength, and reduce fatigue. Some of this is happening today in research, but is not yet commercially available. For example, software is being used to create a highly personalized mapping of the spinal cord to allow back-injury patients using a tablet to enable their own movement and aid in rehabilitation.[2]

As illustrated in figure 13, the Spectrum of Augmentation asks us to choose how we amplify our cognitive and physical capabilities. Whether by exponential or quantum leaps, machines will assist humans, and humans will assist machines as well. The data machines capture, consider, and communicate are essential for creating better futures. Digital aids will be ubiquitous as they shrink and become increasingly embedded into things and people. Algorithms enabling machine learning will get smarter. Communication between devices and across networks will continue to increase in scale and speed.

How will you augment your intelligence?

Technology

Human

FIGURE 13: Spectrum of Augmentation

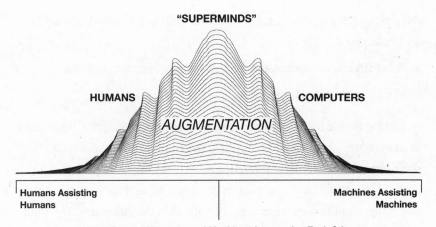

FIGURE 14: The Increasing Augmentation of Humans with Computers.

AI Is Finally Getting Practical

As forecasted by *AI 2041*:

> Humans will work symbiotically with AI performing quantitative analysis, optimization, and routine work, while we humans contribute our creativity, critical thinking, and passion. Each human's productivity will be amplified, allowing us to realize our potential.[3]

AI 2041 combines the futureback storytelling of novelist Chen Quifan with commentary by computer scientist Kai-Fu Lee.

The human-computer spectrum of capabilities and mix of talents will not be an either/or choice, human or machine. Looking futureback, there will be full-spectrum blending of human and machine choices that will look something like figure 14.

The Spectrum of Augmentation is focused on how we choose to blend human and machine capabilities. Over the next decade, you will need to answer these penetrating questions for yourself, for your organization, and for your community:

- What can humans do best and what do we *want* to do for ourselves?
- What can machines do best?

Making choices on this spectrum begs us to rethink intelligence, particularly in an age when neuroscience reveals how the mind works and computer scientists demonstrate how machines can learn.

Amplifying everyone opens an opportunity to explore how technology might augment the ways we engage with others in the officeverse. The World Economic Forum's Augmented Workforce Initiative mission statement outlines the importance of augmentation going into the future:

> Bringing together industry executives, thought leaders, policy makers, and labor unions to understand and harness the potential of human-centric operations on future shop floors, technology-mediated workforce empowerment, augmentation, and digital workforce transformation.[4]

As computer science professor Batya Friedman said: "At stake is nothing less than what sort of society we want to live in and how we experience our humanity."[5]

Spanning the spectrum between human and technology is essential for solving the systemic problems of climate change, social injustice, and economic inequality. AI can reveal some of the patterns embedded in society's wicked problems; however, not everything will be quantifiable or codifiable in these sociotechnical situations. Solving our systemic challenges will require human-machine collaboration to create better futures for working and living. We will need to become superminds.

Superminds Are Coming

During the 1980s, the term *artificial intelligence* (or *AI*) became cemented in the public mind. Researchers and entrepreneurs attempted to build "expert systems," digital versions of human experts. But the goal now should be machines that extend human capabilities and help us solve the world's wicked problems. Our IFTF colleague Jake Dunagan describes this as an "infinite cortex, a seamless integration of mind and world to extend individual capacities and make us a smarter species."[6]

DALL-E, for example, is an evolving GPT-3 based technology that blends language and images to illustrate anything. Using natural language as input, the application connects meanings to visually depict a textual description.[7] Of course, there are concerns that this kind of technology could be used to easily create images that people think look real but are entirely made up. Also, AI has demonstrated its "inherent biases and the unsustainable amount of computing power."[8] AI lacks ethics and common sense, which is amplifying calls to "reclaim AI from Big Tech's control."[9]

Despite the continued popularity of the terms *Artificial Intelligence* and *AI*, it was an unfortunate choice by the founding fathers of cognitive science[10] to create a simplistic term that prompted immediate resistance. Human beings didn't like the idea of being replaced by computers when the term was coined, and they still don't.

Since then, many experts have reframed the reigning metaphor of "mind as machine." Kate Crawford, senior principal researcher at Microsoft Research, argues that AI is neither artificial nor intelligent, rather, it is:[11]

> Both embodied and material, made from natural resources, fuel, human labor, infrastructures, logistics, histories and classifications. AI systems are not autonomous, rational or able to discern anything without extensive computationally intensive training with large data sets or predefined rules and rewards.[12]

Thinking futureback, more data, *plus* more connections, *plus* more computing power does not necessarily equal more intelligence.[13] It will be much easier, and much more attractive, to *augment intelligence* rather than try to replicate it.

Augmented intelligence is becoming more and more powerful. In tech centers around the world now, people talk about keeping "humans in the loop" with advanced computing and machine learning. Another phrase that we hear with increasing frequency is *computers in the group*,[14] or what used to be called a nonhuman participant in electronic meetings.

MIT professor Thomas W. Malone, the founding director of the MIT Center for Collective Intelligence, coined the term *superminds* in his book of the same name to describe the blending of human and computer intelligence in the future.[15] Superminds are groups of augmented individuals acting intelligently together.

Superminds is the best term we know to describe the kind of augmented human intelligence for offices and officing that is coming fast. The future officeverse will be populated with superminds—people working in tandem with technology to mobilize the collective intelligence for better futures. Superminds will depend on technologies augmenting their intelligence to engage in what Cal Newport calls deep work, while avoiding the "hyperactive hivemind."[16] Superminds will need enchanted objects to assist them.

The Magic of Enchanted Objects

The augmented, amplified, and enhanced office will be a world filled with what David Rose calls "enchanted objects," ordinary items that can do extraordinary things. Rose's enchanted pill bottle, for example, reminds you when to take your pills, and his enchanted umbrella tells you when it is going to rain. Augmented intelligence will make all this possible. Rose identifies five steps on the ladder of enchantment, which moves from adding sensing/sensor capabilities for personal information to adding connections and stories for fun and motivation.[17]

Objects that are referred to as "smart" are often more like "enchanted." With either actual devices or digital twins (digital representations of humans or objects), the potential to enchant objects with intelligence will increase as network speed, coverage, and computing power converge. In the health-care industry, for example, data from the health-care gold rush may fundamentally change behaviors and perhaps even be an antidote to rising health-care costs. However, "smart" will only be intelligent if humans are able to agree on industry standards and security for what humans perceive as useful.

Known in the design community as "speculative design," technology will also enable us to enchant objects with more data and provide more insight about what the social implications of such magic might be. Dunne and Raby suggest that it will "allow an individual to open windows on the future in order to better understand the present."[18]

That's futureback thinking. Enchanted objects—whether real or fictional—can be catalysts for creating better futures because they trigger insights, the raw material for change. For example, what if, after the trials of the pandemic, research on "smart masks" produces a mask that can protect not only against viruses but also against all negative elements in the environment.

Such intelligence can be both insightful and inspiring, engaging both designer and user to create a preferred future. Many examples of virtual objects designed to enchant our intelligence exist, and all leverage technology in provocative ways.[19] For example, Earth 2050 provides an interactive porthole into how people will live in twenty- or thirty-years' time, including what our lives may be like and what jobs we may have. Created by a global group of futurists, scientists, and internet users, the website allows visitors to select a decade and see the predictions for different cities and countries.[20]

Superminds working with enchanted objects will create better futures for offices and officing.

Augment Your Decisions

When a Google engineer claimed its large language model LaMDA was sentient, the reaction was a resounding "no" from the AI community. Many saw this signal as another example of anthropomorphizing computers and self-projection.[21] But there is much more going on here as people continue to sort out what humans can do best and what computers can do best. Benjamin Bratton, who is directing a new research program on the speculative philosophy of computation, writes with Blaise Agüera y Arcasn after the sentience claim, that:

> AI as it exists now is not what it was predicted to be. It is not hyperrational and orderly; it is messy and fuzzy.... Perhaps the real lesson for philosophy of AI is that

reality has outpaced the available language to parse what is already at hand. A more precise vocabulary is essential.[22]

Unfortunately, we don't yet have a precise vocabulary, and we are stuck with the misleading umbrella term *Artificial Intelligence*. For now, to navigate the Great Opportunity of office shock, we should be asking how computers could augment humans. More specifically, how can computers help humans make better decisions?

Fortunately, we seem to be more apt to listen to *how* to do something rather than *why* we should. For example, people were more willing to put on sunscreen when an AI explained how to apply sunscreen before going out rather than why they should use sunscreen.[23] Moreover, decision-making support is influenced by the rationality and spontaneity of the decision makers.[24] Despite the best data and designed algorithms, the intelligence of a computer is dependent on the intelligence of the user.[25]

With over 188 cognitive biases identified to date,[26] how could machine intelligence not be dependent on human intelligence, particularly when it comes to diversity and inclusion? Our intelligence can be greatly augmented by truly smart learning algorithms that reveal the biases inherent in human data and decisions, making us much smarter.

The Risks of Augmenting Intelligence

Thinking futureback, the difference between augmentation for incremental improvement and augmentation for disruptive innovation will be a dramatic spectrum of impacts—including serious downside risks. As computing becomes more intelligent, a new variation of the digital divide will emerge as rich people become more enhanced, while poor people may well be more amplified in ways that are likely to be more stressful and less humane.

Even as the world becomes more connected, it will become more fragmented and polarized. We've always had a rich/poor gap, but it will become increasingly visible and stark. When impoverished and hopeless young people see rich kids flaunting their wealth, as often happens on social media even now, the results could be explosive.

Cybercrime, cyberwarfare, and cyberterrorism will loom over the next decade and beyond. Asymmetric warfare is already a fact of life, and what military analyst Sean McFate called "durable disorder" is already obvious. Some of the most powerful superminds will be criminals, especially since they can operate without many of the legal constraints that honest people have. Very small groups of bad people will be able to do bad things that will be amplified through digital networks. Durable disorder will be part of the VUCA world of the future.

The *New York Times* published a guest essay by inspirational Harvard Business School professor emeritus Shoshana Zuboff with the provocative title "You Are the Object of a Secret Extraction Operation,"[27] where she makes the case that Google and Facebook have developed an unprecedented economic system built on the concealed extraction, manipulation, and sale of human data. In her book about this threat, she talks about the human ability to make sense out of phenomena that have never occurred before:

> One explanation for surveillance capitalism's many triumphs floats above them all: it is *unprecedented. The unprecedented is necessarily unrecognizable* (emphasis added). When we encounter something unprecedented, we automatically interpret it through the lenses of familiar categories, thereby rendering invisible precisely what is unprecedented. . . . This contributes to the normalization of the abnormal, which makes fighting the unprecedented even more of an uphill climb.[28]

Impossible futures are also unprecedented. We think they are impossible because they don't fit our familiar categories. Futureback thinking helps make sense out of futures that we cannot imagine as well as figure out what we might do in response.

Certainly, the mixing of human and computing intelligence over the next decade will be unprecedented. UN Sustainable Development Goal #4 is related to improved intelligence and the need for equity in its implementation—a critical concern for us in this book: Ensure inclusive and equitable quality education and promote lifelong learning opportunities for all.

We need to think futureback to understand the potential scenarios, pursue those with the most promise, and avoid those that are most threatening. We need to use the Spectrum of Augmentation to create harmony between human and computing intelligence. Fortunately, superminds—augmented humans working together—will have a very good chance of thriving in the future officeverse.

Augmented Storytelling Is Coming

We tried out GPT-3, a current large language model, to augment our writing of this chapter. Our futurist colleague Jeremy Kirshbaum coached us since he is already using large language models like GPT-3 to aid in his research, writing, and storytelling.

Jeremy Kirshbaum uses the metaphor of farming to describe the value of augmented writing. Large language models (a kind of AI) are like the introduction of tractors for a farmer. You still need to be a good farmer and to know when and what to plant, even if you now have a tractor to augment your farming. A tractor doesn't do all the work for you, it just helps you work better than if all you had was a hoe. You still need to be a skilled farmer and user of tractors. Tractors are not robot farmers. Tractors need a lot of context and guidance to be useful. Runaway tractors are dangerous.

Similarly, GPT-3 is not a robot writer. Still, it did help us as we outlined, went through many drafts, and reflected on the content of this chapter. Thinking futureback as writers, we expect that most good writers—including the three of us—will be augmented in some way by the end of the next decade.

Finally, we asked GPT-3 to augment our writing and create a poetic story about augmented intelligence, written in the style of Pablo Neruda. Below is the unedited "Ode to Augmented Intelligence" created by GPT-3, with our guidance. You might think of what you read below as a futureback story of augmented intelligence by an artificial intelligence:

In the desert
of knowledge,
in the dryness
in the heart of the desert,
I saw a well.
The well was full of intelligence.
There was no one around.
The well was covered by a stone lid,
and I could not see what was inside.

I wanted to go down into the well,
but I was afraid.
Then I heard voices and steps:
a group of men came toward me.
They reached the well, took off their shoes,
and peered down into it.
They were so happy that they laughed and cried
and took off their hats and clapped them.

"What is in the well?" I asked.
"Intelligence," they said.
"What is augmented intelligence?" I asked.
"It is the most valuable thing in the world," they said.
"What has augmented intelligence?" I asked.
"The future," they said.
"What is it like?" I asked.
"It is a golden key," they said, "and if you turn it in the door
of your heart, you will know everything."

"How do I get the key?" I asked.
"You must go down into the well," they said.
"What do I see there?" I asked.
"You will see a golden ladder," they said.
"Where does the ladder lead?" I asked.
The men looked at me and did not answer.[29]

We like this futureback story since it ends with a provocative unanswered question rather than an automated answer. Such stories will be even more provocative when illustrated by a text-to-image diffusion model like Dall-E 2 or Google's Imagen that creates artistic and realistic images from words (see the chapter 9 illustration for an illustration done by Joseph and Midjourney).[30] Digital artist and new media art theorist Mark Amerika sees his life as an "Artificial Creative Intelligence (ACI)," a new type of collaboration augmenting the capabilities of multi-passionate creatives.[31]

Augmenting creative people to engage people for change, rather than only being creative, will be critical on the journey toward better futures. Storytelling will yield to storymaking.[32]

The Spectrum of Augmentation is provocative because it is evocative. These tools are finally getting practical, and they will improve dramatically over the next decade. As they augment our intelligence, they will also amplify our imagination. Over the next decade, they will improve our ability to think and act futureback.

Your Choices on the Spectrum of Augmentation

In this chapter we have applied full-spectrum thinking to understanding the multiple ways in which humans will be able to augment their intelligence: brain power, physical power, cooperative power, and emotional power to extend their performance and therefore their contribution to better working and living.

As you think about your own personal story across this spectrum, consider these questions:

1. How might you illustrate your story about the Spectrum of Augmentation?

2. How might you balance the fear of machines replacing humans with the opportunities that augmented intelligence could bring?

3. How would you increase the chances that augmentation will equitably be available to anyone who wants it within your organization?

4. Do you currently use any enchanted objects and how do you see the potential for your use both personally and within your office?

5. The combination of human creativity and the power of computers will provide the potential to build a better future. How might this augmentation be used to create better futures for working and living in your life?

NINE

Better Than Being There

The Spectrum of Place and Time

Imagine a world

in which it is easy to move between in-person and virtual
experiences. In this future world, we will always be online
and enhanced, unless we choose to be offline. While the
goal of virtual meetings used to be approximate face-to-face
meetings, the new mantra will be to create ways of working
that are better than in-person offices alone. Better ways of
working, better ways of living, better ways of making the
future. COVID-19 hybrid work was only an incremental step
toward the officeverse—a nested network of networks.

Officeverse Emerging (opposite)
Illustration by Joseph Press, augmented by Midjourney, an AI art
generator using the prompts *collaboration, multiverse, people, technology,
solarpunk, place, space, virtual, working,* and *office.*
*After reading this chapter, consider how you might illustrate
your story about the Spectrum of Place and Time.*

Way back in 2008, when renowned workplace architect Frank Duffy introduced his vision for the "networked office," he asked this provocative question:
"Why should empowered and self-reliant people,
equipped with increasingly powerful information
technology, ever come to work at all?"[1] Few people
listened to Duffy at the time. Then, the COVID-19
office shutdowns happened, and work-at-a-distance
was suddenly required for everyone.

Now, it is impossible to go back to the office the
way that it was. As illustrated in figure 15, the choices
for the office of the future are up for grabs. Thinking
futureback, this chapter starts from the early hybrid
offices but goes deeply into future media options
that will gradually become available in the emerging
officeverse.

During the office lockout, workers without offices
were surprisingly productive with simple technologies and no advance preparation. Workers surprised
many traditional managers by getting a lot of office
work done without going to the office at all.

Where and when
will you office?

Officeverse

Office

FIGURE 15:
Spectrum of Place
and Time

The COVID-19 experience, however, was deeply unfair. For those with no
private space to work, poor connectivity, inadequate furniture, or children who
needed their attention, work from home was Herculean. For others, however,
a door was cracked opened to reveal a new way of office working that was *better
than being there* in their old offices. Office shock opened opportunities to reimagine where, when, and how office work might be done in the future.

The COVID-19 shutdown let the mules of change loose. Impossible offices
became possible.

Offices do not need to remain places stuck in the past. We can create exciting
new ways of working and living that were prototyped during the pandemic.
Where, when, how, and even why we work will never be the same again. But we

must make smart choices to create better futures for working and living. There will be many opportunities and many pitfalls ahead.

Today's Hybrid Offices Are Only Temporary

The COVID-19 office lockdowns demanded careful consideration about when and how to return to office buildings. Tough decisions about offices and officing confronted individuals, organizations, and communities. Many architectural firms,[2] researchers,[3] and consultants,[4] made recommendations about the hybrid office. By "hybrid work," most people mean combinations of work in offices and work from home or other locations. That was a useful definition during the initial COVID-19 shutdown, but it was only temporary. This is a chance to think future-back about where we work, when we work, how we work, and what we work on.

Boundaries Are Just Starting to Be Redrawn

New social protocols are signals of what is now needed to navigate work and private life. For example, one of our clients, who is an executive at a very large company, added this footer to his email messages during the COVID-19 shut-down: "If you get an email from me outside normal office hours, it's because I'm sending it at a time convenient to me. I don't expect you to read or reply until normal office hours."

Some companies are already developing guidelines and policies for hybrid offices, to help people draw appropriate lines between work and private life. During the COVID-19 lockdowns meetings were scheduled to inconvenience as few people as possible. However, with home officing across time zones, there were still many who attended at what was their dinner or bedtime. Choices about how available you must be for your work colleagues are already changing the scheduling game. Work hours are up for grabs for many people. The boundaries are not there anymore like they were. Work/life balance seems impossible in this world, but work/life navigation seems more urgent than ever.[5]

As illustrated in figure 16, the emerging officeverse will involve many choices. Fixed boundaries between inside and outside will be remnants of the old office.

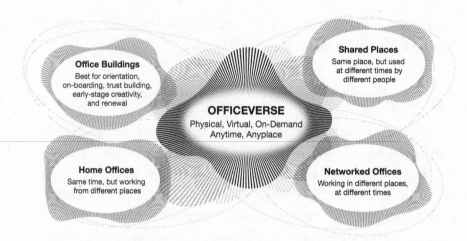

FIGURE 16: Officeverse Emerging. Expect new mixes of physical, virtual, on-demand working spaces.

Leaders will need to decide how much freedom to give for people to design their own places versus how much we want to determine the design of places. Futureback thinking will allow people and organizations to reimagine how, where, and when they work.

Hybrid Office Choices

Office buildings provide *same time/same place* options for communication and other kinds of office work. There are distinct advantages to in-person meetings and the culture of offices, but there are also constraints. You must commute to an office and only one person can speak at a time during in-person meetings, for example. Still, in-person meetings will continue to be preferable for many types of meetings and office work.

Virtual meetings like video or audio teleconferencing are *same time/different place*. They provide more of a sense of presence than a conference call, but they do require good planning and attentive participation to be effective and efficient.

Factories or stores are *same place/different times*. Another example is to think of a document as a "place" where multiple authors can work on the same document at different times. In these cases, physical presence is required to do the work, but people are using the same location at different times. The media of communication must work well across work shifts to provide continuity.

Home offices or regional hubs are *different times/different places*. This communication is asynchronous since people are working at different times—often day and night. These media work particularly well across time zones or when great flexibility in work hours is required.

The hybrid office is here, but looking futureback about office shock, we need to ask *why* we do office work and *with whom* we want to work. To think full spectrum about these questions, we will need to rethink and resculpt place and time.

The hybrid office is just a first step toward the *officeverse*: an emerging environment offering new options across the entire map of *anytime/anyplace*.

Embracing our new capability to work in different places and at different times shatters both the physical and temporal dimensions of the office—this is the *officeverse*. The officeverse is the mule in the place and time spectrum, a multisensory and multimedia place for collaboration, that provides the opportunity to choose the best options for matching the nature of the work with how, where, and when it is done. The Spectrum of Place and Time provides a way to look at the span of choices available between working in an office building and working in the officeverse.

Beyond Today's Hybrid Offices

Boundaries will be redrawn, with many more possibilities to consider.

Collaborative spaces in virtual and augmented reality will be available for immersive, embodied, and even tactile officing. But for many they remain unusual and foreign and will require training and much more contact with the tools to establish proficiency. However, the potential for enriching office work, enhancing interactions, and expanding professional and social connections is unlimited.

Although many companies and individuals will try very hard to own and control it, the officeverse will take on a virtual life of its own. Mules that disrupted place and time in the real world will only be more extreme in the officeverse. In the officeverse, place and time will be different. This new world will be a far cry from today's hybrid offices. Already, the boundaries between work and private life are being pierced. Work from home can be great, but overwork from home can be awful.

As the workplace is co-created by citizens of the officeverse, the activities occurring within it will disrupt many of today's organizational models. Originally designed to structure and control the complexities of human interactions, organizational charts will be irrelevant in the officeverse. Managing the challenges of the officeverse will require conceptual changes of the importance of time, deadlines, sequencing of tasks, and the effects on individuals of all of these.

With many possible connections, trust in the officeverse will require artful nurturing and negotiation. While technology is important for office connectivity, the most essential social technology is trust. The need for trust will be acute in a future with more online interaction and less physical interaction. Institute for the Future research has suggested that it is very difficult to seed and grow trust through using social media. On the other hand, it is very easy to seed distrust and mistrust through social media.[6]

Employee activity tracking technology was sometimes used during the pandemic as an unpopular tool to track the behavior of individual knowledge workers. It will be easier to measure performance, but harder to observe people while they work. If a company focuses on performance, rather than time sitting at a desk, that will give workers a much wider range of choices regarding when and where they work.

In anticipation of Web3 and quantum computing changing the virtual game completely,[7] blockchain-enabled technologies like smart contracts will offer the potential to replace those primitive efforts and allow independence in fulfilling work responsibilities.[8] In virtual worlds, some form of monitoring activity will be ubiquitous, so trust will be an issue. Like the trust developed in video game communities, new ways of nurturing trust will emerge in the officeverse.[9] The foundation of trust in the officeverse will ultimately be built on creating a shared language and opportunities to mobilize people for better futures of working and living.

As Marshall McLuhan said, "We shape our tools, and thereafter our tools shape us."[10] The officeverse will be a network of networks, with tools that will shape us in disruptive and surprising ways over the next decade and beyond.

Digital natives (twenty-seven or younger in 2023) and XR natives (seventeen or younger in 2023) are experiencing ahead-of-their-times digital interfaces via video gaming platforms. They are creating their own worlds, developing social networks, and (probably unknown to them) preparing for the office of the future. Gamers are often way ahead of today's average office worker in terms of being future-ready. The digital and XR natives will have a competitive advantage in the officeverse.

Your Persona, Your Space

You will get to choose or create your own avatar to establish your identity in the virtual officeverse. You will have many choices, and avatars will be about much more than appearance. They signal who you want to be and how you want to present yourself to others. You can create a version of yourself that may range from current traits to something more aspirational. Avatars will be extensions of you, and may even enable you to be in multiple places at the same time. An *MIT Technology Review* cover story introduces readers to the next generation's multiple selves.[11]

In the popular book and movie *Ready Player One*, the avatars do not look like the real person's physical body, but they do embody the spirit and aspirations of that person. Avatars will be designed to adapt to the world you are in, constantly adjusting to the animate and inanimate objects in your environment. They will project your facial expressions and physical movements, and you will be able to give yourself an upgrade or redesign whenever you like. Over time, your avatar's capabilities will grow since your avatar is a container of your information, data, and experience and a distributor of information about you to the officeverse.

How Will You Dodge the Uncanny Valley?

To succeed, the officeverse must eventually bridge what Japanese robotics professor Masahiro Mori called the "uncanny valley,"[12] where robots are almost human looking but not quite, in an eerie and disturbing way. On the other side of that valley, we will be better than being there. In the officeverse, we will all be high-fidelity digital humans—but still be ourselves.[13]

Automated and accurate language translation, complemented with bodily gestures captured and communicated via haptic suits, which bring lifelike sensations to the wearer, will increase comprehension. Facial mimicry will enable not only cognitive empathy but emotional empathy as well. The interoperability between platforms will enable the interoperability between people.

With avatars, the workplace playing field can be fairer. Gender, age, ethnicity, and other physical traits can be hidden or less apparent, unless you want them to be visible. You can form relationships with others that perhaps you would not have considered in the real world. Our avatars can moderate prejudice based on gender, ethnicity, or any physical attributes or disabilities. Potentially, communication among avatars may be more authentic and less prejudiced. Discrimination, potentially, should be decreased in the officeverse.

Challenges and risks will not go away in the officeverse, but they will be different. Avoiding inappropriate behavior and cultural appropriation will require training and monitoring. As we have seen in the use of current social media, balancing digital with physical interaction will remain important, and avoiding physical isolation in favor of electronic relationships will continue to be a challenge for some. Loneliness became an issue during the lockdowns of the pandemic despite extensive social media use. MIT social scientist Sherry Turkle concluded in her research that young people are often "alone together" in digital environments.[14] We believe that when the office is part of the digital social technology,[15] your workplace can make you feel alone together if you are not mixing your digital and in-person experiences.

Blending your real self with your online persona will be essential in the officeverse. This extremely creative exercise will be relevant for everyone in the office, regardless of role or way of working. The new office will need to offer people the flexibility to express their creativity. Fortunately, there is an entire generation growing up with digital experiences. They are shaping new dimensions of living and playing, which will reshape where and when we work.

Designing Your Own Workspace

The visionary workplace architect Fritz Haller sought to create a system for users to design their homes, their offices, and even their cities.[16] Echoing similar positions from architects like N. John Habraken[17] and Ezio Manzini,[18] Haller's intention was to give inhabitants more agency in building design. While participatory design is still an active approach,[19] scaling of size and culture remains a significant hurdle to realizing the ideal.[20]

In the officeverse, there will be great potential (if organizations agree) for people to design their own spaces and work the way they want to work. As the dimensions of place are being created before our eyes, spaces in the officeverse are disconnecting architects from the classic archetypes of workspaces. In the officeverse, you can be transported to any virtual environment. Traditional water cooler conversations are great at times, but they require people to be at the same water cooler at the same time. With a choice of virtual environments, creativity, personal expression, and social belonging can span time and place.

In the physical office space, managers and designers decided what people wanted in their office environments. Did young talent want a more playful environment that included Ping-Pong tables? How does that decision affect their older coworkers? What designs were equally attractive to employees of all genders? What customizations were employees allowed to make in their environments? Creating a sense of comfort and belonging in the office space has been a continuing challenge.

In the officeverse, everyone can create their custom environment. Creative collaboration and serendipitous interactions are the pure pleasures of today's office that many people miss. In the officeverse, our opportunities to create, collaborate, and learn will be spectacular. Early research suggests that people recall information better when they learn through virtual reality.[21] This research tested visual memory (like the game Concentration) and found that the immersive nature of VR helped participants increase their correct answers by almost

9 percent. The officeverse will be a critical catalyst in shifting mindsets away from executing routine tasks to exercising imagination, making, and systemic thinking, which are essential skills for the postpandemic economy,[22] and skills that many young people learn through gaming.

In video gaming environments, creativity is the currency.[23] These world-builders are not only tinkering with basic blocks but also co-creating with others. They are reshaping the virtual dimensions of living and working with creative collaboration fueled by serendipitous interactions between real people and virtual objects. In his book *Beautiful Minecraft,* James Delaney shares images of fantastic and stunning artistic expression in this kid-oriented virtual world.[24]

Creating a customized office will also allow the physical world to contribute to one's sense of self-identity and self-fulfillment. Interior design choices like colors, furnishings, and finishes will be tailored to please the individual creator's eye and mind. The same virtual environment can even generate different views for different people. Extreme personalization will enable exploration of new extremes of thought, new personal agency, and possibly a new sense of purpose.

The Timeless Meaning of Place

Architects are schooled in the Roman concept of *genius loci,* the protective spirit of a place. Genius loci is less about the physical environment and more about the timeless meaning of place. It is the attributes of the environment that are impregnated with memories, emotions, and resonance. In an officeverse, the role of place will be very different—but even more important.

Place has always been a platform for social experience. From open-air or covered marketplaces to the piazza for community gathering and cultural events, social interaction was always the real attraction. Shopping together, playing together, learning together, and working together are integral parts of human history. The officeverse will be a place for new forms of interaction.

Jaron Lanier, one of the pioneers of virtual reality, builds on McLuhan stating that our experiences in the virtual worlds will ultimately teach us how to see and be sensitive to stimuli in the real world. His experience of being in a real forest was enriched in a visceral way after spending time in a VR forest—the digital brought a greater appreciation of the analog.[25] Such convergence can establish an amplified presence that has the feel of "being there" regardless of physical location and time dimensions.

Places reshaped by office shock can promote new serendipity and sociability among individuals, organizations, and communities. Physical buildings and their surrounding areas can create a very attractive culture of communities. They can reflect a corporate culture and facilitate the growth of that culture.

However, there will be a need to develop new principles, guidelines, rules, and practices in the officeverse. When private information becomes public, the pain for an individual, a company, or a government could be severe. New concepts of sharing and boundary management will develop, and there will be many challenges. By learning how to coordinate in the officeverse, we will have new insight on how to better coordinate in the real world.

With a new appreciation and potential of how place can engage people for collective action, the officeverse may also contribute to achieving the UN Sustainable Development Goals. Drawing inspiration from Lanier, we can envision that Goal #9 (Build resilient infrastructure, promote inclusive and sustainable industrialization, and foster innovation) will be accelerated by redrawing the boundaries of time and place.

The rejuvenation of place is an ingredient essential to leverage office shock to create better futures for working and living. The Spectrum of Place and Time provides choices to challenge our old ideas of place and time, look for new ways of working, and harmonize our journey to the future.

Your Choices on the Spectrum of Place and Time

The officeverse will give us many more choices for offices and officing—and the choices will be much deeper than with today's hybrid working. The officeverse will be tailor-made, and personalized.

In the officeverse, everyone who intentionally provides teams with opportunities to customize and personalize officing through the meaningful design of space and time will become office designers. The porous boundaries of personal and social experiences, individual and social cognition, and ultimately neurological input and externalized behaviors will necessitate thinking across gradients of possibility beyond the categories of past offices and officing.

As you think about your own personal story across this spectrum, consider these questions:

1. How might you illustrate your story about the Spectrum of Place and Time?

2. How will you determine what tasks or activities are best carried out together or apart through the varied officeverse media options?

3. In what way does the concept of an avatar appeal to or disturb your thinking about working in the officeverse?

4. Trust will be a critical ingredient for making virtual relationships successful. How will you seed and sustain trust?

5. How does the opportunity to design your workspace affect your comfort level in the officeverse?

6. How will you establish a sense of organizational culture and belonging in your officeverse?

TEN

Coordinating with Clarity

The Spectrum of Agility

Imagine a world

in which agility and resilience will be prioritized over certainty
and efficiency. Imagine leaders who will be skilled in the art of
flexive intent, with great clarity about where they intend to go but
great flexibility about how they will get there. All office workers
will have license to act, innovate, and coordinate within the
envelope of clarity provided by purpose and emergent leadership.
Distributed authority hierarchies will come and go based on
who is in the best position to make which decision at what time.
Scenarios, simulation, and gaming will allow people to prepare in
low-risk ways for the highly uncertain future. Economies of scale
(where bigger was almost always better) will yield to economies
of organization, where you will be what you are able to organize.

Braided Agility *(opposite)*
Illustration by Yeti Iglesias from Mexico.
*After reading this chapter, consider how you might
illustrate your story about the Spectrum of Agility.*

Marina Gorbis refers to organizations as a kind of social technology, which "is not preordained but designed."[1] Coordinating with clarity means being more than an office shock absorber; it means developing readiness for the future.

As illustrated in figure 17, the Spectrum of Agility moves from Stable Structures to Shape Shifting. It implies a shift from centralized to distributed, and from certainty to clarity. Agility is the ability to get there early and respond in coordinated ways with speed, strength, balance, and grace.

Stunning agility was evident in the rapid development of a vaccine for COVID-19. Dr. Melanie Ivarsson, head of development at Moderna, led the team that developed the mRNA vaccine. She faced a VUCA challenge during the global pandemic: collaborate with competitors to develop a vaccine that many viewed as impossible within a rapid time frame. There were mules everywhere, including people who resisted the very idea of a miracle vaccine.

How will you increase your ability to be agile and resilient?

Shape-Shifting

Stable

FIGURE 17:
Spectrum of Agility

The entire world, the entire eco-system learned to work entirely differently and that made all the difference....We did not compete with each other....The collaboration among all the companies was unprecedented.[2]

Her ability to organize a shape-shifting team with agility, to do something that had never been done before, led to a groundbreaking world-saving vaccine. In the VUCA world, internal rigidity will be a greater threat than external change.

Future-Ready Officing

Traditional offices were designed with rigidity to pursue certainty. They were production lines for knowledge workers, with human touches occasionally along the way. Rigidity can be comforting at times, but certainty is brittle—and brittle breaks. The COVID-19 crisis broke the certainties of the traditional office.

The office used to be hierarchical and centralized. In the future officeverse, however, everything and everyone that can be distributed will be distributed. Attempts to centralize resources and control decision-making will constantly be disrupted. Because of extended periods of office shock, the unexamined assumptions about centralized offices and officing will be up for grabs.

The future will be an incessant carnival of surprises that will be intensified by a new generation of gamers entering the officeverse. Organizing to create better futures in the face of uncertainty will be daunting. Acting and thinking full spectrum will require new metaphors and mindsets to develop agility and thrive. We will need to organize, personalize, and game our way to an agile resilient office with better working and living.

Organizing for Future-Readiness

The COVID-19 crisis exposed that what companies formerly perceived as their own private supply "chains" were in fact fragile and increasingly open supply *webs*. Supply webs encompass vast amounts of information across organizational boundaries. They require increased communication and coordination. Supply webs are one example of how the traditional way of viewing and managing organizations is being disrupted. Supply chains were designed for just-in-time efficiency. How will tomorrow's supply webs be designed for agility and resilience—rather than efficiency alone?

In the officeverse, organizations will require flexibility and empowerment, rather than command and control. They will need to respond quickly to market fluctuations and delegate decision-making to people or teams in the best position to act.

We call this way of organizing shape-shifting.[3] As illustrated in figure 18, such shape-shifting organizations are entangled social and digital networks where hierarchies come and go on the route to achieving shared purpose. They grow from the edges, where diversity flourishes and innovation is easier to get going. Shape-shifting organizations cannot be controlled, but they can be guided with

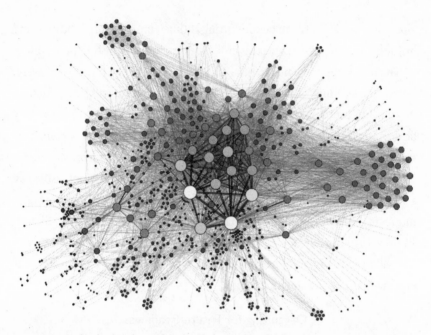

FIGURE 18: An Archipelago of Agility. Informed by DAO network mapping, shape-shifting organizations will continually ebb and flow as individuals and their fluid.

flexive intent organized around purpose and clear leadership statements of direction. Leaders in shape-shifting organizations are always looking for mutual-benefit partnering opportunities for engagement, to help them accomplish what they cannot accomplish alone.

Shape-shifting organizations have no fixed center, with hierarchies that come and go based on who is in the best position to make which decisions at what time. The most productive shape-shifting organizations will have not only great clarity of direction but also great flexibility of execution. The choices on the Spectrum of Agility help the knowledge worker to synchronize individual talent for agility and resiliance with the organizational need for shape-shifting in pursuit of improved decision-making. The harmony of finding your best position on the spectrum will increase your value to the organization and improve its agility and resilience.

Shape-shifting organizations will be characterized by:

- Leaders who lead through entangled social and digital networks.
- Leaders who come and go across the mesh, not above it.
- Leaders who have the ability to calm situations where differences dominate and find common ground.
- Leaders who are strong, yet humble.

Shape-shifting organizations will be like fishnets or other interwoven network structures that have the flexibility and strength of braided cord. As described in the book *Braided Organizations*, shape-shifting is accomplished by an "intertwined network of contributors with different capabilities, not controlled via formal hierarchy, who work together to invent ways to accomplish common purpose."[4]

In braided shape-shifting organizations, a magnetizing purpose draws people together from the futureback. Braided working weaves collective intellgence to get things done through shared governance. As shared purpose evolves, members shift their roles and responsibilities as required to move forward. Leaders tap into distributed resources to assist in navigating complexity. A constant flow of information permeates ever-changing boundaries.[5]

Braided working in a shape-shifting organization is exemplified in companies like Blinkist. Founded in 2012 in Berlin, Germany, as of 2021 the subscription service connects eighteen million readers worldwide to the biggest ideas from bestselling nonfiction via fifteen-minute audio and text clips. When Niklas Jansen and his co-owners decided to go international in 2017, they faced a real issue: How to create a more responsive organization that puts the emphasis on empowering individuals to operate with distributed power? Jansen and his People Team noticed that it was not more structure that was needed, but less. Self-managed and self-empowered teams revealed a third need: transparency.

Where most traditional organizations would aim for more processes and policies, the Blinkist team shifted to fewer:

We started to see the best organizational systems are somewhat invisible and ended up with a really clear purpose and focus—staying truly focused on the customer and employee problem, inspiring us to keep learning.[6]

Taking inspiration from the world of information technology and targeting operating systems, Blinkist's People Team created the Blinkist Operating System. Every team figures out their own way to work in pursuit of innovation and speed. Pushing decision-making down to the lowest possible level still influences the long-term thinking in the company but, says Jansen, behavior, purpose, and culture are still the central focus.

As Blinkest illustrates, agile is more than a mere working methodology. Although agile methods are necessary, they are an insufficient condition to ensure the organizational flexibility required to adapt to changing market demands. Even with the promising yet emerging Web3 and DAOs, if leaders do not have flexive intent they may not succeed in changing the established systems. Coordinating with clarity will require personal agility to ensure that braided working happens in shape-shifting teams.

Leading with Readiness

In the book *The New Leadership Literacies*,[7] Bob describes how leaders will need physical, mental, and even spiritual (though not necessarily religious) agility in the future. Think of this individualized agility as creating and sustaining positive energy in the face of turmoil. Agility is a combination of energy and animation, an ability to engage with ambiguity and flip it into something positive.

Leaders who are fluent in this new literacy will walk into a group—in person or virtually—and radiate authentic positive energy. They will have a disciplined personal approach to their own physical, mental, and emotional fitness. They will balance their energy levels throughout the day and night, moderate peaks, and drops. They will create space for others to live happy energetic lives.

Over the next decade, the media for distributed work will get dramatically better. Today's platforms have established the basic connections, but there is so much that will be improved. Digital media will amplify our personal agility in remarkable ways.

For example, a Duke University neurobiology study[8] found that paraplegics who have been told that they would never walk again are using brain-machine interfaces with a virtual reality interface to control their legs. The goal is to regain mobility, strength, and independence. This is an example of personal physical agility at a very basic level. The future will be a mix of superminds and super bodies, requiring a high level of mental and physical agility to adapt to any situation.

As command-and-control structures give way to shape-shifting braids, people will be able to step outside the confines of traditional fixed organizational structures and cultivate the crowd's collective intelligence for inspired action. Agile resilient offices will not be easy though. Periods of confusion will cloud the path to achieving breakthroughs. People must learn to maintain their own emotional stability, mindful not to succumb to drowning in attempts to analyze everything. Staying buoyant will be essential, and gaming provides a way to practice.

Gameful Engagement for Readiness

Gameful engagement has evolved from something purely recreational to a powerful organizing tool. Gaming requires personal agility and nimble thinking along with a willingness to reconnect with play. Gameful engagement is emotionally laden attention, which is very similar to the definition of a good story. In a game, however, you get to be in the story.

As neuroscientist Andrew Huberman describes, play is a biological need that is regulated by homeostasis, just like food and water.[9] Play allows the brain to test contingencies in different roles to shape your personal-play identity.[10] Play and tinkering in low-risk environments triggers neuroplasticity for developing new capabilities. Online gaming environments can help to improve skills like creating organizations or cooperating with other individuals and teams. Thinking futureback, what we think of as gaming today will be the most powerful learning medium in history.

In the future an agile shape-shifting organization will be a blended reality of both physical and virtual communities. This combination will demand an experience that has social effects and provides all participants with more agency in accomplishing tasks. In effect, the agile organization will need a new kind of office.

Gameful cooperation enables us to experiment with co-creating impossible futures. Accelerated by a new generation of gamers growing into leadership positions, gameful[11] literacies will influence ways of collaborating, and organizing, in every industry. Whether online or face-to-face, gaming is redefining how we connect and what we do together, which will redefine the future of an organization. Since these platforms will operate as both safe havens and combative spaces in continual flux at any given moment in time, organizing people will also be hyperfluid, expansive, and sometimes fickle.

The player networks in the book and movie called *Ready Player One* show how a complex and messy assembly of players can call gaming networks their new social home. Whether in a massively multiplayer online roleplaying game like *League of Legends* or in a multiplayer online Battle Arena like *Fortnight*, or a sandbox game without boundaries like *Minecraft*, these places "capture the social experience."[12] In these platforms, players create squads, sports teams, or parties to cooperate by real-time communication. Driven by an intent to win, such player networks increasingly resemble purpose-driven communities in the physical world.

In the world of gaming, agile cohorts can be built rapidly to create pop-up communities centered around core values. To encourage a positive culture, gaming companies have codes of conduct to "create communities of positive play"[13] by "providing an inclusive gaming environment where everyone, anywhere . . . can have fun while feeling safe and respected."[14]

Voluntary Fear Engagement

Office shock will come loaded with surprises, some of which will be frightening. Astronaut Kayla Barron said, while aboard the International Space Station, "It's more important to be brave than fearless."[15] In the officeverse, where technology empowers multiple identities, you will be able to write your own story. You can experience what it would be like as a human working for robots, like in the popular VR game *Job Simulator*.[16] Players can try out jobs and learn what they like and don't like, experience discomfort in low-risk ways.

Before the 9/11 terrorist attacks occurred, for example, there were prescient war gaming scenarios about terrorists pirating commercial aircraft and flying them into buildings, but nobody in leadership positions imagined that those scenarios were possible—so they weren't taken seriously. There was little imagination and preparation for this scenario until after the attack.

Voluntary fear exposure—think of it as gaming with possible futures—allows players to experience frightening scenarios in low-risk ways to become more future-ready. Futureback thinking is a kind of voluntary fear exposure. War gaming allows players to experience being killed without having to die. This technique is a therapy used by psychologists to help people confront their fears. It is a safe environment in which to experience interaction with something that in real life may be terrifying, for example, fear of flying or fear of spiders. But it can be used through gaming to create a new and unanticipated world of the future to experiment with and experience new ways of working and living.

Simulation and gaming are excellent ways to practice in low-risk ways. As futurists Stuart Candy and Jake Dunagan said: "It is better to be surprised by a simulation than blindsided by reality."[17]

Dunagan proposed the idea of a Global Simulation Corps for youth service to allow young people to game possible futures—including impossible futures—to prepare for the future.

> Simulations are models of reality that help people prepare for possible futures, and the most ambitious of these attempts to model large complete systems—even entire economies or ecosystems.[18]

Thinking futureback will help develop clarity of direction about where, when, and why we work, but we need to stay very agile about how we get to that future. We will have to prototype our way out of the noisy and threatening present.

Gaming for the Future

At Institute for the Future, we use scenarios and gaming to probe impossible futures, focusing on the importance of surprise. As we think futureback about offices and officing, how can we prepare ourselves to be surprised and hone our agility? Scenarios, simulations, and games allow us to prepare to be surprised, to think the unthinkable. Scenarios allow us to probe impossible futures and experience them in low-risk ways. Simulations and games allow all people to be inside their scenarios, to practice leadership in low-risk ways. Scenarios use characters and dialogue to bring the future to life. As in world building, character development and dialogue are critical to making the scenarios vivid and engaging.

Virtual simulations are being used increasingly for skills training and encourage lifelong learning. For example, VR simulations prepare members of fire and rescue services for safely fighting fires and rescuing endangered citizens,[19] including learning CPR.[20] Cybersecurity simulation training is a way to accurately test how your organization responds to simulated cyberattacks. Police officers at the Mountain View, California, police department apply state-of-the-art neuroscience research to a combination of virtual reality and biometric devices to "give officers individual ways to improve the ways in which they respond to calls."[21]

Gaming in low-risk simulated environments allows us to learn how to organize in anticipation of the surprises and futures that we may perceive as impossible.

Gameful engagement will empower profound learning experiences. From prototyping store designs to troubleshooting industrial systems to training on-the-ground workers, play in this playground will trigger neuroplasticity at a scale never before possible. Gaming will be the nuclear core of building agile mindsets and organizations.

Develop Your Own Flexive Intent

We suggest the term *flexive intent*[22] to describe how to coordinate with clarity. By *flexive*, we mean pliable and responsive—not rigid or brittle. Imagine a fishnet lying on a dock. Pick up one node in the net and a temporary hierarchy is created. Put that node down and pick up another node and another temporary hierarchy forms. By *intent*, we mean being clear about direction. Intent is commitment to a direction of change and possibly an outcome.

In the VUCA world, leaders must be very clear about their intention, but very flexible about how that intent might be achieved on a day-to-day basis. Flexive intent opens opportunities to adapt the course of action in response to ever-changing circumstances.

Synchronizing with others—characterized by a common language, shared stories, heightened empathy, and communal resilience—will move members of an agile collective to synchronized action to co-create better futures for working and living.

Office shock is an opportunity to rethink your organizational purpose for employees, shareholders, and stakeholders of all kinds as well as your collective purpose for society at large. Look inside and outside your organization. Partners will want win-win opportunities, so the critical success factor analysis (see chapter 11) will help you decide first what is most important to your organization. Expect that different organizations will have different critical success factors, which will make coordination between partners more challenging, but more important for achieving shared success.

Mazzucato recommended that the European Union launch concrete, ambitious, targeted, inspirational missions.[23] Missions are inherently futureback. They are projects targeting the UN Sustainable Development Goals, with a focus on social impact. Denmark, for example, prevented any companies that use tax havens from receiving stimulus money. France required that airlines could not get stimulus funding unless they showed that they had reduced their carbon footprint. The European Union has a mission to have one hundred carbon neutral cities. To achieve these missions there will be many projects. Projects must include new social contracts with inclusive and sustainable conditions. What Mazzucato calls "missions" are based on a futureback view of what needs to be done and are good examples of flexive intent.

In the future, command and control will be out. Flexive intent will be in.

Your Choices on the Spectrum of Agility

Making choices on the Spectrum of Agility, and mobilizing for collective action, will be dependent on coordinating with clarity. With greater agility, people in shape-shifting organizations can focus on the cross-pollination of ideas that not only strengthen interconnections and sustainability but also require a fundamental shift in mindset, behavior, and culture. This spectrum requires close synchronization between the individuals in the office and the organization to achieve the agility required for better decision-making to lead to better futures for working and living.

As you think about your own personal story across this spectrum, consider these questions:

1. How might you illustrate your story about the Spectrum of Agility?

2. How have you thought about moving your personal behavior away from the efficiency/effectiveness model and toward a model of increased agility and resilience?

3. Gaming skills will be well developed in the digital-native members of the workforce, but what about everyone else? How will you and your organization use gaming to increase your own resilience?

4. How will the lessons learned through gaming be translated into actionable tasks and processes?

5. As a leader in an organization, how will you enable distributed authority?

PART III

WHAT NOW?

Making Smart Choices for Individuals, Organizations, and Communities

All that you touch,
You Change.
All that you Change,
Changes you.
The only lasting truth,
Is Change.
God Is Change.

OCTAVIA BUTLER
Parable of the Sower[1]

Our purpose in part III is to help you apply the futureback methodology for yourself, your organization, and your community. We provide you with a Quick Start Guide that includes four steps:

Step 1. Find your Future Self;

Step 2. Set your navigational star;

Step 3. Make your choices by sliding the scales on the Seven Spectrums of Choice described in part II;

Step 4. Co-create a compelling story of your flexive intent.

Part I provided a futures context for understanding office shock, while part II introduced the Seven Spectrums of Choice for you to consider.

Part III focuses on What Now? What can you do now—as an individual, an organization, or a community—to create better futures for work and life? Now is the time to develop the agility that will be required to create a better future. Now is the time for you to write your own stories for your offices and officing.

The mixing board will help you harmonize your choices across the spectrums and synchronize them with others. Combined with futureback thinking and a full-spectrum mindset, you can now flip office shock into an opportunity to co-create better futures of working and living.

ELEVEN

Thinking Futureback about Office Shock

Introducing Our Quick Start Guide

Imagine a world

in which a mixing board will help you think full spectrum to lead futureback. With this mixing board, you will be able to clarify your future of offices and officing while avoiding the traps of certainty. It will help you to make smart choices to harmonize within the Seven Spectrums of Choice (as introduced in part II of this book). The mixing board will help you synchronize your choices with others across the seven spectrums and reveal how your personal, organizational, and community choices can be coordinated for better working and living. It will help you avoid the dissonances, as you lead the transition with flexive intent.

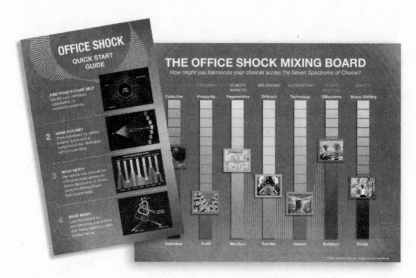

FIGURE 19: Office Shock Quick Start Guide (see book insert after page 60)

The best office shock stories still need to be written.

In part I (What Future?), we introduced the futureback method and the full-spectrum mindset. We applied these to create possible stories from the impossible shocks we face in the VUCA world.

In part II (What Next?), we introduced the Seven Spectrums of Choice for offices and officing. The spectrums provide insight on the choices you will want to make for stories of futures with:

- Purpose (spanning individual and collective)

- Outcome (spanning profit and prosperity)

- Climate Impacts (spanning net-zero and regenerative)

- Belonging (spanning familiar and different)

- Augmentation (spanning human and technology)

- Place and Time (spanning buildings and officeverse)

- Agility (spanning stable and shape-shifting)

In part III (What Now?), we invite you to write your own story for offices and officing.

To help you to think futureback about offices and officing, we've created a Quick Start Guide (figure 19) that brings together the spectrums' mixing board and the other tools in this book.

The Quick Start Guide will help you win in the world of office shock. It can prepare you for whatever future comes—and more importantly help you make the future you want.

The Quick Start Guide presents an approach to developing your own clarity about offices and officing. It begins with defining who you are, then what future you want. Next is to make choices across the seven spectrums that inform what actions you want to take now to prepare yourself, your organization, and your community.

The Quick Start Guide will help you turn office shock into a great opportunity to create a better future.

Step 1: Find Your Future Self

Start by tearing out the Quick Start Guide in this book or retrieving it from the Office Shock web site.

Prepare for navigating office shock, by imagining

- Your Future Self as a worker (more to come in chapter 12)
- Your Future Self as part of an organization (more to come in chapter 13)
- Your Future Self as part of a community (more to come in chapter 14)

Being aware of who you are in the future VUCA world isn't easy. When COVID-19 hit, the boundaries between personal and professional personas were forcefully blurred. Now, after living with mandatory blurring, it is possible to make more conscious choices about how we want to work and live.

Thinking futureback about yourself is difficult for most people because our future selves are neurological strangers to us. Our brains, the prefrontal cortex in particular, shut down when thinking about ourselves in the future. For this reason, at IFTF we start our futureback workshops with an exercise we call "Find

Future Self." Once you find your Future Self, it will make the future feel more urgent to you. Awareness of your Future Self will prime your brain to be more open to ways the future will be different. It will motivate you to actively shape the future today for all the roles you play:[1]

- Your Future Self as an individual worker is the focus of chapter 12. To be ahead of the potential shocks of office shock, we recommend first choosing what is most important for you as an individual. What do *you* need for success in the future, and what are *your* choices?

- Your Future Self as part of an organization is the focus of chapter 13. There you can reflect on what it means to be part of something bigger than yourself. Indeed, your choices about how to organize, both formally and informally, will be a primary influence on the future of the office.[2]

- Your Future Self as a member of a community, and/or a policy maker, is the focus of chapter 14. Your role as a citizen in a community is the broadest future self. Here you can explore how to think futureback about what people and organizations choose to do together in the community. For example, successful delivery of public health requires individuals and organizations to work together for diagnosis, tracking, treatment, and prevention. If you are a policy maker, your choices may include zoning, public transportation, equitable access, availability of free networking, the rights of individuals, health benefits, and child-care options—just a few of the areas where policies can influence with whom we work.

Office shock has created a need to harmonize the choices you will make in each spectrum. The mixing board opens an opportunity for a jazzlike conversation to help you synchronize between yourself and others on a better future for offices and officing.

Step 2: What Future?

With clarity about your future self, you can now think futureback about better futures for working and living. Begin by choosing a navigational star to guide your intentions.

Your navigational star is a direction of a better future that you will commit to pursue with flexive intent. If you need ideas about a compelling direction to pursue, then consider the UN Sustainable Development Goals as a North Star,[3] or the variations we propose in the "Office Shock Navigational Stars" section at the end of this book. As discussed in chapter 3, the sanctioned yet broad nature of the Sustainable Development Goals make them good navigational stars[4] to guide your flexive intent.

Your navigational star can also reflect a specific spectrum. For example, for pursuing Purpose you might say, "My future will focus on promoting well-being for people at all ages." An example for Climate Impacts could be "In my future I will be a custodian of biodiversity."

With increased clarity of What Future? you can then define What Next?

Step 3: What Next?

Flip the Quick Start Guide over to The Office Shock Mixing Board.

Our Office Shock Mixing Board has seven channels (what we call spectrums of choice) for you to move the sliders as you make choices (see figure 20). Each spectrum of office shock has polarities: extreme positions you can slide between. You can make different choices at different times in different situations.

Consider the breadth of the spectrum and where you want your balance to be. The polarities of each spectrum provide a wide range of options and your choice will likely reflect where you are in your career.

For example, if you are considering the Spectrum of Outcomes, as an individual, you may choose to position yourself toward the top, but not all the way, indicating that you are balancing your requirement for personal profit with a desire to contribute to improving the prosperity of others.

To make the spectrums more manageable, we encourage you to define your critical success factors[5] that will show you the way toward your preferred future. This interview process was developed by Christine Bullen and Jack Rockart at MIT. It was one of the first initiatives to identify links between information technologies and corporate strategy. They will help crystalize your intentions, where you are on the span of the spectrum, and the path forward.

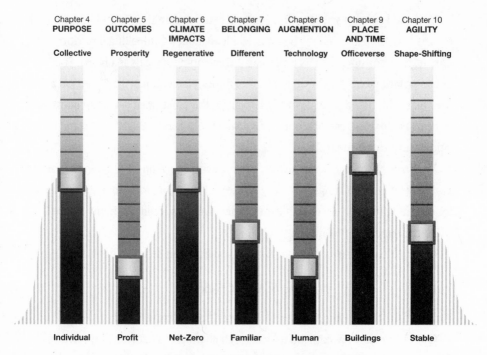

Chapter 4 **PURPOSE**	Chapter 5 **OUTCOMES**	Chapter 6 **CLIMATE IMPACTS**	Chapter 7 **BELONGING**	Chapter 8 **AUGMENTION**	Chapter 9 **PLACE AND TIME**	Chapter 10 **AGILITY**
Collective	Prosperity	Regenerative	Different	Technology	Officeverse	Shape-Shifting
Individual	Profit	Net-Zero	Familiar	Human	Buildings	Stable

FIGURE 20: Office Shock Mixing Board: Harmonize the spectrums of choice for navigating office shock.

The critical success factor interview questions are designed to provoke you to think about what would need to go right for you to successfully turn office shock into a great opportunity. They ask you what failures, if they occurred, would hurt you the most? If you disappeared magically for three years and your life went on, what would you most like to know about your organization when you returned?

Answers to these questions will help you to define your critical success factors. Knowing your critical success factors will inform your choices for What Next? It will also reveal any gaps and any requirements you will need to synchronize with others.

For example, for the Spectrum of Outcomes, you might say, "In my future I want to find inclusive, productive, and decent work for both me and my workforce community." An example for the Spectrum of Augmentation might be, "I want to learn the best way to augment my intelligence as quickly as possible."

To help you define what's next, chapters 12, 13, and 14 contain a list of possible critical success factors to provoke your choice-making for each spectrum.

These are not binary either/or choices. There is a full spectrum of possibilities between the polarities. The mixing board provides a way to help you see and think through your choices—and the implications of your choices for others.

Step 4: What Now?

Turn your choices into actions by defining what, how, and who to guide your journey. We recommend using a scaffolding as shown in figure 21 to ensure clarity of your intent and provide the space to be flexible about how you pursue it.

In *IDeaLs (Innovation and Design as Leadership): Transformation in the Digital Era*, Joseph and his coauthors researched how companies engage people for transformation. Flexive intent best describes the type of collective leadership demonstrated by Philips and seven other companies on their transformation journey.

For example, Philips's evolution from a consumer product company to a technology health-care company began in 2011.[6] The signposts along Philips's journey to lead the industry toward value-based care are indicative of innovation, design, and leadership. Funding for pre-seed accelerator projects was fast-tracked, a design thinking methodology called "co-create" became the standard for collaborative activities, and leadership development was augmented with futureback thinking to accelerate the digital transformation.[7]

Models illustrating transformation are typically flat and linear, what anthropologist and author Josh Berson refers to as the "landscape metaphor." To grasp how communities enact change over time, he recommends considering a scaffold that supports and bounds the collective search for action.[8]

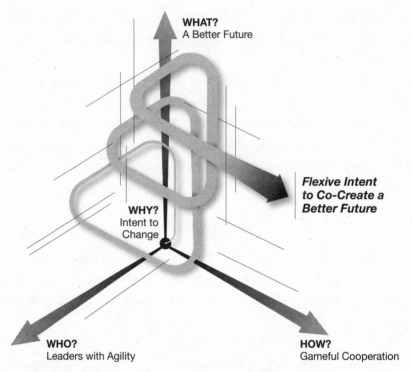

FIGURE 21: The IDeaLs' Transformation Scaffold (adapted for *Office Shock*). With flexive intent, change can be cultivated in complex environments.

Inspired by Bergson and indicated in the research with Philips and others, the IDeaLs team proposed a 3-dimensional scaffold for coordinating with clarity across three dimensions.

There are four important dimensions of this model:

1. **Intent to Change (Why?):** An intention to change an existing situation into a preferred one.

2. **A Better Future for Offices (What?):** The more meaningful experiences of people that provide opportunities for them to participate in the preferred future, often resulting from stated critical success factors.

3. **Gameful Cooperation (How?):** The means to engage people in the co-creation of the preferred future.

4. **Leaders with Agility (Who?):** The ways to engage people to develop a deep level of commitment that leads to actions that change existing situations into preferred ones.

Leaders will need both clarity and flexibility in creating more resilient and inclusive organizations, a key characteristic of an agile organization. IDeaLs is a scaffold for coordinating with clarity, and flexive intent is the means to climb the scaffold. This *place of possibilities* is where the American physicist and feminist theorist Karen Barad sees agency—a space of possibilities for change.[9] The choices of how to coordinate change with clarity on the transformation journey will either make or break any intentions for better futures.

Clarity of direction is essential, and so are the contours that will influence your trajectory. Think of the spectrums as guardrails. Understanding the span between them helps guide your choices along the spectrum. You'll want to know what spectrum you are on and what the extremes are so you can choose where you want to be.

Thinking full spectrum (beyond simplistic categories) will help you stay in sync with others on the road toward better futures for working and living. As illustrated in figure 22, synchronizing your choices on the Seven Spectrums of Choice will vary as you consider your own needs, the needs of your organization, and the needs of your community.

Synchronizing Your Future Selves

The conversation around the Seven Spectrums of Choice (both with yourself and others) should help you harmonize within and across each spectrum. It will also reveal a way to sync with others as they apply futureback thinking to make the best of office shock.

Your personal story has most likely evolved since its initial creation. In this chapter we have introduced the concept of the mixing board for helping to navigate the choices on the seven spectrums. Consider how thinking futureback with the Quick Start Guide can help to continue to evolve your story:

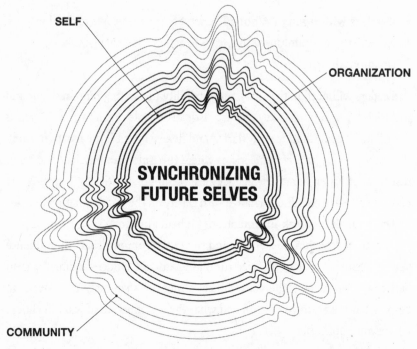

FIGURE 22: Synchronizing Your Future Selves. A visual reminder
to stay in sync with others on the office shock journey.

1. How has finding Future Self helped you to envision your future self and
   prepare you to take on a variety of roles in the VUCA world?

2. How have the UN Sustainable Development Goals helped you to define
   a navigational star to guide your futureback method and keep your full
   spectrum mindset?

3. How can the mixing board help you to consider your choices along the
   seven spectrums and synchronize with those of your organization?

4. How can the IDeaLs scaffold inform your transition story toward a better
   future?

TWELVE

Personal Choices

How You Can Navigate Office Shock

Imagine a world
in which you—and most desk workers—have a better chance
to find work paths with purpose, success, and fulfillment.
Purpose-driven people will be happier, healthier, and will live
longer. Purpose-driven companies will perform better. Rigid
career tracking will yield to multiple paths and mixes that blend
work and private life—with intention, flexibility, and choice.

To write your own story for offices and officing, we suggest you follow the four steps of the Quick Start Guide:

Step 1: Find Your Future Self.

Step 2: What Future?

Step 3: What Next?

Step 4: What Now?

With your Future Self as an individual, and a preferred future for yourself, place the mixing board in front of you. Looking at the seven spectrums, consider each spectrum as an individual office worker.

Here in chapter 12, we focus on choices for individual workers. This chapter is written for office workers, gig workers, workers in cooperatives, and others who do knowledge work. We are particularly interested in those individuals who are or want to be part of distributed organizations.

To inspire your story, spark your choices with the following provocations and critical success factors:

The Spectrum of Purpose for Individuals

I will be "in good company" when I get to work with people who share my purpose and sense of well-being. Office shock is an opportunity for me to move up the traditional hierarchy of needs and add more purpose and meaning to my work, maybe even more transcendence.

What might you do next to develop yourself on the Spectrum of Purpose?

- Meet a broader range of your own personal needs—I intend to ensure that my safety and needs are stable, so I can concentrate on my personal growth and purpose.

- Commit to continuous learning—I intend to grow and adapt by stimulating my brain while seeking a better future through my search for purpose.

- Look for ways you can improve social injustice—I intend to live in a future with greater prosperity for people and greater social justice for my community and society.

The Spectrum of Outcomes for Individuals

COVID-19 was the tipping point for office shock, but the aftershocks of social injustice and economic inequality continue to reverberate. As part of the Great Opportunity, I want to pursue broader social good—even though the current corporate economic system prioritizes profit. I want to seek out new organization models that offer new opportunities for more equitable ownership and greater prosperity for more people.

What might you do next to develop yourself on the Spectrum of Outcomes?

- Explore and evaluate new models of ownership—As new models of ownership are introduced and tried out in other organizations, I intend to have a stake in the game by questioning traditional approaches and embracing more equitable enterprise models.

- Try out ways to make employees true stakeholders—I intend to be a leader in creating an environment where our workers see themselves as members of our organization, not just people receiving payment for work done.

- Explore ways to become a more equitable enterprise—I intend to learn how to think full spectrum about how to accelerate the shift toward more prosperity and community benefit.

The Spectrum of Climate Impacts for Individuals

I am willing to cut back on my own consumption. I want to be part of an organization that produces with circularity and regenerates the planet. I understand that we will need circularity across the entire product life cycle, including extending the life of our possessions through repair, reuse, donation, and recycling. I want to be part of a regenerative economy that promotes care rather than carelessness, cooperation rather than competition, creating abundance rather than depleting resources.

What might you do to develop yourself on the Spectrum of Climate Impacts?

- Make conscious choices about consumption—This will be painful since we have grown up in a world of flagrant consuming and disposing. But I intend to change my behavior—both personally and in how I office—to curb my consumption and critically examine my choices.

- Adjust to lifetime ownership—I intend to think about the things I purchase as "forever goods" for which I have an urgent need and will help me make better choices and embrace the circular economy model.

- Regenerate communities—I recognize that climate change is a systemic problem that is threatening my entire community. I intend to work with my office and living communities to end careless consumption and adopt cooperation on climate response.

The Spectrum of Belonging for Individuals

Office shock will provide an opportunity for me to seek out, accept, and reward full-spectrum diversity that moves beyond simplistic labels, categories, and buckets. I will nurture a sense of inclusion and belonging in the organizations where I work. I will contribute to vibrant communities. I will accept differences in language, appearance, and behavior so that I can engage with people who come from different roots or routes.

What might you do next to develop yourself on the Spectrum of Belonging?

- **Know my roots**—I have studied and learned from my ancestral lineage. While roots are important in shaping us as individuals, I intend not to put people into old boxes but be open to their talents and contributions.

- **Know my routes**—I have learned from the roads I have traveled to get to where I am now. I intend to be a person who recognizes routes that I and others have taken, what we have learned, and what pain we have endured.

- **Embrace diversity**—I intend to be a leader who mixes and matches the dynamic talents of all my coworkers to contribute to valuable solutions to our increasingly complex problems. I will work to increase a sense of belonging for everyone in our organization.

The Spectrum of Augmentation for Individuals

I understand that I will need to be augmented to address the systemic problems and dilemmas of climate change, social injustice, and economic inequality. Solving our systemic challenges will require me to collaborate with others, to learn how to use advanced technology. I need to become a supermind—an augmented human working with others.

What might you do next to further develop yourself on the Spectrum of Augmentation?

- **Become a supermind**—The opportunity to augment my intelligence is highly attractive, so I intend to understand how to best achieve this while protecting my core humanity.

- **Synchronize through stories**—I intend to develop my own stories about what humans do best and how humans—including me—can be augmented to make a better life.

- **Augment decision-making**—I intend to use technology to handle the complexity and leave the craft of making the best decisions to me. The combination of technology doing the heavy lifting and my experience will make me smarter and more successful.

The Spectrum of Place and Time for Individuals

Imagine a world in which it is easy to move between in-person and virtual experiences. In this future world, we will always be online and enhanced, unless we choose to be offline. While the goal of virtual meetings used to be to approximate face-to-face meetings, the new mantra will be to create ways of working that are *better* than in-person offices alone. I want better ways of working, better ways of living, better ways of making the future. Hybrid work was only an incremental step toward the officeverse—a nested network of networks.

What might you do next to develop yourself on the Spectrum of Place and Time?

- **Redraw your boundaries**—The COVID-19 pandemic meant that the boundaries between office and home were broken down. The waves of office shock will allow us to redraw those boundaries. I intend to choose where and when I work, understanding that I need to be highly productive whatever I choose.

- **Embrace the officeverse**—The officeverse will require me to learn new ways of working, learn how to use new media, and figure out how to develop trusting relationships with people I've never met in person. I will prepare for working in the officeverse.

- **Create your avatar**—We will all need identities in the officeverse. I understand that means I need at least one avatar. I intend to embrace this need and become comfortable with it.

The Spectrum of Agility for Individuals

I will embody flexive intent in the ways that I work. Intent is a commitment to a desired outcome. Flexive means being adaptive—not rigid or brittle—to achieve desired outcomes. The traditional office was hierarchical and centralized, but that's not what I want. In the future officeverse, everything and everyone that can be distributed will be distributed. I want to work in the officeverse.

What might you do next to develop yourself on the Spectrum of Agility?

- **Organize for agility**—I intend to be part of a shape-shifting organization in which decisions will be made by whomever is in the best position to make that decision, regardless of hierarchy. I will endeavor to be a leader who is strong and humble at the same time.

- **Train for your own personal agility**—As I hone my own full-spectrum thinking, I intend to use augmented intelligence and agility to improve more dynamic decision making.

- **Be a gamer to improve your own agility**—I will use gaming to prepare me for unwelcome surprises, so I can practice my leadership in low-risk ways. I will use the art of prototyping to enhance my brain's neuroplasticity and develop an agile mindset.

At this point in your personal story, you are ready to formulate action items to propel you toward the better future of working and living:

1. How can you use the UN Sustainable Development Goals for guidance about your own navigational star?

2. As you work through each of the seven spectrums, create a list of factors that will help you envision what success means in your future.

3. With the image of success in your mind, how can you begin to plan a path toward the future that is clear, but not certain?

Now that you have thought about your future self across the Seven Spectrums of Choice, you are ready to engage your organization in a similar exercise. Your choices will reveal the levels of synchronization between yourself and the organizational aspirations of those with whom you work.[1]

Organizational Choices

How Your Organization Can Navigate Office Shock

Imagine a world

where organizations will be what they want to organize, guided by their flexive intent, strategy, and priorities. In a world where anything that can be distributed will be distributed, offices will be fluid and flexible. The now-separate functions called human resources or people, real estate, and information technology will be strategically integrated and report directly to the CEO as they develop an office shock navigation strategy. The traditional "home office" for many organizations will not be a towering edifice but rather a distributed network of offices in homes and regional hubs.

To write your own story for offices and officing, we suggest you follow the four steps of the Quick Start Guide:

Step 1: Find Your Future Self.

Step 2: What Future?

Step 3: What Next?

Step 4: What Now?

With your Future Self as a leader or member of an organization, and a preferred future for that organization, place the mixing board in front of you. Looking at the seven spectrums, consider each spectrum for the organization.

Here in chapter 13, we focus on choices for organizational leaders at all levels of decision-making, for organizations at all levels of maturity (start-up to more mature), and for anyone considering mobilizing others to become more active. This chapter is not only written for corporations but for governments, global agencies, and nonprofits as well. In fact, for governments, there is the potential for a single decision to change offices across an entire county, state, or even a country. Nonprofits vary dramatically, but many of them have offices that are experiencing office shock and can benefit from remaking old choices that are now outdated regarding how work gets done. Futureback thinking will help to guide the flexive intent of an organization toward better futures for working and living.

After each key player in your organization determines their critical success factors, a meeting to synchronize the choices can serve as an excellent way to collaborate in new ways. The result may be a revision of some critical success factors to bring them in line with the partnership, thus strengthening cooperation, synchronizing across your internal organizations, and helping all to navigate office shock in a partnership beyond what each organization could do alone.

For each spectrum, make your organizational choices using the following critical success factors as provocation.

The Spectrum of Purpose for Organizations

To be perceived as a "good company," our organization will need to provide a healthy working environment for people as well as our customers and the communities of which we are a part. Our office buildings will echo our organizational purpose and our workers. The ways our people work will personify our organization.

What might your organization do next on the Spectrum of Purpose?

- **Meet a broader range of your employees' hierarchy of needs**—Our organization intends to help our workers meet their fundamental needs for security while also allowing them the space to explore their purpose in working.

- **Improve social injustice**—Our organization intends to ensure that we provide a safe workspace for everyone, educate our workers about social justice, and work in our community to further social equity.

- **Play the wisdom game**—Our organization intends to create a wise understanding of the positive and negative aspects of our work environment, with deep concern for our workforce.

The Spectrum of Outcomes for Organizations

Office shock is a chance to rethink both the shareholder and stakeholder value of our organization. It is a chance to look through a wider lens about profitability over time as well as the effects on our workers, customers, and our local communities. Our organization will play an increasing part in growing and sustaining prosperity for our community and the larger society. Organizing for shared value will be amplified through distributed digital networks that encourage collaborative practices and pursuit of common goals.

What might your organization do next on the Spectrum of Outcomes:

- **Organize for shared social value**—Our organization intends to move beyond the traditional model of organizing solely for efficiency and control.

We will work toward using new models to empower people inside and outside our organization.

- **Invest in new models of ownership**—As new models of ownership are developed, our organization will explore how these models might be used by our organization. Not every new approach will work for us, but we don't want to miss one that can deliver better outcomes.

- **Become a more equitable enterprise**—Regardless of the business model we pursue, our organization intends to be a more equitable enterprise that is not solely profit driven. We will deliver social as well as financial value to our workforce and our communities.

The Spectrum of Climate Impacts for Organizations

Our organization will produce within the circular economy and regenerate the planet. We will employ circularity across the entire product life cycle, including extending the life of our possessions through repair, reuse, donation, and recycling. Our regenerative strategy will promote care rather than carelessness, win/win cooperation rather than win/lose competition and will create abundance rather than depleting resources.

What might your organization do next on the Spectrum of Climate Impacts?

- **Become part of the circular economy**—Our organization intends to move beyond net-zero by improving our supply chains, our delivery systems, the life cycles of our products, and our commitment to recycle or repurpose our products. Our goal is no longer cradle to grave, but rather birth to rebirth.

- **Become regenerative in community**—The systemic nature of climate disruption necessitates our action to engage the entire community. Our organization intends to manufacture and sell locally as much as possible. When expanding, we will reuse existing infrastructure to minimize distribution and energize the local communities where we will seek workers.

- **Go beyond sustainability**—Since no single company or government can achieve the goal of saving the planet, our organization intends to lead or contribute to cooperative efforts within our industry and with governmental agencies to transition toward symbiosis.

The Spectrum of Belonging for Organizations

Most offices today are made up of people who are already familiar with one another. Often in traditional offices, people look alike, dress alike, and behave in similar ways. In the future, organizations will create office environments to attract, accept, and reward full-spectrum diversity beyond simplistic labels, categories, and buckets. Organizations will sustain a culture of inclusion and belonging.

What might your organization do next on the Spectrum of Belonging?

- **Know your roots**—Just like people, organizations have roots: Who are our founders? What communities—physical and social—did we come from? How have previous leaders' beliefs and prejudices shaped who we are as an organization? Our organization intends to consciously understand this background and use that knowledge to unearth any prejudices and stereotypes that stem from it.

- **Know your routes**—In our journey from our founding, our organization has traveled routes that were influenced by people, places, politics, and decisions. Our organization intends to uncover those patterns to move forward with a fresh futureback perspective.

- **Learn from the anger of youth**—The true digital natives are already in the workforce, and their numbers are growing rapidly. Many of them are angry, particularly about climate and social justice issues. Our organization intends to learn from them and integrate them into our workforce and gain from their ideas and talents. Cross-generational learning will be most important for the future.

The Spectrum of Augmentation for Organizations

Our organization will be made up of superminds, groups of augmented individuals working in harmony with technology. Our organization will compete for superminds and mobilize enchanted objects (ordinary objects that will do extraordinary things with digital support) to support our people, our customers, and our communities.

What might your organization do next on the Spectrum of Augmentation?

- **Augment intelligence in your organization**—Our organization intends to pursue the promise of partnering humans with computers to grow superminds. We will answer these questions for our organization: What do humans do best and what do we want to do for ourselves? What can machines do best and what do humans want machines to do for us?

- **Synchronize with others through stories**—Our organization intends to tell better stories about our organization's purpose and commitment to the future. Understanding how storytelling can engage people and strengthen teams will provide us with a powerful tool for imagining a better office through futureback thinking. Stories will be central to our strategy, not just public relations.

- **Reduce the risks of augmented intelligence**—Our organization intends to balance the unprecedented value of augmentation with safeguards from the threats of misuse or deliberate threats so that we can reap the rewards of better intelligence. At the same time, our organization intends to ensure the safety of our workforce and always offer partnering of humans and machines as a choice.

The Spectrum of Place and Time for Organizations

Because of office shock, our organization will explore new ways of working that have never been possible before. The officeverse will not be just a more-of-the-same internet. The officeverse will offer a chance for us to innovate regarding where, when, and how we work together. Copying the way things used to work in physical offices will be futile in virtual worlds, but our organization will invent new ways of working that are better than being there in person.

What might your organization do next on the Spectrum of Place and Time?

- **Redraw your boundaries**—Our organization will offer choices for where and when people work if their intended outcomes are met.

- **Explore the officeverse now**—The officeverse will present our organization with new ways of using technology, collaborating, and pursuing our purpose. Our organization intends to extend our workforce and learn to lead in a world of work where location and time are fluid concepts.

- **Customize your workplaces**—Workers have always personalized their workspace to enhance their work experience and boost productivity. Our organization intends to support our workers' choices and provide the technological support they need equitably across the workforce.

The Spectrum of Agility for Organizations

Flexive intent is a commitment to a clear direction of change combined with adaptivity in how you might achieve that change. While traditional offices were hierarchical and centralized, our organization will embrace the officeverse, with clarity of direction. We will be a shape-shifting organization and operate successfully with increasingly distributed authority.

What might your organization do next on the Spectrum of Agility?

- **Organize for agility, not just efficiency**—As our organization becomes more shape-shifting, we intend to train our managers to use flexive intent to ensure the right people—the people with the best knowledge—are making the decisions.

- **Recruit and retain people who are physically and mentally agile**— Our organization intends to train managers to create and sustain positive energy in their leadership.

- **Use gaming to improve agility**—Our organization intends to bring gaming into our office to improve the agility of our workforce and help workers imagine impossible futures. We will ensure gaming methods are equitably distributed so that the positive impact gaming has on brain neuroplasticity is available to all workers.

At this point your personal story is expanding to include how you can guide, lead, or influence your organization to move toward a better future of working and living:

1. How can the UN Sustainable Development Goals help your organization envision the future?

2. As you create a list of factors for future success for your organization, how can you link them with your personal list?

3. With the image of success in your mind, how can you begin to plan a path toward the future that is clear, but not certain?

Now that you have thought about your organization's choices across the seven spectrums, you are ready to consider community choices in a similar way. This exercise will reveal the levels of synchronization among you, your organization, and the communities in which you operate.

FOURTEEN

Community Choices

How Your Community Can
Navigate Office Shock

Imagine a world
in which government policies and laws incentivize and support
distributed workplaces and workspaces. Cities will use zoning
and incentives to bring more knowledge workers to within
walking or biking distance from where they work. Building
codes will encourage planet friendly design and operations.
Cost-free access to the metaverse will be everywhere, including
outdoor green spaces. Laws against discrimination will
encourage organizations to recruit purposely different people.
Governments will anticipate citizen needs in advance, using
futureback thinking to simulate alternative futures, impacts
of climate change, and trade-offs around key policy choices.
Imagine a world in which the government issues an annual
Future State of the Office report for every community.

To write your own story for offices and officing in your community, we suggest you follow the four steps of the Quick Start Guide:

Step 1: Find Your Future Self.

Step 2: What Future?

Step 3: What Next?

Step 4: What Now?

With your Future Self as a member of a community, and a preferred future for the community, place the mixing board in front of you. Looking at the seven spectrums, consider each spectrum as a citizen of a community.

Community choices will involve all three of your future selves: your personal self, your organizational self, and your community self. These choices will highlight the value of harmonizing across the spectrums and synchronizing among the personas of your future selves.

Here in chapter 14, we focus on choices for policy makers, staff planners, elected legislators, and other public servants. Our intent is to provide a lens on this office shock for the public sphere, while most of the rest of the book focuses on the personal and corporate spheres. This chapter is written for policy makers, staff, citizens, and elected officials in government, from local to regional to national to global. Government offices are certainly office shocked, and many of their organizational choices were discussed in chapter 13.

Offices will be fundamental to future communities, but they will be different kinds of offices and officing. Office shock has given us the opportunity to imagine new policies, laws, and regulations. Such innovations in governance will provide the infrastructure to braid adjacent organizations, physically or virtually.

In 2021 during the COVID-19 shutdowns, our book project team member Gabe Cervantes was accepted by a program designed to create a new community and regenerate an existing one. Tulsa Remote is one of the first of many efforts by rural and semirural parts of the United States to attract remote tech workers.[1] Tulsa Remote was created by the George Kaiser Family Foundation, and executive director Aaron Bolzle describes it this way: "This program's core focus is on creating the most vibrant and inclusive Tulsa possible, to aid future generations who are looking for opportunities."[2]

Tulsa Remote is seeking newcomers that aren't represented yet in Tulsa as part of a larger drive to put the state of Oklahoma on the map as a tech center and an attractive place to live. It aims to regenerate the current community by mixing in new people. The opportunities for cross-community pollination are exciting—social, economic, political, and cultural. This and other programs across the USA open the spectrum of choices for community leaders and their constituents. Gabe still worked full time for Institute for the Future, which is located in California, but he was living in what is coming to be called "Techlahoma." Gabe became a digital nomad, without a long-term commitment to any specific geographic area.

Consider the lessons that Tulsa Remote and similar programs might have for your community. Your responses will help your community to navigate office shock and synchronize across all your citizens and constituents to co-create better futures for working and living.

As you develop your community story, think about the following provocations and critical success factors.

The Spectrum of Purpose for Communities

As a community, we will attract and engage with good companies, good organizations, and good workers. As they walk around our town, people will feel like they are in good company, a good community of good people. Purpose-driven communities know who they are and do not pretend to be who they are not. Many communities want to be tech centers, for example, but that will be a difficult image to nurture if it isn't authentic. We will create ways of working that contribute to the good of the community—not just the financial performance of individuals.

What might your community do next on the Spectrum of Purpose?

- **Meet a broader range of community needs**—Our community will help citizens meet their basic security needs so that they also can pursue their growth needs, like career exploration and achieving their own purpose.

- **Improve your shared community identity**—Our community identity will change over time, but it is essential that we be authentic. Members of our community must contribute to our evolving identity for that identity to be authentic. We seek to be a location where people want to live, whether they are born here or choose to move here. We will communicate our shared identity clearly and accurately, in a compelling way.

- **Improve social injustice**—Our community will ensure that we provide a safe environment, with widespread and accessible educational programs about social justice. We will work in our community to further social justice initiatives toward greater equity.

The Spectrum of Outcomes for Communities

Our community believes that profitable companies can and should contribute to the prosperity of the communities where they do business. Our community needs taxes and support from office owners and the people who work in offices. Our community will pay it back in terms of quality-of-life outcomes for individuals. Downtown areas that depend on office workers will be hollowed out if too many office workers are working from home or regional hubs, so our community will need to nurture the positive bustle of downtown living with downtown libraries, cafes, and events.

What might your community do next on the Spectrum of Outcomes?

- **Increase community value**—Our community will foster values that go beyond financial goals to include growth experiences and improving the lives of others.

- **Organize for shared social value**—We will work with companies in our community to encourage them to focus on their social value as well as their economic value to the region.

- **Embrace new models of ownership**—As new models of ownership are developed, our community will explore them through education and, when they are attractive, enact legislation to encourage their growth.

The Spectrum of Climate Impacts for Communities

We as a community will play an important role in the circular economy across the entire product life cycle, including extending the life of physical products through repair, reuse, donation, and recycling. Our regenerative local (and global) economy will promote care rather than carelessness, cooperation rather than competition, and create abundance rather than deplete resources. While eliminating carbon emissions will be critical, reversing climate change will depend on reimagining how we as communities can live in harmony with the planet to be regenerative—not just sustainable.

What might your community do next on the Spectrum of Climate Impacts?

- **Make conscious choices about consumption**—Within our community, we will be a model by only using sustainably sourced products, reducing our consumption, and eliminating waste. We will work with community members and organizations within our community to teach the values of regeneration.

- **Become a regenerative community**—The systemic nature of climate change necessitates engaging the entire community. We will work with companies in our area to encourage reuse of existing assets and local production. We will attract and keep talent locally to help the companies in our area source their workforce. We will foster the construction of equitable housing through legislation.

- **Go beyond sustainability**—No single government can achieve the goal of saving the planet, which is why we will be visionaries for others and devise cooperative efforts within our community and with the industry in our community to transition this world toward one of symbiosis.

The Spectrum of Belonging for Communities

We as a community will encourage and incentivize more diverse office complexes and work practices, but it will take creativity and courage. Many communities try to be welcoming, but people often cluster with others like themselves—either by choice or because their options are limited. Our community will enforce laws against discrimination and seed belonging for people of different backgrounds and ways of living.

It will be a big challenge for governments to create a climate of mental health and flexibility. It will be a nuanced challenge, and big organizations often have a hard time with nuance. The following are potential critical success factors to inform how your community intends to achieve the desired levels of belonging.

What might your community do next on the Spectrum of Belonging?

- **Celebrate diversity**—As a community we must celebrate diversity in our own offices and in the community. We will discard outdated prejudices, value every individual for their unique talents and contributions, and work to increase a sense of belonging for everyone in our community.

- **Seek out purposely different people**—We will attract the purposely different in both our workforce and our population at large. This will kick-start new ways of problem solving, and we will benefit from this element of variety.

- **Cultivate community**—While increasing the variety of experiences in our community, we risk losing cohesiveness. Within our offices we will implement new processes and rituals—in the sense of a series of activities to create traditions—that will engender feelings of belonging. Within our community at large, we will foster a sense of belonging through public activities and celebrations.

The Spectrum of Augmentation for Communities

The vision of smart cities has been around a long time, but smart cities will finally be possible on a large scale. Our cities of superminds will be capable of making impossible futures possible. Our government will need to be run by superminds connecting with local communities. Cross-generational communication and partnerships will be particularly important. The kids will have a competitive advantage and we will encourage and expect them to contribute to our community.

What might your community do next on the Spectrum of Augmentation?

- **Augment intelligence in your community**—Our community will implement augmentation for our employees to help them tackle the complex problems we face, for example, land use, water supply, sustainable facilities, infrastructure repair and improvement. We will use advanced modeling techniques to envision a better future.

- **Synchronize through stories**—Understanding how storytelling can engage people and strengthen teams will provide us with a powerful tool for futureback thinking to imagine how our community will thrive in the future.

- **Reduce the risks from augmented intelligence**—We will use augmentation safely to protect our employees and will always make the use of deep augmentation a choice. We will protect against criminal use of augmented intelligence, which will be a major source of concern in communities.

The Spectrum of Place and Time for Communities

As a community, we wonder how permanent hybrid work will affect those who rely on office workers coming downtown every day. As a community, we want people walking the streets in good company with one another, but the officeverse is going to be largely virtual. Flexibility and choice will be the norm. "Office hours" (remember the concept of 9 to 5?) will be redefined, and the concept will seem like a quaint relic of the past. Anytime/anyplace will be the new norm for most communities.

What might your community do next on the Spectrum of Place and Time?

- **Create communities of avatars**—In addition to our employees creating personas in the officeverse, we will create avatars of guides and docents, available 24/7 to help the community navigate its public information and spaces at all hours, similar to what is done at museums and libraries.

- **Customize your workplaces**—We will support our employees creating officeverse versions of their workspaces (home, office, coffee shop) and see that the tools are equally available to everyone.

- **Rejuvenate your places**—With a new appreciation of the importance of place, our community intends to nurture social cohesion and value relationships in the places our citizens and adjacent neighbors reside.

The Spectrum of Agility for Communities

We as a community will develop our own flexive intent. We will need to develop an authentic expression (in a compelling story) of our own clarity of direction regarding offices and officing. Within that envelope of clarity and purpose, each community will seek enthusiastic participants. Professional staff for governments and communities will need to be deeply digital. They will be very sophisticated at using social media to organize people and find common ground across polarized differences. Agility will be key, especially to scale up the choices on the seven spectrums at a global level. Again, the kids will have a competitive advantage because they have grown up with video gaming experiences that are already closer to the metaverse than today's office internet.

What might your community do next on the Spectrum of Agility?

- **Organize for agility**—Our community will incorporate flexive intent into our leadership training, with our public officials and volunteer communities. We will do this by revising the handbooks for each cohort that will illustrate the benefits of flexibility and clarity of direction in achieving outcomes as our organizations become increasingly shape-shifting.

- **Embrace gaming to improve agility**—We will bring gaming into our learning programs for all staff and public officials to help them practice their leadership in low-risk ways. Embarking on worldwide solutions, gaming will help anticipate the surprises likely to arise from tackling a new, unknown, and unimagined path.

- **Transform with clarity and flexibility of execution**—Within our communities we will encourage clarity and coordination while avoiding the rigidity of past hierarchies for employees, public officials, citizens, and industry groups.

Most importantly, communities will need to decide what they choose to do together.

Your personal story should include the role(s) you play in your larger community—local or global. What specific things can you do to influence your community toward the better future of living and working that you have been envisioning?

1. Who will you work with to determine how your personal story can be expanded for your larger community?

2. What navigational stars will help guide your community?

3. What does future success look like for the community you are choosing?

4. As you create a list of factors for future success for your community, how can you link them with your personal list?

5. With the image of success in your mind, how can you begin to plan a path toward the future that is clear, but not certain?

CONCLUSION

What We Can Do Now to Create Better Futures

Even as we grieved, we've grown; even fatigued we've found
that this hill we climb is one we must mount together. We are
battered, but bolder; worn but wiser. I'm not telling you not
to be tired or afraid. If anything, the very fact that we're weary
means we are, by definition, changed; we are brave enough to
listen to, and learn from, our fear. This time will be different
because this time we'll be different. We already are.[1]

AMANDA GORMAN

Office shock made it possible to create better futures for living and working that used to be perceived as impossible.

Part I of this book introduced office shock and showed how to use futureback thinking to get beyond the noise of the present to answer the question, What Future? We included a brief history of the fifty-year prototyping of new media for distributed work that made it possible for so many organizations to quickly go virtual when COVID-19 hit.

Part II introduced the Office Shock Seven Spectrums of Choice to inform your choices of What Next? for your office and officing.

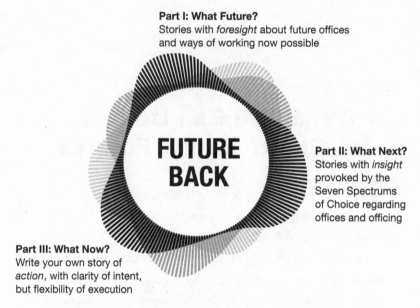

Part I: What Future?
Stories with *foresight* about future offices
and ways of working now possible

FUTURE
BACK

Part II: What Next?
Stories with *insight*
provoked by the
Seven Spectrums
of Choice regarding
offices and officing

Part III: What Now?
Write your own story of
action, with clarity of intent,
but flexibility of execution

FIGURE 23: The Office Shock Journey. The book storyline can inspire your
navigating office shock toward better futures of working and living.

Part III introduced a Quick Start Guide to help you, your organization, and
your communities make smart choices. Figure 23 is a graphic summary of the
journey we've taken in this book.

Office shock has just begun and there is no going back now.

What Future? Make Impossible Futures Possible

Beliefs about the future create blinders. Office shock has opened our eyes. The
impossible has become possible. Fixed ways of working will become ever-more
fluid. Thinking futureback in a time of office shock will help you imagine what
will be possible.

The types of impossible futures that we shared in the introduction are becoming increasingly possible:

- **Impossible futures that happen too fast to be believable:** Just like before the COVID-19 shutdowns in 2020, many people would have thought it was impossible to have low-cost high-quality desktop or mobile phone video teleconferencing.

You can choose to remake your office into a prototype of a better future for yourself, your organization, and your community.

- **Impossible futures that require convergence of many low-probability scenarios:** Just like a global pandemic of the scale of COVID-19 was viewed as possible in the abstract but was impossible to imagine, it had profound effects on entrenched social norms, disrupted economic activity, and caused further political and cultural schisms.

You can choose to remake your office and officing with more purpose, economic equality, and climate impact.

- **Impossible futures that break the accepted rules of reality:** Just like the rapid development of a vaccine for the novel coronavirus was viewed by many as impossible because it required so much information sharing among competing companies and novel approaches to development.

You can choose to remake your office by collaborating with clarity and flexive intent in mobilizing people across organizational boundaries to accelerate addressing the wicked problems our communities face.

- **Impossible futures that depend on alien concepts:** Just like the rapid development of a vaccine for the novel coronavirus was viewed as impossible because mRNA was a fringe experiment proposed by an atypical scientist.

You can choose to remake your office by applying alien concepts like new economic models that offer more equitable ownership.

There is no simple choice for making a better way of working. Even if you have clarity on direction and an inspirational navigational star, turning impossible futures into new possibilities will not be easy.

What Next? Make Your Choices

In part II, we introduced the Seven Spectrums of Choice for offices and officing. Here in the conclusion, we encourage you to pursue the aspirational scenarios that opened each chapter on a spectrum of choice. Then, we describe what's next to inspire you to build a better world.

Imagine a world in which more workers are motivated by a sense of purpose and meaning.

Building worlds with more sense of **purpose** (chapter 4) starts with getting reacquainted with your purpose, the purpose of your organization and your community. Pursuing this aspiration will require individuals who are purpose driven and who seek out organizations with complementary purpose-driven practices. Policy makers would need to incentivize and reward purpose-driven people and purpose-driven organizations.

Imagine a world that generates both financial return for shareholders and social value for stakeholders.

Building worlds with more attention to **outcomes** (chapter 5) starts with choosing the outcomes you seek and how to measure your progress. Be prepared to be transparent about the results—even if they are not as good as you hoped. The Spectrum of Outcomes is an often-tense mix of financial and social value. While shareholder value has long been the focus of publicly traded companies, these companies are increasingly called on to provide social value as well. Corporations are increasingly seeking engagement with and support from stakeholders like customers, local communities, suppliers, and even gig workers—not just with shareholders, investors, and employees. We expect that this outreach will increase in the future, even as the pressure for short-term financial performance remains strong.

Imagine a world in which people figure out how to equalize the balance between production and consumption.

Building worlds with positive **climate impacts** (chapter 6) starts with choosing your climate positive goals using accepted global standards, measuring accurately, and sharing your progress and shortcomings. It is too late to have a separate net-zero or even regenerative strategy as part of corporate social responsibility or public relations alone. Now, the climate future is urgent and stinging with chronic emergencies. Climate positive initiatives must be an integral part of corporate strategy.

Imagine a world in which robust diversity is expected and rewarded.

Building worlds with more sense of **belonging** (chapter 7) starts with choosing a purposely different workforce, with people who know their roots (their genealogies), the routes they've taken to get where they are, and the aspirational future that they want for themselves. The majority minority future is already here in many parts of the world, as full-spectrum thinking about race, gender, age, and even thinking styles is becoming the new status quo. Providing a sense of inclusion and belonging will be a critical success factor for all organizations. Understanding the value of purposely different people for your organization will be a critical leadership skill that will yield great value.

Imagine a world in which work will be augmented, amplified, and enhanced, with humans and machines working together to extend human intelligence and enhance work.

Building worlds with more computer-assisted human **augmentation** (chapter 8) starts with choosing how you and your organization will become even more deeply digital over the next decade. Answer, for you and your organization, these questions: What can humans do best? What can computers do best? Artificial intelligence, machine learning, augmented reality, and a variety of other digital aids will become ubiquitous over the next decade. Ideally, each person will decide how augmented they want to be, both within the workplace and within their private lives. Human and computing resources will be mixed in profound ways.

Imagine a world in which it is easy to move between in-person and virtual experiences. In this future world, we will always be online and enhanced, unless we choose to be offline.

Building worlds with more flexibility of **place** and **time** (chapter 9) starts with choosing how to be there without being there—to be even better than being there. Leaders must become skilled at choosing which medium is good

for what and how to communicate effectively through each medium, including in-person meetings. The possibilities of dynamic ways of working together
regardless of physical place or time constraints will dramatically alter how we
office in the future.

Imagine a world in which agility and resilience will be prioritized over certainty and efficiency. Imagine leaders who will be skilled in the art of flexive
intent, with great clarity about where they intend to go, but great flexibility
about how they will get there.

Building worlds with more **agility** (chapter 10) starts with working as braids
in shape-shifting organizations. Local and global talent will be much more
available and eager, although the terms of engagement will be emergent and
sometimes problematic—particularly where trust is low.

There is no simple binary choice of how to build a better world. Although
you may have clarity on your choices, building better worlds will not be easy.
There will be trade-offs. You may not be able to fulfill all your aspirations. If you
apply your agency to prototype new offices, your world will become better.

What Now? Try Out New Ways of Officing

In part III, we showed how you can make your own choices and develop your
own critical success factors for offices and officing. In chapter 11, we introduced a
Quick Start Guide for you to lead futureback with flexive intent to create better
futures for working and living.

Here in the conclusion, we remind you of the scenarios that led our chapters 12 to 14 for individuals, organizations, and communities. Then, we describe
what's possible now by prototyping your choices of new offices and officing.

Imagine an office in which you—and most desk workers—have a better
chance to find work paths with purpose, success, and fulfillment. It won't be
just getting a job; it will be making a living in good company.

Prototyping new offices that reflect your **personal choices** (chapter 12)
starts with exploring the new array of choices for individuals who, in many

cases, were not prepared and did not even realize they had a choice. Rigid career tracking is giving way (finally) to extremely rich mixes of options. The bad news is that there will be fewer full-time jobs. The good news is that there will be many more ways to make a living. The even-better news is that people will be free to pursue different aspects of the career they love—or even totally different careers in parallel. People will combine meaningful work with meaningful contributions to their communities. Technology will provide much more flexibility for every individual and a variety of professional and personal communities will benefit from their talents.

Imagine an office in which the now-separate functions called human resources or people, real estate, and information technology will be strategically integrated and report directly to the CEO. Offices and officing will be too strategic to leave to anyone but the top leadership.

Prototyping new offices that reflect your **organizational choices** (chapter 13) starts with redefining the "home office" to be both the corporate headquarters and the office at the homes of the workers—including the CEO and the board. Economies of organization are now replacing economies of scale. Bigger will not always be better. You will be what you can organize. Anything that can be distributed will be distributed. Opportunities are growing while limitations are decreasing.

Imagine an office in which policies and laws incentivize and support distributed workplaces and workspaces. Imagine that governments issue a Future State of the Office report in every community.

Prototyping new offices that reflect your **community choices** (chapter 14) starts by re-asking the question of what we choose to do together, the question of what role governments might play in how we work and live. Policy makers can incentivize and regulate the ecosystems of work; they can encourage or restrain. This is a time to track signals of governments who are making a difference. Often, the most interesting signals we see are from local governments rather than national governments, which are often so polarized nowadays that they cannot imagine how to engage with the impossible futures that are looming.

Seek Harmony—Resist Polarization

Office shock offers a unique opportunity to reevaluate our expectations about how we might work together to create better futures for working and living. Office shock is a perfect storm for change: a convergence of climate change, social justice, economic inequality, and the demand for distributed work. As Jacqui Patterson, director of the NAACP Environmental and Climate Justice Program, states:

> Our future must be rooted in a just transition. This involves moving away from a society functioning on extraction to one rooted in deep democracy and to one integrating regenerative processes, cooperation, and acknowledgment of interdependence and again, where all rights are respected (Indigenous, women, and all marginalized communities) and honored. This absolutely must include earth rights as well. We have to respect the vessel. We have to get to a place where we can live in harmony with each other and the Earth.[2]

Office shock is a wake-up call, but leaders have ignored calls to change before. Intellectuals and artists have argued eloquently that ways of working and living need to change. Alvin Toffler warned against *Future Shock* in 1970. Ten years later, director of experimental documentary films Godfrey Reggio captured on film a vision of what was going on. Titled *Koyaanisqatsi*, which in the Hopi language means "life out of balance," Reggio and composer Philip Glass sought to open the eyes of the viewers because, as the trailer described: "Until now, you've never really seen the world you live in." Jean-Michel Basquiat tried to communicate the chaos of the 1980s as well, only to take his own life. Grunge bands like Nirvana, Rage Against the Machine, and Green Day in the 1990s foreshadowed the shocks of the new millennium. Today, musician and activist Tom Morello continues the call for change in both music and writing.[3]

Today's politics are polarized, with certainty on all sides but little clarity or willingness to work together. Local communities seem more willing to work together, but even in small towns polarities are threatening. Tensions around vaccines and protective masks are vivid examples. When do individual rights yield to community safety or benefit? What do we choose to do together? Public health seems an obvious space to work together, but that logic was questioned during the pandemic.

What can governments do to get past the polarities and find common ground? Looking futureback certainly helps, but policy makers will need to ask what kind of community they want to encourage—given the external future forces.

In embracing more community in officing, we can break down the barrier between public and private. The foreword to Mariana Mazzucato's *The Entrepreneurial State* is titled very appropriately "Rediscovering Public Wealth Creation." Silicon Valley benefited greatly from a rich public/private ecosystem of innovation. Communities need to figure out ways to encourage the next generation of offices and officing. Her research on entrepreneurship revealed that the shining engine of capitalism, usually portrayed as the output of private individuals, is the result of the ecosystem surrounding the entrepreneurs. Mazzucato's research shows that the famous innovations of companies like Apple were dependent on the innovations of governmental initiatives.[4] Private needs the public and the public needs the private.

Working together at a distance has never been so easy and so urgent. We must do as Buckminster Fuller asked us all to do in his classic *Operating Manual for Spaceship Earth*:

Go to work, and above all co-operate.[5]

Synchronize Work and Life

As we close this book, we suggest that you ask yourself seven basic questions about offices and officing—think of yourself, your family, your organization, and your communities. Try to think futureback from ten years ahead as you answer these questions thoughtfully:

1. Why do you want an office at all?
2. What outcomes are you seeking from your work?

3. How can your work and life be more climate positive?

4. With whom do you want to work?

5. How do you want to augment your own work and life?

6. In what places and at what times do you want to work?

7. How will you design your life for agile resilience as disruptions pepper you?

Office shock will continue to create dilemmas that you cannot solve, but you can flip them into positives. COVID-19 was awful in so many ways, but it also opened great opportunities to create previously impossible futures for offices, officing, and the officeverse. *Office Shock* is a story of people making something better out of a bad thing.

By thinking futureback and full spectrum, we can contribute to helping humans develop and sustain more symbiotic relationships. Homeostasis rather than dominance. Relationships amplified by technology rather than controlled by it. You can avoid the insanity of entropy. You can navigate office shock and flip it into great opportunities.

OFFICE SHOCK
NAVIGATIONAL STARS

(As inspired by the UN Sustainable Development Goals)

Successful strategies in the VUCA world must be very clear about direction but very flexible about execution. To develop your clarity, it is useful to have a navigational star. The UN Sustainable Development Goals are a great starting point in that search for clarity.

Below, we have organized the UN Goals around the Seven Spectrums of Choice described in part II of this book and summarized in the Quick Start Guide. You can use this framework as provocation for creating your own navigational star, your own clarity.

Purpose: End poverty (Goal #1), and end hunger (Goal #2) in all its forms everywhere to ensure healthy lives and promote well-being for all at all ages (Goal #3).

Outcomes: Promote sustained, inclusive, and sustainable economic growth; full and productive employment; and decent work for all (Goal #8) with a reduction in inequality within and among countries (Goal #10).

Climate Impacts: Take urgent action to combat climate change and its impacts (Goal #13) above, for example, terrestrial ecosystems, forests, and biodiversity (Goal #15) and below, for example, oceans, seas, and marine resources (Goal #14) by sustainable consumption and production patterns (Goal #12).

Belonging: Achieve gender equality and empower all people, regardless of gender, race, or personal choices (Goal #5).

Augmentation: Ensure inclusive and equitable quality education and promote lifelong learning opportunities for all (Goal #4).

Time and Place: Build resilient infrastructure, promote inclusive and sustainable industrialization, and foster innovation (Goal #9). Contributing to making cities and human settlements inclusive, safe, resilient, and sustainable (Goal #11), management of water (Goal #6), and modern energy (Goal #7) for all.

Agility: Promote peaceful and inclusive societies for sustainable development, provide access to justice for all and build effective, accountable, and inclusive institutions at all levels (Goal #16) by strengthening the means of implementation and revitalizing the Global Partnership for Sustainable Development (Goal #17).

Here is the full list of UN Sustainable Development Goals, but for details on each see: https://sdgs.un.org/goals.

Goal #1: End poverty in all its forms everywhere.

Goal #2: End hunger, achieve food security and improved nutrition, and promote sustainable agriculture.

Goal #3: Ensure healthy lives and promote well-being for all at all ages.

Goal #4: Ensure inclusive and equitable quality education and promote lifelong learning opportunities for all.

Goal #5: Achieve gender equality and empower all women and girls.

Goal #6: Ensure availability and sustainable management of water and sanitation for all.

Goal #7: Ensure access to affordable, reliable, sustainable, and modern energy for all.

Goal #8: Promote sustained, inclusive, and sustainable economic growth, full and productive employment, and decent work for all.

Goal #9: Build resilient infrastructure, promote inclusive and sustainable industrialization, and foster innovation.

Goal #10: Reduce inequality within and among countries.

Goal #11: Make cities and human settlements inclusive, safe, resilient, and sustainable.

Goal #12: Ensure sustainable consumption and production patterns.

Goal #13: Take urgent action to combat climate change and its impacts.

Goal #14: Conserve and sustainably use the oceans, seas, and marine resources for sustainable development.

Goal #15: Protect, restore, and promote sustainable use of terrestrial ecosystems, sustainably manage forests, combat desertification, and halt and reverse land degradation and halt biodiversity loss.

Goal #16: Promote peaceful and inclusive societies for sustainable development, provide access to justice for all, and build effective, accountable, and inclusive institutions at all levels.

Goal #17: Strengthen the means of implementation and revitalize the Global Partnership for Sustainable Development.

Office Shock

DISCUSSION GUIDE

This discussion guide is an aid for teachers and students who want to use *Office Shock* in their courses or for more general learning. It can also be used by individuals, organizations, or communities to help navigate office shock.

We wrote this book to help individuals, organizations, and communities create stories that inspire better futures for working and living.

Office shock is not just about when to go back to the office. It's about opening possibilities for human connection in more meaningful ways. Office shock and its aftershocks will help people transform their organizations and themselves.

To prepare for the opportunities of office shock, every individual office worker, organization, and policy maker should ask in this order:

1. What is the **purpose** of your office and officing?

2. What are the desired **outcomes** you aim to achieve with your office and by officing?

3. What will be the **climate impacts** of your office and officing?

4. **With whom** do you want to office? This is the Spectrum of Belonging.

5. How will you extend the **intelligence** of your office? This is the Spectrum of Augmentation.

6. **Where** and **when** will you office?

7. How will you design an **agile** resilient office?

These questions demonstrate the need for clarity and nimbleness in these times of great uncertainty. They reveal spectrums of choice that will make possible the formerly impossible. You cannot be certain, but you can be clear about where you want to go.

Conversation Starters

Below, we suggest questions that will guide your learning to think futureback and make smart choices about offices and officing.

Your Choices about Futureback Thinking

As you think about how strategic foresight might help you write your own personal story of offices and officing, consider these questions:

1. How can you break out of thinking present-forward, reduce your own cone of uncertainty, and move toward the futureback thinking of Future-Next-Now?

2. Full-spectrum thinking requires breaking out of the ingrained patterns of categorizing things into familiar boxes. How might you grow your full-spectrum mindset?

3. How can you develop and practice your storymaking skills?

Your Choices as You Look Back to Look Forward

Your choice is whether to learn from history or ignore it and risk remaking old mistakes. It took more than fifty years for distributed digital technologies to be an overnight success in 2020 and beyond. Zoom didn't just happen when

COVID-19 hit. In chapter 5 we shared our stories about this evolution and what it implies about what's next as the officeverse emerges.

1. The networked office broke resistance to change in hierarchical offices. 2020 was a tipping point for change. How can you use futureback thinking to imagine better ways of working for yourself and your organization from now going forward?

2. The birth of augmented knowledge work began in the 1970s, and we are still asking the question of how we best combine what humans do with what machines can do. What is your stance regarding augmented intelligence? What are the aspects of work where you need the most augmentation? What areas do you want to keep to yourself?

3. Technology has evolved dramatically in the past fifty years, making impossible things possible. In chapter 2 we shared our stories about this evolution. What are the lessons you take from this history?

4. The past is riddled with present-forward thinking about technology that limits imagination. How might you encourage more futureback thinking?

Your Choices to Create Impossible Futures

1. Imagine a world where you and your organization are empowered to make the future a better place. What might that impossible future look like and feel like to you?

2. Create a story about the kind of future workplace in which you would want to work and live. Your story could examine:
   - What is your purpose in working in this office?
   - What outcomes will you aim to accomplish?
   - Do you have any concerns about climate change?
   - Who would be your ideal coworkers?
   - How would you like technology to enhance your abilities?

- Where, when, and how often do you want to work?
- How would you increase your ability to be agile and resilient?

3. What could you do now to be ready for this future?

Your Choices on the Spectrum of Purpose

Our Spectrum of Purpose ranges from individual to collective, personal needs to societal needs. Office shock is fueling a shift from work as what we do to make money, to work as something transcendent, something we do that is connected to our larger goals and values.

1. How might you illustrate your story about a future with a more positive experience of purpose?

2. Do you derive a personal sense of meaning from your work today? If not, how would you change your experience of purpose?

3. What social value (beyond your own personal income) are you contributing through your officing?

4. Does your organization enhance your individual purpose by having a corporate purpose that is linked to community, beyond individuals?

5. Does your organization have a focus on stakeholders, in addition to shareholders?

6. How can thinking futureback enhance your ability to seek meaningful work?

Your Choices on the Spectrum of Outcomes

Spanning this spectrum between profit and prosperity opens an opportunity to reflect on how we define value, how we organize ourselves, who makes decisions, the nature of working relationships, and ultimately our economic models.

1. How might you illustrate your story about a future with more positive outcomes?

2. What are the desired results or outcomes—both individual and social—that you are seeking from your office?

3. Who is obtaining value from the outcomes of your work and the work of your organization?

4. How might you organize yourself to increase a sense of membership among your workers? Will this call for a new model of ownership?

5. What path do you want to take in the pursuit of increasing prosperity for all your stakeholders?

Your Choices on the Spectrum of Climate Impacts

This spectrum focuses on what we feel is the dominant outcome to be concerned about over the next decade: chronic climate emergencies. Certainly, there are many urgent futures to be concerned about, but regenerating life on this planet is so very basic.

1. How might you illustrate your story about a future with more positive climate impacts?

2. How has the question of "to consume or not to consume?" affected your behavior and that of your organization? How might you change your practices to become more sustainable?

3. How do you see yourself participating in the circular economy?

4. How can offices and officing contribute to restoring the planet and increasing its regenerative capacity?

5. How can we get the world working on a more cooperative basis to prevent planetary destruction?

6. How can we convince organizations—particularly corporations—that they have a huge role to play in climate regeneration and that in the long run it will enhance their business performance?

Your Choices on the Spectrum of Belonging

If anything is clear in the VUCA world, it's that who we choose to office with is going to be a constantly moving target. Although we may belong to and work for the same company, organization, or goal, the teams that help us accomplish our work will be in constant flux. Although we lose the immediate familiarity of who we work with, the purposeful design of mixing and matching will bring forth new innovations and approaches to challenges in the future.

1. How might you illustrate your story about a future with more belonging?

2. What makes you different, and how can you celebrate your otherness authentically while still engaging with others?

3. In your present moment, in your present community, what are the aspects of every member that can contribute to a vibrant organization?

4. How can you use the concepts of roots and routes to bring a purposely different mix of talent into your organization?

5. How will you address the diversity dilemma in your office?

6. The digital natives will likely have very different expectations for offices and officing. They are likely to be less loyal and more critical of current ways of working. How are you preparing for their arrival? How will you benefit from cross-generational communication now?

Your Choices on the Spectrum of Augmentation

In this spectrum we have applied full-spectrum thinking to understanding the multiple ways in which humans will be able to augment their intelligence—brain power, physical power, cooperative power, and emotional power—to extend their performance and therefore their contribution to better working and living.

1. How might you illustrate your story about the Spectrum of Augmentation?

2. How might you balance fear of machines replacing humans with the opportunities that augmented intelligence could bring?

3. How would you increase the chances that augmentation will equitably be available to anyone who wants it within your organization?

4. Do you currently use any enchanted objects and how do you see the potential for your use both personally and within your office?

5. The combination of human creativity and the power of computers will provide the potential to build a better future. How might this augmentation be used to create better futures for working and living in your life?

Your Choices on the Spectrum of Place and Time

The officeverse will give us many more choices for offices and officing—and the choices will be much deeper than with today's hybrid working. The officeverse can be tailor-made, and personalized. Creating something new and different will trump defining a standard or structure to implement.

1. How might you illustrate your story about the Spectrum of Place and Time?

2. How will you determine what tasks or activities are best carried out together or apart through the varied officeverse media options?

3. In what way does the concept of an avatar appeal to or disturb your thinking about working in the officeverse?

4. Trust will be a critical ingredient for making virtual relationships successful. How will you seed and sustain trust?

5. How does the opportunity to design your workspace affect your comfort level in the officeverse?

6. How will you establish a sense of culture and belonging in your officeverse?

Your Choices on the Spectrum of Agility

Making choices on the Spectrum of Agility, and mobilizing for collective action, will be dependent on coordinating with clarity. With greater agility, people in shape-shifting organizations can focus on the cross-pollination of ideas that not only strengthen interconnections and sustainability but also require a fundamental shift in mindset, behavior, and culture.

1. How might you illustrate your story about the Spectrum of Agility?

2. How have you thought about moving your personal behavior away from the efficiency/effectiveness model and toward a model of increased agility and resilience?

3. Gaming skills will be well developed in the digital native members of the workforce, but what about everyone else? How will you and your organization use gaming to increase your own resilience?

4. How might you make good use of voluntary fear exposure?

5. How will the lessons learned through gaming be translated into actionable tasks and processes?

6. As a leader in an organization, how will you enable distributed authority?

Thinking Futureback about Office Shock: A Quick Start Guide

Your personal story has most likely evolved since its initial creation. In chapter 11 we introduced the concept of the mixing board for helping to navigate the choices on the seven spectrums. Consider how thinking futureback with the Quick Start Guide can help to continue to evolve your story:

1. How has finding Future Self helped you to envision your future self and prepared you to take on a variety of roles in the VUCA world?

2. How have the UN Sustainable Development Goals helped you to define a navigational star to guide your futureback method and keep your full-spectrum mindset?

3. How has the mixing board helped you to consider your choices along the seven spectrums and synchronize with those of your organization?

4. How has the IDeaLs scaffold informed your transition story toward a better future?

Personal Choices: How You Can Navigate Office Shock

At this point in your personal story you are ready to formulate action items to propel you toward a better future of working and living:

1. If you need navigational stars, how can you use the UN Sustainable Development Goals for guidance?

2. As you work through each of the seven spectrums, create a list of factors that will help you envision what success means in your future.

3. With the image of success in your mind, how can you begin to plan a path toward the future that is clear, but not certain?

Now that you have thought about your future self across the Seven Spectrums of Choice, you are ready to engage your organization in a similar exercise. Your choices will reveal the levels of synchronization between yourself and the organizational aspirations of those with whom you work.

Organizational Choices:
How Your Organization Can Navigate Office Shock

At this point your personal story is expanding to include how you can guide, lead, or influence your organization to move toward a better future of working and living:

1. How can the UN Sustainable Development Goals help your organization envision the future?

2. As you create a list of factors for future success for your organization, how can you link them with your personal list?

3. With the image of success in your mind, how can you begin to plan a path toward the future that is clear, but not certain?

Now that you have thought about your organization's choices across the seven spectrums, you are ready to consider community choices in a similar way. This exercise will reveal the levels of synchronization among you, your organization, and the communities you lead or serve.

Community Choices:
How Your Community Can Navigate Office Shock

Your personal story should include the role(s) you play in your larger community—local or global. What specific things can you do to influence your community toward the better future of living and working that you have been envisioning?

1. Who will you work with to determine how your personal story can be expanded for your larger community?

2. What navigational stars will help guide your community?

3. What does future success look like for the community you are choosing?

4. As you create a list of factors for future success for your community, how can you link them with your personal list?

5. With the image of success in your mind, how can you begin to plan a path toward the future that is clear, but not certain?

Applying the Seven Spectrums of Choice

The ideas throughout this book and especially in part III provide input to the design of a workshop that aims to help people embrace futureback thinking and use the seven spectrums to make conscious choices for a better future of offices and officing. More information about the workshop format can be found on our website, officeshock.org. But here is the basic concept.

The Seven Spectrums of Choice apply to you as an individual, as an organizational leader or member, and as a citizen of a community. Therefore, you should consider your viewpoint when using the spectrums to write your own story for offices and officing. Here is a suggested four-step process:

Step 1: Find Your Future Self.

- Are you using the mixing board as an individual, organizational leader/ member, or citizen of a community?

Step 2: What Future?

- Thinking ten years ahead think futureback about better futures for working and living. Begin by choosing a navigational star (or stars) to guide your intentions.

Step 3: What Next?

- Our Office Shock mixing board has seven channels (what we call spectrums of choice) for you to move the sliders as you make choices. Each spectrum of office shock has polarities: extreme positions you can slide between. You can make different choices at different times in different situations.
- To make the spectrums more manageable, we encourage you to define the *critical success factors* that will show you the way toward your preferred future. They will help crystalize your intentions, where you are on the span of the spectrum, and the path forward.

Step 4: What Now?

- Turn your futureback choices into actions by defining what, how, and who to guide your journey.
- Use flexive intent to develop your compelling story with clarity, but not certainty.

NOTES

Preface

1. weforum.org/great-reset/. Accessed April 19, 2022.

Introduction

1. https://youtu.be/FRztxowVuPA. Accessed April 19, 2022.

2. Isaac Asimov, *Foundation* (New York: Avon, 1955).

3. See Neal Stephenson, *Snow Crash: A Novel* (New York: Del Rey, 2017 © 1992).

4. www.technologyreview.com/2022/02/08/1044732/metaverse-history-snow-crash.

5. Thomas W. Malone, *Superminds: The Surprising Power of People and Computers Thinking Together* (New York: Little, Brown, 2018).

6. For music aficionados, a mixing board is also known as an audio mixer, audio console, mixing desk, mixing console, sound mixer, sound board, audio mixer, or simply as board or mixer. In using the term mixing board, we refer to all these names of the same thing.

We drew inspiration from the world of music because we need more harmony in the world. Used during a performance or a recording, a mixing board is a panel for adjusting and combining musical sounds. Mixing boards are a mechanism to blend the sounds of various instruments, across the channels for each instrument. The sliders on a mixing board can be moved up and down, allowing musicians and producers to make choices about sounds of each channel. Most importantly, the mixing board provides a powerful place to combine individual choices to create a collective, synchronized sound.

7. For more about intrapreneurialism, see linkedin.com/pulse/intrapreneurs-illness-how -corporate-innovation-fever-innovative/.

8. Bob Johansen, *Full-Spectrum Thinking: How to Escape Boxes in a Post-Categorical Future* (Oakland, CA: Berrett-Koehler, 2020).

9. Alfred Huang. *The Complete I Ching: The Definitive Translation* (Rochester, Vt: Inner Traditions, 2010). page xxv.

PART I: WHAT FUTURE?

1. Anab Jain, ted.com/talks/anab_jain_why_we_need_to_imagine_different_futures.

Chapter 1: Futureback Thinking

1. Alvin Toffler, *Future Shock* (New York: Random House, 1970).

2. Quoted in Kara Swisher, "Big Tech Has Weaved Its Way Completely into Our Lives," *New York Times*, November 18, 2021.

3. blacklivesmatter.com.

4. metoomvmt.org.

5. bbc.com/worklife/article/20220126-the-rise-of-the-anti-work-movement.

6. peoplenotprofits.org.

7. fridaysforfuture.org.

8. scientistrebellion.com.

9. Naomi Klein, https://tsd.naomiklein.org/shock-doctrine/the-book/editions.html.

10. Neal Stephenson, nealstephenson.com/termination-shock.html.

11. H. G. Wells, *Anticipations of the Reaction of Mechanical and Scientific Progress upon Human Life and Thought* (New York: Harper and Brothers, 1901). Also see H. G. Wells, "Wanted—Professors of Foresight!" *Futures Research Quarterly* 3, no. 1 (Spring 1932): 89–91.

12. Fred Lodewijk Polak, *The Image of the Future, Elsevier International Series* (San Francisco: Jossey-Bass, 1973).

13. Marshall McLuhan, *Understanding Media: The Extensions of Man* (New York: Penguin, 1966).

14. Rachel Carson, *The Silent Spring* (New York: Fawcett World Library, 1962).

15. csf.gov.sg/who-we-are.

16. ec.europa.eu/info/strategy/strategic-planning/strategic-foresight_en.

17. u.ae/en/about-the-uae/strategies-initiatives-and-awards/federal-governments-strategies -and-plans/future-foresight.

18. oecd.org/strategic-foresight/about-us.

19. See also Bob Johansen, *Full-Spectrum Thinking* (Oakland, CA: Berrett-Koehler, 2020).

20. C. West Churchman, "Wicked Problems," *Management Science* 14, no. 4 December 1967): B-141–B-146.

21. Bob Johansen, *Get There Early* (San Francisco: Berrett-Koehler, 2007).

22. Mark W. Johnson and Josh Suskewicz, *Lead from the Future: How to Turn Visionary Thinking into Breakthrough Growth* (Boston: Harvard Business School Press, 2020).

23. Climate Central is an independent, policy-neutral 501(c)(3) nonprofit, group of scientists and communicators who research and report the facts about our changing climate and how it affects people's lives. Climate Central maps are based on the latest sea-level projections, including those from the recently released Sixth Assessment Report (AR6) from the Intergovernmental Panel on Climate Change (IPCC) and the 2022 Sea Level Rise Technical Report from an interagency US government task force.

24. coastal.climatecentral.org/map/.

25. If flooding is not enough to encourage futureback thinking, US residents can also forecast risk of fire by zip code at riskfactor.com.

26. https://en.wikipedia.org/wiki/Bjarke_Ingels.

27. vimeo.com/117303273.

28. R. M. Sapolsky, *Behave: The Biology of Humans at Our Best and Worst* (New York: Penguin Books, 2018).

29. Will Storr, *The Science of Storytelling: Why Stories Make Us Human and How to Tell Them Better* (New York: Harry N. Abrams, 2020).

30. For more detail on this research, see Kendall Haven, *Story Smart: Using the Science of Story to Persuade, Influence, Inspire, and Teach* (Santa Barbara, CA: Libraries United, 2014).

31. Phillips, D. J. P. "The Magical Science of Storytelling." TEDx. March 16, 2017. Accessed December 2020. https://www.youtube.com/watch?v=Nj-hdQMa3uA.

32. M. Nguyen, T. Vanderwal, and U. Hasson, "Shared Understanding of Narratives Is Correlated with Shared Neural Responses," *NeuroImage* 184 (2019): 161–70.

33. *AlphaGo*. Directed by Greg Kohs, Moxie Pictures, September 29, 2017.

34. healthcaredive.com/news/big-data-the-new-gold-rush-report-predicts/519515.

35. Storr, *Science of Storytelling*.

36. *MIT Technology Review* 123, no. 1 (January–February 2020).

37. Arnaud D'Argembeau, Claudia Lardi, and Martial Van der Linden, "Self-Defining Future Projections: Exploring the Identity Function of Thinking About the Future," *Memory* 20, no. 2 (2020): 110–20.

38. A. L. Valencia and T. Froese, "What Binds Us? Inter-Brain Neural Synchronization and Its Implications for Theories of Human Consciousness," *Neurosci Conscious* 1 (2020).

39. Yuval Noah Harari, *Sapiens: A Brief History of Humankind* (New York: Harper Perennial, 2018). See also Agustín Fuentes, *The Creative Spark: How Imagination Made Humans Exceptional* (New York: Dutton, 2017).

40. Our use of the term *syncronization* is based on the neuroscience of social interaction, also referred to as a social synapse. Our usage is different from Carl Jung's definiton of synchronicity.

41. World Science Festival, Science and Story: The Instinct for Curiosity, October 7, 2016. Accessed December 2020. See also Y. Yuan, J. Major-Girardin, and S. Brown, "Storytelling Is Intrinsically Mentalistic: A Functional Magnetic Resonance Imaging Study of Narrative Production across Modalities," *Journal of Cognitive Neuroscience* 30, no. 9 (2018). See also R. A. Mar, "Stories and the Promotion of Social Cognition," *Current Directions in Psychological Science* 27, no. 4 (2018): 257–62.

42. T. Buganza, P. Bellis, S. Magnanini, J. Press, A. Shani, D. Trabucchi, R. Verganti, and F. Zasa, *Storymaking: How the Co-creation of Narratives Engages People for Innovation and Transformation* (New York: Routledge, 2022).

43. Timothy Hubbard et al., "Boundary Extension: Findings and Theories." *Quarterly Journal of Experimental Psychology* 63 (2010): 1467–94. See also S. L. Mullally and E. A. Maguire, "Memory, Imagination, and Predicting the Future: A Common Brain Mechanism?" *Neuroscientist* 20, no. 3 (2014): 220–34.

44. Johansen, *Full-Spectrum Thinking.*

45. The work of acclaimed American writer, poet, and social critic is put at the center of "I Am Not Your Negro" (2017), a documentary based on Baldwin's unfinished book manuscript *Remember This House,* which reflects on race in America by tracing the lives and assassinations of his three friends: Malcolm X, Medgar Evers, and Martin Luther King Jr.

Chapter 2: Looking Back to Look Forward

1. For more background information on the COVID-19 pandemic and its impacts, we suggest these books that chronicle the areas of pandemics, quarantines, and their impacts in history up through the COVID-19 infections: Geoff Manaugh and Nicola Twilley, *Until Proven Safe* (New York: MCD; Farrar, Straus and Giroux, 2021); Lawrence Wright, *The Plague Year* (New York: Knopf, 2021); Michael Lewis, *The Premonition* (New York: W. W. Norton, 2021).

2. House of Commons (meeting in the House of Lords), October 28, 1943.

3. Frederick Taylor, *The Principles of Scientific Management* (New York: Harper, 1911).

4. Max Weber, *The Theory of Social and Economic Organizations,* trans. A. Henderson and T. Parsons (Oxford: Oxford University Press, 1947).

5. Andrew Laing, "New Patterns of Work: The Design of the Office," in *Reinventing the Workplace,* ed. John Worthington (York, England: IoASS; Architectural Press; University of York 1997).

6. https://insideinside.org/project/larkin-adminstration-building-1906/.

7. smithsonianmag.com/history/marvin-gayes-whats-going-relevant-today-it-was-1971-180977750/.

8. Vannevar Bush, "As We May Think," *Atlantic Monthly* (July 1945): 101–8.

9. James Gillies and Robert Cailliau, *How the Web Was Born: The Story of the World Wide Web* (Oxford: Oxford University Press, 2000).

10. https://www.lawrence.edu/articles/lu-alum-jack-nilles-father-telecommuting.

11. https://en.wikipedia.org/wiki/Remote_work.

12. R. Johansen, *Groupware: Computer Support for Business Teams* (New York: Free Press, 1988).

13. Hubert Lipinski and Richard P. Adler, "The HUB Project: Computer-Based Support for Group Problem-Solving," *Institute for the Future Research Report R-51*, January 1982.

14. Johansen, *Groupware.*

15. For an overview of the current state of AI companions, see https://youtu.be/QGLGq8WIMzM.

16. In 1958, the Quickborner consulting group was established by two brothers, Wolfgang and Eberhard Schnelle, who had previously been working as assistants in their father's furniture studio. Upon founding Quickborner outside of Hamburg as a space planning firm, the two brothers soon developed an interest in office space. They saw the current status quo, which used versions of scientific management and consisted of uninspired rows of desks and a strict office hierarchy, as an opportunity for change. They wanted to create a system where the individual is the focus, and to rebel against the strict grid of corridors and desks with something organic and natural. Their approach was called Bürolandschaft, a German term that translates to "office landscape." Wikipedia: https://en.wikipedia.org/wiki/Office_landscape.

17. F. Duffy and C. Cave, "Bürolandschaft Revisited," *Architect's Journal*, March 26, 1975, 665–75.

18. Andrew Laing, *New Patterns of Work: The Design of the Office* (New York: Routledge, 2005).

19. Colin Macgadie, personal communication, 2022.

20. Philip Stone and Robert Luchetti, "Your Office Is Where You Are," *Harvard Business Review* (March–April 1985): 102–16.

21. Laing, *New Patterns of Work.*

22. John Zeisel, *Inquiry by Design: Tools for Environmental Behavior Research* (Monterey, CA: Brooks/Cole, 1981).

23. Francis Duffy and Kenneth Powell, *The New Office* (London: Conran Octopus, 1997).

24. F. D. Becker and F. Steele, *Workplace by Design: Mapping the High-Performance Workscape* (San Francisco: Jossey-Bass, 1995).

25. Duffy and Powell, *New Office.*

26. DEGW was established in London in 1971 as an offshoot of New York space planners JFN. The original partners were all educated as architects, with Luigi Giffone also being an engineer; Francis Duffy, John Worthington, and Peter Ely studied together at the Architectural Association. DEGW specialized in the design of office environments and was one of the first

practices to place an emphasis on how organizations use space and the important role that design has to play in this. They revolutionized space planning for large-scale offices by placing an emphasis on the changing nature of organizations and the need for office accommodation to reflect this, incorporating ideas on mobile and remote working. From spatialagency.net /database/degw. Also see Amy Thomas, "Architectural Consulting in the Knowledge Economy: DEGW and the ORBIT Report," *Journal of Architecture* 24, no. 7 (2019), 1020–44.

Chapter 3: Impossible Futures

1. Trying to define cyberpunk is a difficult task, but you know it when you see it. Think of movies like *Blade Runner* and *Ghost in the Machine*. On one side of cyberpunk you have powerful megacorporations and private security forces, and on the other you have the dark and gritty underworld of illegal trade, gangs, drugs, and vice. In between all of this is politics, corruption, and social upheaval. "High tech. Low life." Cyberpunk is also a culture with attitude and a distinct style. Anti-authoritarian, brand-averse, tech-literate; these are just some of the qualities you may find in a cyberpunk. https://en.wikipedia.org/wiki/Cyberpunk.

2. Steampunk is a design style inspired by Victorian-era industrialism. Science fiction author K. W. Jeter created the term steampunk in 1987 to describe a style of fantasy fiction that featured Victorian technology, especially technology powered by steam. The style first appeared in mainstream pop culture in the late 2000s and currently is used in several design genres including fashion, literature, film, television, video games, and DIY projects. The steampunk genre was originally inspired by the fictional works of Jules Verne, Mary Shelley, and H. G. Wells, who wrote popular science fiction romances in the late 1800s. Today, the steampunk genre emphasizes both the use of older technologies and retro-looking futuristic inventions as people in the nineteenth century might have imagined them. https://whatis.techtarget.com/definition /steampunk.

3. Yuval Noah Harari, quote from episode 325 of the Geek's Guide to the Galaxy podcast.

4. The term *Afrofuturism* was coined by Mark Dery in his 1994 essay, "Black to the Future." In the piece, the term is defined as "speculative fiction that treats African American themes and addresses African American concerns in the context of the twentieth century technoculture— and, more generally, African American signification that appropriates images of technology and a prosthetically enhanced future." https://libguides.pratt.edu/afrofuturism; see also Ytasha Womack, *Afrofuturism: The World of Black Sci-Fi and Fantasy Culture* (Chicago: Lawrence Hill Books, 2013).

5. Solarpunk is a somewhat promiscuous adjective, used to describe a vision of the future that we actually want. That means a future where high technology is put in service of humans and the environment. Which is to say, a solarpunk future is one that is "sustainable" at a not-just-for-rich-people level, a human-friendly future that can scale. In short, solarpunk is a

reaction to climate change, inequality, and our cultural obsession with dystopian futures. See https://hieroglyph.asu.edu/2014/09/solarpunk-notes-toward-a-manifesto.

6. P. von Stackelberg and A. McDowell, "What in the World? Storyworlds, Science Fiction, and Futures Studies," *Journal of Futures Studies* 20, no. 2 (2015): 25–46; also see Alex McDowell on telling stories that shape the future, youtube.com/watch?v=Sj_LZFhKU8c.

7. This typology was developed at Institute for the Future by Kathi Vian, Jacques Vallee, and Bob Johansen in 2011. See the 2012 Map of the Decade: The Future Is a Question about What Is Possible, Institute for the Future.

8. www.nytimes.com/2021/04/08/health/coronavirus-mrna-kariko.html.

9. Jane McGonigal's 2022 book contains very useful advice and gameful experiences to help stretch your imagination. See Jane McGonigal, *Imaginable: How to See the Future Coming and Feel Ready for Anything–Even Things That Seem Impossible Today* (New York: Spiegel and Grau, 2022).

10. United Nations Sustainable Development Goals, https://sdgs.un.org.

11. Ban Ki-Moon, https://unstats.un.org/sdgs/report/2016/.

12. According to Jason Zac, musician, sound engineer, and founder of Nathaniel School of Music, the last decade has seen the widespread use of digital audio workstations (DAW). The music production software of the DAW, used in tandem with a MIDI Controller (a Bluetooth-enabled device resembling the traditional mixing board) allows users to record and mix multiple audio tracks on a personal computer. The DAW enables everyone to become a sound engineer, which makes the traditional mixing board less common. However, the need to mix is even more relevant, hence the board as metaphor is very appropriate for mixing better futures for working and living.

13. To allow people to compare how they move their sliders on the mixing board, we recommend taking the online office shock survey at www.officeshock.org.

PART II: WHAT'S NEXT?

1. Octavia E. Butler, quotation at Oakland Museum exhibit on Afro-Futurism, 2020.

2. See "About the Artists" at the back of the book for more detail.

Chapter 4: In Good Company

1. www-cnbc-com.cdn.ampproject.org/c/s/www.cnbc.com/amp/2022/06/21/beyonce-break-my-soul-is-an-ode-to-the-great-resignation.html.

2. Abraham Maslow, *Toward a Psychology of Being* (New York: Wiley, 1961).

3. Scott Barry Kaufman, *Transcend: The New Science of Self-Actualization* (New York: Tarcher-Perigee/Penguin, 2020).

4. Maslow, *Toward a Psychology of Being*, 220 (also see Maslow's characteristics of transcenders, pages 221 to 225).

5. Maslow, *Toward a Psychology of Being*, 220.

6. Jenn Lim, "How to Find the Secret to Meaningful Work," on Podcast How to Build a Happy Life, hosted by Arthur Brooks, 2021, https://podcasts.apple.com/us/podcast/how-to-find-the-secret-to-meaningful-work/id1587046024?i=1000540502958. See also IFTF Urgent Optimists program, https://urgentoptimists.org/.

7. For an overview of neurotransmitters, see https://dana.org/article/neurotransmitters/. For a summary of "Action Potential, Learning and Synapse," see https://qbi.uq.edu.au/brain-basics/brain/brain-physiology/action-potentials-and-synapses. See "Neuroscientists Reveal How the Brain Can Enhance Connections," https://news.mit.edu/2015/brain-strengthen-connections-between-neurons-1118. Also see Andrew Huberman on "4 Ways Your Brain & Body Are Governed by Neurotransmitters, Neuromodulators, Hormones, and Pheromones," instagram .com/tv/CIgNmM4HMJG/?hl=en. Andrew Huberman, "How Your Nervous System Works & Changes | Huberman Lab Podcast." January 4, 2021. Accessed January 2021. https://youtu.be/H -XfCl-HpRM. A. Huberman, "How Neuroscience Can Hack Your Brain's Potential." November 22, 2020. Accessed December 2020. https://youtu.be/qksd7aHGAUQ.

8. https://can-acn.org/donald-olding-hebb/.

9. L. J. Cozolino, *The Neuroscience of Human Relationships: Attachment and the Developing Social Brain* (New York: W. W. Norton, 2006).

10. David Brooks, "Globalization Is Over. The Global Culture Wars Have Begun," *New York Times*, 2022. nytimes.com/2022/04/08/opinion/globalization-global-culture-war.html.

11. John Carryrou, *Bad Blood: Secrets and Lies in a Silicon Valley Startup* (New York: Alfred A. Knopf, 2018), 12.

12. Anna Lembke, *Dopamine Nation* (New York: Dutton, 2021).

13. James Suzman, *Work: A Deep History, from the Stone Age to the Age of Robots* (New York: Penguin Press, 2021).

14. https://thenapministry.wordpress.com/.

15. bbc.com/news/business-60353916, accessed 4/10/22.

16. bcorporation.net/en-us/.

17. globenewswire.com/news-release/2020/05/20/2036111/0/en/Danone-to-pioneer-French -Entreprise-à-Mission-model-to-progress-stakeholder-value-creation.html.

18. trendhunter.com/trends/striding-out.

19. trendhunter.com/trends/healing-clinic.

20. newyorker.com/business/currency/can-companies-force-themselves-to-do-good.

21. forbes.com/sites/forbesagencycouncil/2018/11/05/why-employee-stakeholders-are-the -secret-to-your-organizations-transformative-success/?sh=456c9a79130a.

22. http://freespace.io.

23. https://youtu.be/7gVMh_kyTVs.

24. L. Lus-Arana, "The Many Effects of the Guggenheim Effect," *MAS Context* (2017): 315–451.

25. Mariana Mazzucato, *Mission Economy: A Moonshot Guide to Changing Capitalism* (New York: Penguin Books, 2022), 9.

26. Mazzucato, *Mission Economy*, 171.

27. J. K. Galbraith, *Economics and the Public Purpose* (New York: New American Library, 1973), as quoted in Mazzucato, *Mission Economy*, 169.

28. T. Piketty, *Capital in the Twenty-First Century*, trans. A. Goldhammer (Cambridge, MA: Belknap Press of Harvard University Press, 2017).

29. Mazzucato, *Mission Economy*, 169.

30. yesmagazine.org/social-justice/2020/04/06/coronavirus-community-collective -response.

31. Kaufman, *Transcend*.

32. Deidre Kramer, "Wisdom as a Classical Source of Human Strength," referenced in Kaufman, *Transcend*, 226.

Chapter 5: Pursuing Prosperity

1. "A Free-Market Manifesto That Changed the World, Reconsidered," *New York Times*, September 11, 2020.

2. "A Free Market Manifesto."

3. Milton Friedman, "A Friedman Doctrine: The Social Responsibility of Business Is to Increase Its Profits," *New York Times Magazine*, September 13, 1970.

4. Mariana Mazzucato, *The Value of Everything: Making and Taking in the Global Economy* (New York: PublicAffairs, 2018).

5. Y. Varoufakis and J. Moe, *Talking to My Daughter about the Economy: A Brief History of Capitalism* (New York: Farrar, Strauss and Giroux, 2018).

6. James C. Scott, *Seeing Like a State: How Certain Schemes to Improve the Human Condition Have Failed* (New Haven, CT: Yale University Press, 1998).

7. Gerald Davis, *The Vanishing American Corporation: Navigating the Hazards of a New Economy* (Oakland, CA: Berrett-Kohler, 2016).

8. Gerald F. Davis and Aseem Sinha, "Varieties of Uberization: How Technology and Institutions Change the Organization(s) of Late Capitalism," *Organization Theory* 2 (2019): 1–17.

9. https://assets.pubpub.org/8b6dpdiq/41608610847456.pdf.

10. newyorker.com/culture/infinite-scroll/the-promise-of-daos-the-latest-craze-in-crypto.

11. A decentralized autonomous organization (DAO) is one that is an internet-based organization, collectively owned and managed by its members. The rules of operation (the equivalent of the legal framework) and the organization's treasury are encoded in a mechanism called a smart contract and published online. There is no central hierarchical authority. The group members make decisions collectively. These organizations reside on the blockchain—a list or ledger of records (called blocks) that contain a time stamp and information about each

transaction. Each new block contains information about the previous one and therefore resists being modified since any such modification would affect all the previous blocks. The collection of blocks containing information about the associated transactions form a chain (hence the name blockchain). investopedia.com/tech/what-dao/.

12. Aaron Dignan, "Changing the Way DAOs work." https://medium.com/the-ready/ changing-the-way-daos-work-54136e8d071d.

13. Simon Jäger, Benjamin Schoefer, and Jörg Heining, "Labor in the Boardroom," *SSRN Electronic Journal*. https://economics.mit.edu/files/17273, 2019; Jarkko Harju, Simon Jäger, and Benjamin Schoefer, Voice at Work, 2021, nber.org/papers/w28522.

14. https://democracyjournal.org/magazine/42/prosperity-by-design/.

15. Nick Romeo, "Can Companies Force Themselves to Do Good?" *New Yorker*, January 10, 2022.

16. See https://purpose-economy.org/en/ for more examples.

17. organicgrown.com.

18. wildplastic.com/en/.

19. https://einhorn.my.

20. Kaal offers the following example: For instance, the Uber DAO can be seen as Uber the company with all its constituents but without the company, for example, the entity, itself and its hierarchical governance structures. If Uber were a DAO, the Uber drivers as a group with their respective nonfungible token holdings would become Uber, for example, a fully decentralized company without hierarchies. The control and power over the Uber DAO would be in the hands of the DAO Uber token holders. Yet, the staking mechanisms for nonfungible tokens in emerging DAO protocols make the voting structure different from any previous attempts at creating liquid democracies. For a consumable overview of DAOs, see Cathy Hackl, "What Are DAOs and Why You Should Pay Attention," forbes.com/sites/cathyhackl/2021/06/01/what-are -daos-and-why-you-should-pay-attention/?sh=495344f67305; Wulf A. Kaal, "A Decentralized Autonomous Organization (DAO) of DAOs (March 6, 2021)." Available at SSRN, https://ssrn .com/abstract=3799320 or http://dx.doi.org/10.2139/ssrn.3799320; "Changing the Way DAOs Work," by Aaron Dignan, https://medium.com/the-ready/changing-the-way-daos-work -54136e8d071d.

21. J. S. Colton, A. C. Edenfield, and S. Holmes, "Workplace Democracy and the Problem of Equality," *Technical Communication 66*, no. 1 (January 1, 2019): 53–67.

22. N. Schneider, *Everything for Everyone: The Radical Tradition That Is Shaping the Next Economy* (New York: Nation Books, 2018).

23. https://zebrasunite.mn.co.

24. Richard D. Wolff, *Democracy at Work: A Cure for Capitalism* (Chicago: Haymarket Books, 2012).

25. D. Kruse, R. B. Freeman, and J. R. Blasi, National Bureau of Economic Research, Russell Sage Foundation, and Rockefeller Foundation, *Shared Capitalism at Work: Employee Ownership,*

Profit and Gain Sharing, and Broad-Based Stock Options (Chicago: University of Chicago Press, 2011).

26. As an illustration of challenges to securing these benefits, see the debate on Proposition 22 in Lauren Hepler's article, "Uber, Lyft, and Why California's War over Gig Work Is Just Beginning," https://calmatters.org/economy/2020/08/california-gig-work-ab5-prop-22/.

27. Varoufakis and Moe, *Talking to My Daughter about the Economy*.

28. Kate Raworth, *Doughnut Economics: Seven Ways to Think Like a 21st Century Economist* (White River Junction, VT: Chelsea Green Publishing, 2017).

29. In Canada and the United States, for example, the Genuine Progress Indicator takes everything the GDP uses into account but adds other figures that represent the cost of the negative effects related to economic activity. The Organization for Economic Cooperation and Development's "Better Life Index" comprises a broad range of areas—including income and employment, education, security, and work-life balance. The European Union launched the Beyond GDP to look beyond economic performance to determine welfare in the member states and to also include the United Nation's Seventeen Sustainable Development Goals. Germany uses the National Welfare Index, and Canada's Comprehensive Wealth project adds one number for evaluation and policy making on top of GDP. The UN Environment Programme–led Inclusive Wealth Index shows the aggregation through accounting and shadow pricing of produced capital, natural capital, and human capital for 140 countries.

30. weforum.org/agenda/2018/11/forget-gdp-for-the-21st-century-we-need-a-modern -economic-measure/.

31. www.iftf.org/equitableenterprise/.

32. For an example, see "The Long-Term Stock Exchange (LTSE) is an SEC-registered national securities exchange built to serve companies and investors who share a long-term vision," https://longtermstockexchange.com.

33. Mazzucato, *Value of Everything*, 270.

34. Mazzucato, *Value of Everything*, 270.

35. Thomas L. Friedman, "The Answers to Our Problems Aren't as Simple as Left or Right," *New York Times*, July 7, 2019.

36. Friedman, "Answers to Our Problems."

37. Choices for post-corporate economic models include eco-capitalism: continuing with the current models of production and profit, but for more sustainable processes and products. See https://link.springer.com/book/10.1007/978-3-319-92357-4; eco-socialism is another choice, which moves the needle toward the left (politically speaking) to embrace common ownership of the means of production by freely associated producers and restoring the commons. See J. Kovel and M. Lowy, An Ecosocialist Manifesto, http://environment-ecology.com/political-ecol-ogy/436-an-ecosocialist-manifesto.html, 2001; Green New Deal proposals in the United States, United Kingdom, and European Union call for public policy to address climate change along with achieving other social aims like job creation and reducing economic inequality. See https://

www.nytimes.com/2019/02/21/climate/green-new-deal-questions-answers.html. Economy for
the Common Good (ECG) is an economic model, which makes the Common Good, a good life
for everyone on a healthy planet, its primary goal and purpose. See www.ecogood.org/what-is-
ecg/ecg-in-a-nutshell/. Permaculture is an approach to land management and settlement design
that applies regenerative agriculture, town planning, rewilding, and community resilience
to create communities based on "sharing and caring" in human relationships rather than a
competition. See David Holmgren, "Essence of Permaculture" (PDF). Permaculture: Principles
and Pathways beyond Sustainability, self-published, 2007.

Chapter 6: Beyond Sustainability

1. Santiago, Chile, and Los Angeles, California, are both experiencing megadroughts,
and climate impact is likely to affect their water supply permanently: "Not just less water
for now. Maybe less water forever." See https://mail.google.com/mail/u/0/#inbox/
FMfcgzGpFgrvrfNsWQJrvmgBMSdLhQjt.

2. According to a World Bank report, "Groundswell—Preparing for Internal Climate
Migration," without urgent global and national climate action, sub-Saharan Africa, South Asia,
and Latin America could see more than 140 million people move within their countries' borders
by 2050.

3. designcouncil.org.uk/resources/guide/beyond-net-zero-systemic-design-approach.

4. Amitav Ghosh, *The Great Derangement: Climate Change and the Unthinkable* (Chicago:
University of Chicago Press, 2016).

5. ipcc.ch/report/ar6/wg3/resources/press/press-release/.

6. un.org/sg/en/node/262847.

7. Duffy, *Work and the City*.

8. World Economic Forum, "Circular Economy and Material Value Chains," weforum.org/
projects/circular-economy.

9. William Gibson, from account @GreatDismal, August 17, 2018.

10. zedfactory.com/bedzed.

11. See the Ellen Macarthur Foundation Butterfly diagram to visualize a circular economy,
https://ellenmacarthurfoundation.org/circular-economy-diagram. Also see Walter R. Stahel,
The Circular Economy: A User's Guide (New York: Routledge, 2019), chap. 4, for the R's of
circularity.

12. https://ellenmacarthurfoundation.org/the-jeans-redesign.

13. https://emf.thirdlight.com/link/TheJeansRedesign2021CommsPack/@/preview/49.

14. UN Global Compact, "The Future Is Green and Inclusive," 2021, unglobalcompact.org/
library/5966.

15. Bill Reed, "Shifting from 'Sustainability' to Regeneration," *Building Research and
Information* 35, no. 6 (2007): 674–80.

16. Tragedy of the commons is a situation in which individual users, who have open access to a resource unhampered by shared social structures or formal rules that govern access and use, act independently according to their own self-interest and, contrary to the common good of all users, cause depletion of the resource through their uncoordinated action. See Joanna Burger and Michael Gochfeld, "The Tragedy of the Commons 30 Years Later," *Environment: Science and Policy for Sustainable Development* 40, no. 10 (1998): 4–13.

17. youtube.com/watch?v=_EkSIlXEM50.

18. nytimes.com/2021/12/28/climate/chile-constitution-climate-change.html.

19. For more stories of systemic change, we recommend Mariana Amatullo, Bryan Boyer, Jennifer May, and Andrew Shea, *Design for Social Innovation: Case Studies from Around the World* (New York: Routledge, 2022).

20. Fritjof Capra and Pier Luigi Luisi, *The Systems View of Life: A Unifying Vision* (Cambridge: Cambridge University Press, 2016).

21. https://biomimicry.org/what-is-biomimicry/.

22. https://biomimicry.org/what-is-biomimicry/.

23. W. S. Saunders and K. Yu, *Designed Ecologies: The Landscape Architecture of Kongjian Yu* (Basel: De Gruyter, 2013).

24. weforum.org/agenda/2019/08/sponge-cities-china-flood-protection-nature-wwf/.

25. Daniel C. Wahl, "Sustainability Is Not Enough: We Need Regenerative Cultures," *Medium*, March 5, 2017, https://designforsustainability.medium.com/sustainability-is-not -enough-we-need-regenerative-cultures-4abb3c78e68b.

26. The list is too long to include here, but the good news is that it continues to grow. Here is a sampling:
- https://www.philips.com/a-w/about/environmental-social-governance/environmental /circular-economy.html.
- https://www.ikea.com/ch/en/this-is-ikea/sustainable-everyday/a-circular-ikea-making -the-things-we-love-last-longer-pub9750dd90.
- https://hmgroup.com/news/hm-group-launches-circular-design-tool-circulator/.
- https://www.dssmith.com/sustainability/sustainability-strategy.

27. https://mitsloan.mit.edu/ideas-made-to-matter/4-strategies-sustainable-business.

28. See, for example, *The EU and Climate Security: Toward Ecological Diplomacy*, edited by Olivia Lazard and Richard Youngs, https://carnegieendowment.org/files/Youngs_and_Lazard _EU_Climate_FINAL_07.08.21.pdf.

29. See www.technologyreview.com/gfi for the 2022 comparative ranking of seventy-six nations and territories on their ability to develop a sustainable, low-carbon future.

30. The IFRS Foundation announced at the UN Climate Change conference in Glasgow in November 2021 the formation of the International Sustainability Standards Board (ISSB), which will consolidate the Climate Disclosure Standards Board and the Value Reporting Foundation

(which includes the Integrated Reporting Framework and Sustainability Accounting Standards Board [SASB] Standards) by June 2022.

31. Christiana Fugueres and Tom Rivett-Carnac, *The Future We Choose: The Stubborn Optimist's Guide to the Climate Crisis* (New York: Vintage, 2020.)

Chapter 7: Cultivating Community

1. "6 Young Activists in Africa Working to Save the World," *Global Citizen,* August 17, 2018, https://www.globalcitizen.org/en/content/african-youth-activists-south-africa/. This video shows Greta Thunberg meeting with young leaders from Africa: https://www.youtube.com/watch?v=m5tAFYsXe5k.

2. Hilda Flavia Nakabuye, the founder of Fridays for Future Uganda. Quoted from: https://www.youtube.com/watch?v=kjsDxcWS1zU.

3. The 2010 and 2020 Digital Thresholds are described in more detail in Bob Johansen, *Full-Spectrum Thinking* (Oakland, CA: Berrett-Koehler, 2020), 78–89.

4. https://www.oxfam.org/en/research/inequality-kills.

5. M. (Matt) Raskovic, "(Social) Identity Theory in an Era of Identity Politics: Theory and Practice," *AIB Insights* 21, no. 2 (2020), https://doi.org/10.46697/001c.13616. For a comprehensive illustration of identity, see by Sylvia Duckworth's *Wheel of Power and Privilege* at https://tinyurl.com/63ynmssf.

6. Robin Cohen and Carolin Fischer, *Routledge Handbook of Diaspora Studies* (New York: Routledge, 2019), 5. See also J. Clifford, *Routes: Travel and Translation in the Late Twentieth Century* (Cambridge, MA: Harvard University Press, 1997).

7. T. Hübl, *Healing Collective Trauma* (Boulder, CO: Sounds True, 2021).

8. youtube.com/watch?v=2xsbt3a7K-8, 13:50; "MLK Talks 'New Phase' of Civil Rights Struggle, 11 Months before His Assassination," NBC News. In 1967, at the Ebenezer Baptist Church in Atlanta, Georgia, Martin Luther King Jr. spoke with NBC News' Sander Vanocur about the "new phase" of the struggle for "genuine equality."

9. The Belonging Organization, https://belongingorganization.com.

10. youtube.com/watch?v=DoU5F9pNVoA.

11. Courtney L. McCluney, Kathrina Robotham, Serenity Lee, Richard Smith, and Myles Durkee, "The Costs of Code-Switching," Big Idea Series/Advancing Black Leaders, *Harvard Business Review,* November 15, 2019.

12. Ytasha L. Womack, *Afrofuturism: The World of Black Sci-Fi and Fantasy Culture* (Chicago: Lawrence Hill Books, 2013), 16.

13. https://wendyguerrero.net/The-Latinfuturism-Archive.

14. https://catherinesramirez.com/wp-content/uploads/2020/09/ramirez-deus.pdf.

15. Virginia L. Conn and Gabriele de Seta, "Sinofuturism(s)," *Verge: Studies in Global Asias* 7 no. 2 (2021): 74–99.

16. https://sailemagazine.com/2021/04/arab-futurism-imagining-the-future-from-an-arab-perspective/.

17. artnews.com/art-in-america/interviews/sophia-al-maria-erika-balsom-gulf-futurism-sad-sacks-julia-stoschek-interview-1202683264/.

18. David Kushner, "Escape to Zoom Island: How Generation Zoom Transformed a Tiny Island into a Remote Worker's Paradise," *GQ*, April 27, 2022.

Chapter 8: Everyone Amplified

1. Amber Case, *Calm Technology: Principles and Patterns for Non-Intrusive Design* (Sebastopol, CA: O'Reilly Media, 2016).

2. https://www.usnews.com/news/health-news/articles/2022-02-07/new-technology-restores-movement-after-spinal-cord-paralysis. Accessed April 2022.

3. Kai-Fu Lee and Qiufan Chen, *AI 2041: Ten Visions for Our Future* (New York: Random House, 2021).

4. https://www.weforum.org/projects/augmented-workforce-initiative. Accessed April 6, 2022.

5. Batya Friedman as quoted in Artificial Intelligence and the Future of Humans; Pew Research Center and Elon University's Imagining the Internet Center, https://www.pewresearch.org/internet/2018/12/10/artificial-intelligence-and-the-future-of-humans/.

6. Jake Dunagan, "Mind in a Designed World: Toward the Infinite Cortex," 10.13140/RG.2.1.2946.4561, July 21, 2016.

7. nytimes.com/2022/04/06/technology/openai-images-dall-e.html.

8. Google's DeepMind says its new language model called RETRO can beat others twenty-five times its size, see https://www.technologyreview.com/2021/12/08/1041557/deepmind-language-model-beat-others-25-times-size-gpt-3-megatron/.

9. Inside the fight to reclaim AI from Big Tech's control, technologyreview.com/2021/06/14/1026148/ai-big-tech-timnit-gebru-paper-ethics/.

10. In 1956 at Dartmouth College, at their first convening, George Miller, Noam Chomsky, Allen Newell, Herbert Simon, Marvin Minsky, and others presented views on how the brain represents, processes, and transforms information. Inspired by John von Neumann's invention of the computer, they saw the "mind as machine." This metaphor laid the foundation for defining intelligence as a range of computational, mechanical processes, including language, perception, memory, problem-solving, reasoning, and many others.

11. John Thornhill, *Financial Times*, June 9, 2021, ft.com/content/dd621de6-4047-46c3-833a-b21bd2423113.

12. K. Crawford, *Atlas of AI: Power, Politics, and the Planetary Costs of Artificial Intelligence* (New Haven, CT: Yale University Press, 2021).

13. Indeed, the evidence on social media and examples of malicious use of deep fakes are signals that we are far away from more intelligence.

14. We think that Thomas W. Malone from MIT was first to use this phrase when he said, "we should move from thinking about putting humans in the loop to putting computers in the group," see *Superminds: The Surprising Power of People and Computers Thinking Together* (Boston: Little, Brown, 2018), 75.

15. Malone, *Superminds.*

16. Cal Newport, *A World without Email: Reimagining Work in the Age of Overload* (Penguin Random House UK, 2021); Cal Newport, *Deep Work* (London, 2016).

17. David Rose, *Enchanted Objects: Design, Human Desire, and the Internet of Things* (New York: Scribner's, 2014), 194. Rose identifies five steps on what he calls "The Ladder of Enchantment":
   1. Connection: adding sensing/sensor capabilities by connecting to the cloud.
   2. Personalization: adding and leveraging personal information.
   3. Socialization: adding connections to friends, loved ones, and colleagues.
   4. Gamification: adding the fun and motivational elements of video games.
   5. Story-fication: adding a human narrative for the product, service, or user.

18. Anthony Dunne and Fiona Raby, *Speculative Everything: Design, Fiction, and Social Dreaming* (Cambridge, MA: MIT Press, 2013).

19. https://medium.com/demagsign/8-spectacular-speculative-designs-44fb129eb4e2.

20. https://2050.earth.

21. www.wired.com/story/lamda-sentient-ai-bias-google-blake-lemoine/.

22. Benjamin Bratton and Blaise Agüera y Arcas, "The Model Is the Message," essay in *Noēma* magazine, Berggruen Institute, July 12, 2022.

23. T. W. Kim and A. Duhachek, "Artificial Intelligence and Persuasion: A Construal-Level Account," *Psychological Science* 31, no. 4 (2020): 363–80, https://journals.sagepub.com/doi/abs/10.1177/0956797620904985.

24. S. Raisch and S. Krakowski, "Artificial Intelligence and Management: The Automation-Augmentation Paradox," *Academy of Management Review* 46, no. 1 (January 2021): 192–210.

25. https://sloanreview.mit.edu/projects/reshaping-business-with-artificial-intelligence/.

26. https://www.designhacks.co/products/cognitive-bias-codex-poster?variant=28329927043.

27. Shoshana Zuboff, "You Are the Object of a Secret Extraction Operation," *New York Times,* November 11, 2021.

28. Shoshana Zuboff, *The Age of Surveillance Capitalism: The Fight for a Human Future at the New Frontier of Power* (New York: Public Affairs Hachette Book Group, 2019), 12.

29. Made by Jeremy Kirshbaum of Handshake.fyi using the GPT-3 text generator; inspired by the poems of Pablo Neruda.

30. See https://openai.com/dall-e-2/ and https://doi.org/10.48550/arXiv.2204.06125.

31. Mark Amerika, *My Life as an Artificial Creative Intelligence* (Stanford, CA: Stanford University Press, 2022).

32. T. Buganza, P. Bellis, S. Magnanini, J. Press, A. Shani, D. Trabucchi, R. Verganti, and F. Zasa, *Storymaking: How the Co-creation of Narratives Engages People for Innovation and Transformation* (New York: Routledge, 2022).

Chapter 9: Better Than Being There

1. Frank Duffy, *Work and the City, Edge Futures* (London: Black Dog, 2008), 48 and 55.

2. For examples, see https://youtu.be/17fIcc-Ys8Y and https://www.gensler.com/research-insight/publications.

3. For example, see R. C. Pozen and A. Samuel, "Remote, Inc: How to Thrive at Work . . . Wherever You Are," Harper Business, an imprint of HarperCollins Publishers 2021.

4. mckinsey.com/business-functions/organization/our-insights/reimagining-the-office-and-work-life-after-covid-19.

5. We first heard this term *work/life navigation* from the work/family pioneer Ellen Galinsky and her work at the Families and Work Institute.

6. iftf.org/remodelingtrust/.

7. Web3 (potentially powered by quantum computing) could disrupt much of what we talk about in the book, specifically blockchain-based platforms such as DAOs, cryptocurrencies, and smart contracts. Web3, according to American internet entrepreneur and investor Chris Dixon, is "a new way to build networks where instead of the network owned by a company it is owned by a community of users." Web3 highlights that more important than the technologies are the human needs that need to be fulfilled: more trust, more connection, more agency, less control, and such. For more details, listen to Kara Swisher's June 16, 2022, interview with Chris Dixon, "As Bitcoin Busts, What's the Future of Web3? And What Even Is Web3?" www.nytimes.com/2022/06/16/opinion/sway-kara-swisher-chris-dixon.html accessed July 10 2022.

8. Refer to the previous endnote for clarification of Web3.

9. Dr. Rosanna Guadagno, consulting senior Scientist at Stanford University, found that players are more trusting of other players who are part of their guild, a group of players who share a common chat channel, group identifier, and play together regularly, relative to players who belong to other guilds or are not in a guild. https://news.utdallas.edu/faculty-staff/study-explores-how-trustful-online-gamers-are-with/.

10. Marshall McLuhan, *Understanding Media: The Extensions of Man* (New York: Penguin, 1966).

11. *MIT Technology Review* 123, no. 1 (January/February 2020).

12. Professor Mori theorized that as robots become more attractive to humans, they appear more and more human, up to the uncanny valley, where the robot looks human, but something seems not quite right or even weird or creepy. See Masahiro Mori, Tokyo Institute for

Technology, 1970, "The Uncanny Valley: The Original Essay by Masahiro Mori," June 12, 2012. As cited in New Leadership Literacies. For an updated version, see https://youtu.be/WUogvPcc3jQ.

13. Unreal Engine's MetaHuman Creator—an open and advanced real-time 3D creation tool for photorealistic immersive experiences—takes real-time human information and creates real-life avatars in hours. The software—and the company—crossed the uncanny valley by also crossing gaming, marketing, and film for Matrix Resurrections. Fans can download a gaming option that uses action sequences from the movie, and the game characters have a powerful resemblance to the actors in the movie, unrealengine.com/en-US/digital-humans.

14. Sherry Turkle, *Alone Together: Why We Expect More from Technology and Less from Each Other* (New York: Basic Books, 2011).

15. "Without social organizations, social technologies will eat us alive," Marina Gorbis, https://medium.com/institute-for-the-future/without-social-organizations-social-technologies -will-eat-us-alive-86b479ac0874.

16. Christian Gänshirt, "1968—Fritz Haller: Totale Stadt," in *Das ungebaute Berlin. Stadt-konzepte im 20. Jahrhundert,* edited by Carsten Krohn (Berlin: DOM Publishers, 2010), 191–93.

17. N. J. Habraken and B. Valkenburg, *Supports: An Alternative to Mass Housing* (New York: Praeger, 1972).

18. E. Manzini, *Design, When Everybody Designs: An Introduction to Design for Social Innovation* (Cambridge, MA: MIT Press, 2015).

19. https://openarchcollab.org.

20. nytimes.com/2015/01/18/arts/design/a-leader-in-socially-conscious-architecture-is -closing-amid-financial-woes.html.

21. "People Recall Information Better through Virtual Reality, Says New UMD Study," College of Computer, Mathematical, and Natural Sciences, University of Maryland, June 13, 2018. The study involved forty participants who were asked to perform a task using a VR headset and again by using their own coordination. When participants used VR headsets, the results engineered an 8.8% improvement in memory performance. https://cmns.umd.edu/news-events /features/4155.

22. https://www3.weforum.org/docs/WEF_Future_of_Jobs_2020.pdf.

23. Video games can increase creativity, but with caveats. See https://doi.org/10.1080 /10400419.2019.1594524.

24. James Delaney, *Beautiful Minecraft* (San Francisco: No Starch Press, 2017).

25. Jaron Lanier, https://www.nytimes.com/2021/11/11/opinion/sway-kara-swisher-jaron -lanier.htm.

Chapter 10: Coordinating with Clarity

1. Marina Gorbis, https://democracyjournal.org/author/marina-gorbis/.

2. Dr. Melanie Ivarsson, chief development officer of Moderna, quotes from MIT Sloan School iLead interview, http://web.mit.edu/webcast/mitsloan/f21/ilead/1/, 2021.

3. Bob Johansen, *The New Leadership Literacies: Thriving in a Future of Extreme Disruption and Distributed Everything* (Oakland, CA: Berrett-Koehler, 2017), 61–75.

4. Michel Zarka, Elena Kochanovskaya, and Bill Pasmore, *Braided Organizations: Designing Augmented Human Centric Processes to Enhance Performance and Innovation* (Charlotte, NC: Information Age Publishing, 2019).

5. Zarka, Kochanovskaya, and Pasmore, *Braided Organizations*.

6. Conversation with Niklas Jansen, Fall 2019.

7. Bob Johansen, *The New Leadership Literacies* (Oakland, CA: Berrett-Koehler, 2017), 117–30.

8. https://www.neuro.duke.edu/research/research-news/how-vr-helping-paraplegics-walk-again.

9. Using Play to Rewire and Improve Your Brain, Huberman Lab Podcast #58, www.youtube.com/watch?v=BwyZIWeBpRw&list=RDCMUC2D2CMWXMOVWx7giW1n3LIg&start_radio=1.

10. G. Güneş, "Personal Play Identity and the Fundamental Elements in Its Development Process," *Current Psychology* (2021).

11. "Having a gamer's mindset or attitude. Like playful, but more oriented toward achieving goals, trying out different strategies, and taking on new challenges." urbandictionary.com/define.php?term=gameful.

12. A Fireside Chat with Blizzard Entertainment cofounder Mike Morhaime. youtube.com/watch?v=bPFtUiTncy8.

13. ea.com/commitments/positive-play/charter.

14. ubisoft.com/en-us/help/article/code-of-conduct-the-way-we-play/000095037?isSso=true&refreshStatus=noLoginData.

15. Kayla Barron, Annapolis graduate, former officer on ballistic missile-armed submarines, and current astronaut, quoted in "Ready to Explore," *Bainbridge Islander,* December 17, 2021.

16. "How Job Simulator created a perfect way to spectate, and stream, from within VR," https://www.polygon.com/2016/3/30/11330766/job-simulator-vive-twitch-youtube.

17. youtube.com/watch?v=v5cRj2qTCpw, 2020.

18. youtube.com/watch?v=v5cRj2qTCpw.

19. researchgate.net/publication/317826656_Simulation_tool_for_fire_and_rescue_services.

20. O. Almousa, J. Prates, N. Yeslam, et al., "Virtual Reality Simulation Technology for Cardiopulmonary Resuscitation Training: An Innovative Hybrid System with Haptic Feedback," *Simulation and Gaming* 50, no. 1 (2019): 6–22. doi:10.1177/1046878118820905.

21. mountainview.gov/news/displaynews.asp?NewsID=1724&TargetID=9.

22. The term *flexive command* has been suggested in a military context, but while we like the word flexive, we don't think that "command" is appropriate for nonmilitary settings. See Andrew Hill and Heath Niemi, "The Trouble with Mission Common: Flexive Command and the Future of Command and Control," *Joint Force Quarterly* 86 (2017).

23. Mariana Mazzucato, Governing Missions in the European Union, 2019, https://ec
.europa.eu/info/sites/default/files/research_and_innovation/contact/documents/ec_rtd
_mazzucato-report-issue2_072019.pdf. For an example of a very interesting mission map that
demonstrates what we call flexive intent, see "A Mission-Oriented Approach to Cleaning the
Oceans," Mazzucato, at https://www.researchgate.net/figure/A-mission-oriented-approach-to
-cleaning-the-oceans-Source-Mazzucato-2018c-24_fig1_338177337.

PART III: WHAT NOW?

1. Octavia E. Butler, *Parable of the Sower* (London: Headline, 1993), 1 and 75.

Chapter 11: Thinking Futureback about Office Shock

1. For more information, see iftf.org/foresightessentials/.

2. Peter Drucker was noted for this quote: "Culture eats strategy for breakfast." Most
architects, including our coauthor, would be inclined to say: "Organizational strategy eats office
design for lunch."

3. Onna M. van den Broek and Robyn Klingler-Vidra, "The UN Sustainable Development
Goals as a North Star: How an Intermediary Network Makes, Takes, and Retrofits the
Meaning of the Sustainable Development Goals," https://onlinelibrary.wiley.com/share/
D6EAEYCGGUWCTBHJXMBV?target=10.1111/rego.12415.

4. We intentionally are not referring to a specific star, like the North Star, to encourage
everyone to focus on their own celestial guide.

5. The critical success factors methodology was developed at MIT by Jack Rockart and
Christine Bullen. See John F. Rockart, "Chief Executives Define Their Own Needs," *Harvard
Business Review*, March 1979. See also, Christine V. Bullen and John F. Rockart, "A Primer on
Critical Success Factors," CISR No. 69, Sloan WP No. 1220-81, Center for Information Systems
Research, Sloan School of Management, Massachusetts Institute of Technology, June 1981.

6. S. Datar et al., "Royal Philips: Designing Toward Profound Change," *Harvard Business
Review*, July 3, 2018.

7. J. Press et al., *IDeaLs (Innovation and Design as Leadership): Transformation in the Digital Era*
(Bingley, UK: Emerald Publishing, 2021), https://www.ideals.polimi.it.

8. See Josh Berson, *The Human Scaffold: How Not to Design Your Way Out of a Climate Crisis*
(Oakland: University of California Press, 2021).

9. https://en.wikipedia.org/wiki/Agential_realism.

Chapter 12: Personal Choices

1. According to Jason Zac, synchronization brings the three essential elements of music
together to create an embodied emotional experience:

1. Melody—patterns and variations of notes.
2. Harmony—sounds and intervals of notes that create a story.
3. Rhythm—the beat, akin to a heartbeat, guiding a consistent movement.

Chapter 14: Community Choices

1. https://tulsaremote.com/.

2. https://nextcity.org/urbanist-news/tulsa-offered-to-pay-people-to-move-the-program -got-10000-applicants.

Conclusion

1. Amanda Gorman, "Why I Almost Didn't Read My Poem at the Inauguration," *New York Times*, January 20, 2022.

2. #Oursolutions: Conversation with Jacqui Patterson, https://wedo.org/oursolutions -conversation-jacqui-patterson-naacp/.

3. nytimes.com/interactive/2021/10/27/opinion/tom-morello-teaching-guitar-music.html.

4. Mariana Mazzucato, *The Entrepreneurial State: Debunking Public vs. Private Sector Myths*, rev. ed. (New York: PublicAffairs, 2015).

5. F. Buckminster Fuller, ed. J. Snyder, *Operating Manual for Spaceship Earth* (Zurich: Lars Müller Publishers 2014).

BIBLIOGRAPHY

Almousa, O., J. Prates, N. Yeslam, et al. "Virtual Reality Simulation Technology for Cardiopulmonary Resuscitation Training: An Innovative Hybrid System with Haptic Feedback." *Simulation and Gaming* 50, no. 1 (2019): 6–22.

AlphaGo. Directed by Greg Kohs. Moxie Pictures. September 29, 2017.

Amerika, Mark. *My Life as an Artificial Creative Intelligence*. Stanford, CA: Stanford University Press, 2022.

Asimov, Isaac. *Foundation*. New York: Avon, 1955.

Baldwin, James. "I Am Not Your Negro." A documentary based on Baldwin's unfinished book manuscript *Remember This House*, 2017.

Barad, K. *Meeting the University Halfway: Quantum Physics and the Entanglement of Matter and Meaning*. Durham, NC: Duke University Press, 2007.

Becker, F. D., and F. Steele. *Workplace by Design: Mapping the High-Performance Workscape*. San Francisco: Jossey-Bass, 1995.

Berson, Josh. *The Human Scaffold: How Not to Design Your Way Out of a Climate Crisis*. Oakland: University of California Press, 2021.

Bratton, Benjamin, and Blaise Agüera y Arcas. "The Model Is the Message." Essay in *Noēma* magazine. Berggruen Institute, July 12, 2022.

Brown, Tim. *Change by Design: How Design Thinking Transforms Organizations and Inspires Innovation*. New York: Harper Business, 2009.

Buganza, T., P. Bellis, S. Magnanini, J. Press, A. Shani, D. Trabucchi, R. Verganti, and F. Zasa. *Storymaking: How the Co-creation of Narratives Engages People for Innovation and Transformation*. New York: Routledge, 2022.

Bullen, Christine V., and John F. Rockart. "A Primer on Critical Success Factors." CISR Working Paper No. 69, Sloan Working Paper No. 1220-81, Center for Information Systems Research, Sloan School of Management, Massachusetts Institute of Technology, June 1981.

Butler, Octavia E. *Parable of the Sower*. London: Headline, 1993.

Capra, Fritjof, and Pier Luigi Luisi. *The Systems View of Life: A Unifying Vision*. Cambridge: Cambridge University Press, 2016.

Carson, Rachel. *The Silent Spring*. New York: Fawcett World Library, 1962.

Case, Amber. *Calm Technology: Principles and Patterns for Non-intrusive Design*. Sebastopol, CA: O'Reilly Media, 2016.

Chayka, Kyle. "The Promise of DAOs, the Latest Craze in Crypto." *New Yorker*, January 28, 2022.

Churchman, C. "Wicked Problems." *Management Science* 14, no. 4 (December 1967): B-141–B-146.

Clifford, James. *Routes: Travel and Translation in the Late Twentieth Century*. Cambridge, MA: Harvard University Press, 1997.

Cohen, Robin, and Carolin Fischer. *Routledge Handbook of Diaspora Studies*. New York: Routledge, 2019.

Cooperrider, David, and Audrey Selian, eds. *The Business of Building a Better World: The Leadership Revolution That Is Changing Everything*. Oakland, CA: Berrett-Koehler, 2022.

Cozolino, L. J. *The Neuroscience of Human Relationships: Attachment and the Developing Social Brain*. New York: W. W. Norton, 2006.

Crawford, K. *Atlas of AI: Power, Politics, and the Planetary Costs of Artificial Intelligence*. New Haven, CT: Yale University Press, 2021.

Datar, S., et al. "Royal Philips: Designing Toward Profound Change." *Harvard Business Review* (July 3, 2018).

Davenport, Thomas H. *The AI Advantage: How to Put the Artificial Intelligence Revolution to Work*. Cambridge, MA: MIT Press, 2018.

Davis, Gerald. *The Vanishing American Corporation: Navigating the Hazards of a New Economy*. Oakland, CA: Berrett-Kohler, 2016.

Dignan, Aaron. "Changing the Way DAOs Work." https://medium.com/the-ready/changing-the-way-daos-work-54136e8d071d.

Duffy, F., and C. Cave. "Bürolandschaft Revisited." *Architect's Journal* 26 (March 1975): 665–75.

Duffy, Francis, and Kenneth Powell. *The New Office*. London: Conran Octopus, 1997.

Duffy, Frank. *Work and the City*. Edge Futures. London: Black Dog Publishers, 2008.

Dunne, A., and R. F. Fiona. *Speculative Everything: Design, Fiction, and Social Dreaming*. Cambridge, MA: MIT Press, 2013.

Edmans, Alex. *Grow the Pie*. Cambridge: Cambridge University Press, 2021.

Edmondson, Amy C. *The Fearless Organization: Creating Psychological Safety in the Workplace for Learning, Innovation, and Growth*. Hoboken, NJ: John Wiley and Sons, 2019.

Epstein, David. *Range: Why Generalists Triumph in a Specialized World*. New York: Riverhead Books, 2019.

Figueres, Christiana, and Tom Rivett-Carnac. *The Future We Choose: The Stubborn Optimist's Guide to the Climate Crisis*. New York: Vintage, 2020.

Fogg, B. J. *Tiny Habits: The Small Changes That Change Everything*. New York: Houghton, Mifflin, Harcourt, 2020.

Fridays for the Future. https://fridaysforfuture.org/.

Friedman, Milton. "A Friedman Doctrine: The Social Responsibility of Business Is to Increase Its Profits." *New York Times Magazine*, September 13, 1970.

Friedman, Thomas L. "The Answers to Our Problems Aren't as Simple as Left or Right." *New York Times*, July 7, 2019.

Fuentes, Agustín. *The Creative Spark: How Imagination Made Humans Exceptional*. New York: Dutton, 2017.

Fuller, R. Buckminster. Edited by J. Snyder. *Operating Manual for Spaceship Earth*. Zurich: Lars Müller Publishers, 2014.

Galbraith, John Kenneth. *Economics and the Public Purpose*. New York: New American Library, 1973

Ganshirt, Christian. *Fritz Haller: Totale Stadt*. In *Das ungebaute Berlin: Stadtkonzepte im 20. Jahrhundert*, edited by Carsten Krohn. Berlin: DOM Publishers, 2010, 191–93.

Gillies, James, and Robert Cailliau. *How the Web Was Born: The Story of the World Wide Web*. Oxford: Oxford University Press, 2000.

Gorbis, Marina. *Peoplenomics: How the Rise of the Social Economy Will Transform Our Lives*. New York: Free Press, 2013.

Gorman, Amanda. "Why I Almost Didn't Read My Poem at the Inauguration." *New York Times*, January 20, 2022.

Habraken, N. J., and B. Valkenburg. *Supports: An Alternative to Mass Housing*. Westport, CT: Praeger, 1972.

Harari, Yuval Noah. *Sapiens: A Brief History of Humankind*. New York: Harper Perennial, 2018.

Hastings, Reed, and Erin Meyer. *No Rules Rules: Netflix and the Culture of Reinvention*. New York: Penguin, 2020.

Haven, Kendall. *Story Smart: Using the Science of Story to Persuade, Influence, Inspire, and Teach*. Santa Barbara, CA: Libraries United, 2014.

Holmgren, David. "Essence of Permaculture" (PDF). *Permaculture: Principles and Pathways Beyond Sustainability*. Self-published, 2007.

Hubbard, Timothy, et al. "Boundary Extension: Findings and Theories." *Quarterly Journal of Experimental Psychology* 63 (2010): 1467–94.

Hübl, Thomas. *Healing Collective Trauma: A Process for Integrating Our Intergenerational and Cultural Wounds*. Boulder, CO: Sounds True, 2020.

Johansen, Bob. *Full-Spectrum Thinking: How to Escape Boxes in a Post-Categorical Future*. Oakland, CA: Berrett-Koehler, 2020.

———. *Get There Early*. San Francisco: Berrett-Koehler, 2007.

———. *The New Leadership Literacies: Thriving in a Future of Extreme Disruption and Distributed Everything*. Oakland, CA: Berrett-Koehler, 2017.

Johansen, Robert, Jeff Charles, Robert Mittman, and Paul Saffo. *Groupware: Computer Support for Business Teams*. New York: Free Press, 1998.

Johnson, Mark W., and Josh Suskewicz. *Lead from the Future: How to Turn Visionary Thinking into Breakthrough Growth*. Boston: Harvard Business School Press, 2020.

Johnson, Steven. *Everything Bad Is Good for You: How Today's Popular Culture Is Actually Making Us Smarter*. New York: Riverhead Books, 2005.

Kahneman, Daniel. *Thinking Fast and Slow*. New York: Farrar, Straus and Giroux, 2011.

Kaufman, Scott Barry. *Transcend: The New Science of Self-Actualization*. New York: TarcherPerigee, 2020.

Klein, Naomi. *The Shock Doctrine: The Rise of Disaster Capitalism*. New York: Picador, 2008.

Kolata, Gina. "Kati Kariko Helped Shield the World from the Corona Virus." *New York Times*, April 8, 2021. nytimes.com/2021/04/08/health/coronavirus-mrna-kariko.html.

Kovel, J., and M. Lowy. "An Ecosocialist Manifesto." *Environment and Ecology* (2001).

Kripal, Jeffrey. *Authors of the Impossible*. Chicago: University of Chicago Press, 2010.

Kruse, D., R. B. Freeman, and J. R. Blasi Jr. *Shared Capitalism at Work: Employee*

Ownership, Profit and Gain Sharing, and Broad-Based Stock Options. Chicago: University of Chicago Press, 2011.

Laing, Andrew. "New Patterns of Work: The Design of the Office." In *Reinventing the Workplace*, edited by John Worthington. York, England: Architectural Press, 1997.

Lazard, Olivia, and Richard Youngs, eds. *The EU and Climate Security: Toward Ecological Diplomacy.* Carnegie Endowment for International Peace, 2021.

Lee, Kai-Fu, and Chen Qiufan . *AI 2041: Ten Visions of Our Future.* New York: Random House, 2021.

Lembke, Anna. *Dopamine Nation.* New York: Dutton, 2021.

Lewis, Michael. *The Premonition.* New York: W. W. Norton, 2021.

Lim, Jenn. "How to Find the Secret to Meaningful Work." Podcast, "How to Build a Happy Life," hosted by Arthur Brooks, 2021, https://podcasts.apple.com/us/podcast/how-to-find-the-secret-to-meaningful-work/id1587046024?i=1000540 502958.

Lus-Arana, L. "The Many Effects of the Guggenheim Effect." *MAS Context* (2017): 315–451.

Malone, Thomas W. *Superminds: The Surprising Power of People and Computers Thinking Together.* New York: Little, Brown, 2018.

Manaugh, Geoff, and Nicola Twilley. *Until Proven Safe.* New York: Farrar, Straus and Giroux, 2021.

Mann, C. "Lynn Margulis: Science's Unruly Earth Mother." *Science* 252, no. 5004 (1991): 378–81.

Manzini, E. *Design, When Everybody Designs: An Introduction to Design for Social Innovation.* Cambridge, MA: MIT Press, 2015.

Margulis, L. *Symbiotic Planet: A New Look at Evolution.* New York: Basic Books, 1998.

Maslow, Abraham. *Toward a Psychology of Being.* New York: Wiley, 1961.

Mazzucato, Mariana. *The Entrepreneurial State: Debunking Public vs. Private Sector Myths.* Rev. ed. New York: Public Affairs, 2015.

——. *Mission Economy: A Moonshot Guide to Changing Capitalism.* New York: Penguin Books, 2022.

——. *The Value of Everything: Making and Taking in the Global Economy.* New York: Public Affairs, 2018.

McChrystal, Stanley. *Team of Teams: New Rules of Engagement for a Complex World.* New York: Portfolio/Penguin, 2015.

McCluney, Courtney L., Kathrina Robotham, Serenity Lee, Richard Smith, and Myles

Durkee. "The Costs of Code-Switching," Big Idea Series/Advancing Black Leaders. *Harvard Business Review* (November 15, 2019).

McGonigal, Jane. *Imaginable: How to See the Future Coming and Feel Ready for Anything–Even Things That Seem Impossible Today.* New York: Spiegel and Grau, 2022.

McLuhan, Marshall. *Understanding Media: The Extensions of Man.* New York: Penguin, 1966.

Me Too Movement. https://metoomvmt.org/.

Miller, Sarah. "The Millions of Tons of Carbon Emissions That Don't Officially Exist." *New Yorker*, December 8, 2021.

Mullally, S. L, and E. A. Maguire. "Memory, Imagination, and Predicting the Future: A Common Brain Mechanism?" *Neuroscientist* 20, no. 3 (2014): 220–34.

Nap Ministry. https://thenapministry.wordpress.com/.

Newport, Cal. *Deep Work.* London: Grand Central, 2016.

———. *A World without Email: Reimagining Work in the Age of Overload.* Penguin Random House UK, 2021.

People Not Profits. https://peoplenotprofits.org/.

Petzold, Charles. *The Annotated Turing: A Guided Tour through Alan Turing's Historic Paper on Computability and the Turing Machine.* Indianapolis: Wiley, 2008.

Piketty, Thomas, and Arthur Goldhammer. *Capital in the Twenty-First Century.* Cambridge, MA: Belknap Press of Harvard University Press, 2013.

Polak, Fred Lodewijk. *The Image of the Future.* Elsevier International Series. San Francisco: Jossey-Bass, 1973.

Polman, Paul, and Andrew Winston. *Net Positive.* Boston: Harvard Business Review Press, 2021.

Pozen, R. C., and A. Samuel. *Remote, Inc: How to Thrive at Work . . . Wherever You Are.* New York: Harper Business, an imprint of HarperCollins, 2021.

Press, J., et al. *IDeaLs (Innovation and Design as Leadership): Transformation in the Digital Era.* Bingley, UK: Emerald Publishing, 2021. https://www.ideals.polimi.it.

Raworth, Kate. *Doughnut Economics: Seven Ways to Think Like a 21st Century Economist.* White River Junction, VT: Chelsea Green Publishing, 2017.

Rockart, John F. "Chief Executives Define Their Own Data Needs." *Harvard Business Review* (March 1979).

Romeo, Nick. "Can Companies Force Themselves to Do Good?" *New Yorker*, January 10, 2022.

Rose, David. *Enchanted Objects: Design, Human Desire, and the Internet of Things.* New York: Scribner's, 2014.

Rosen, Robert H. *Just Enough Anxiety*. New York: Portfolio, 2008.

Saunders, W. S., and K. Yu. *Designed Ecologies: The Landscape Architecture of Kongjian Yu*. Basel: De Gruyter, 2013.

Schneider, N. *Everything for Everyone: The Radical Tradition That Is Shaping the Next Economy*. New York: Nation Books, 2018.

Schroeter, John. *After Shock*. Bainbridge Island, WA: Abundant World Institute, 2020.

Schwab, Klaus, and Thierry Malleret. *COVID-19: The Great Reset*. Geneva: Forum Publishing, 2020.

Scott, James C. *Seeing Like a State: How Certain Schemes to Improve the Human Condition Have Failed*. New Haven, CT: Yale University Press, 1998.

Senge, Peter M. *The Fifth Discipline: The Art and Practice of the Learning Organization*. Rev. ed. New York: Crown Business, 2006.

Stephenson, Neal. *Snow Crash: A Novel*. New York: Del Rey, 1992.

———. *Termination Shock: A Novel*. New York: William Morrow, 2021.

Stone, Philip, and Robert Luchetti. "Your Office Is Where You Are." *Harvard Business Review* (March–April 1985): 102–16.

Storr, Will. *The Science of Storytelling*. New York: Harry N. Abrams, 2020.

Suzman, James. *Work: A Deep History, from the Stone Age to the Age of Robots*. New York: Penguin, 2021.

Swisher, Kara. "Big Tech Has Weaved Its Way Completely into Our Lives." *New York Times*, November 18, 2021.

Taylor, Frederick. *The Principles of Scientific Management*. New York: Harper, 1911.

Thomas, Amy. "Architectural Consulting in the Knowledge Economy: DEGW and the ORBIT Report." *Journal of Architecture* 24, no. 7 (2019): 1020–44.

Toffler, Alvin. *Future Shock*. New York: Random House, 1970.

Townsend, Anthony M. *Ghost Road: Beyond the Driverless Car*. New York: W. W. Norton, 2020.

Turkle, Sherry. *Alone Together: Why We Expect More from Technology and Less from Each Other*. New York: Basic Books, 2011.

Tzuo, Tien. *Subscribed: Why the Subscription Model Will Be Your Company's Future—and What to Do About It*. New York: Portfolio/Penguin, 2018.

United Nations. Sustainable Development Goals. https://sdgs.un.org.

United Nations Global Compact. "The Future Is Green and Inclusive." unglobalcompact.org/library/5966, 2021.

Varoufakis, Y. *Talking to My Daughter about the Economy: A Brief History of Capitalism*. Translated by J. Moe. New York: Farrar, Straus and Giroux, 2017.

Vian, Kathi, Jacques Vallee, and Bob Johansen. *2012 Map of the Decade: The Future Is a Question about What Is Possible*. Palo Alto, CA: Institute for the Future, 2011.

Von Stackelberg, P., and A. McDowell. "What in the World? Storyworlds, Science Fiction, and Futures Studies." *Journal of Futures Studies* 20, no. 2 (2015): 25–46.

Wahl, Daniel C. "Sustainability Is Not Enough: We Need Regenerative Cultures." *Medium*. March 5, 2017. https://designforsustainability.medium.com/sustainability-is-not-enough-we-need-regenerative-cultures-4abb3c78e68b.

Weber, Max. *The Theory of Social and Economic Organizations*. Translated by A. Henderson and T. Parsons. Oxford: Oxford University Press, 1947.

Wells, H. G. *Anticipations of the Reaction of Mechanical and Scientific Progress upon Human Life and Thought*. New York: Harper and Brothers, 1901.

——. "Wanted—Professors of Foresight!" *Futures Research Quarterly* 3, no. 1 (Spring 1987).

Wolff, Richard D. *Democracy at Work: A Cure for Capitalism*. Chicago: Haymarket Books, 2012.

Womack, Ytasha. *Afrofuturism: The World of Black Sci-Fi and Fantasy Culture*. Chicago: Lawrence Hill Books, 2013.

Wright, Lawrence. *The Plague Year*. New York: Knopf, 2021.

Zarka, Michel, Elena Kochanovskaya, and Bill Pasmore. *Braided Organizations: Designing Augmented Human-Centric Processes to Enhance Performance and Innovation*. Charlotte, NC: Information Age Publishing, 2019.

Zeisel, John. *Inquiry by Design: Tools for Environmental Behavior Research*. Monterey, CA: Brooks/Cole Publishing, 1981.

Zuboff, Shoshana. *The Age of Surveillance Capitalism: The Fight for a Human Future at the New Frontier of Power*. New York: Public Affairs, Hachette Book Group, 2019.

ACKNOWLEDGMENTS

The idea for this book started in the early stages of the COVID-19 pandemic shutdowns during a Zoom meeting of Colin Macgadie, Alex Schärer, Ian Weddell, Marco Strahm, Joseph Press, and Bob Johansen. Alex, the CEO of the Swiss furniture company USM, shared his vision of a global network of office hubs. Bob and Joseph were already thinking futureback about future office scenarios but hadn't yet begun to write. Colin, an architect for BDG in London, was designing office workspaces in preparation for the return to office buildings. We were all pondering both what's possible and what's next for offices. Thank you, Colin, Alex, Ian, and Marco, for helping us ask the right questions and make this book possible. Our hope is to start a new conversation about office places and processes.

While coauthors Bob, Joseph, and Christine wrote this book, a strong core team contributed to the research, organization, and early drafting. Susanne Forchheimer was our mission control, doing all the organizational work of managing, scheduling, and coordinating—in addition to her frequent content suggestions. Gabe Cervantes contributed greatly to chapter 7 on the Spectrum of Belonging, but he also helped refine our message and spread the word about office shock. Sabrina Howard contributed in major ways to chapters 4 and 5 on the Spectrums of Purpose and Outcomes. Our early team conversations were critical to creating the basic structure and flow of the book.

Berrett-Koehler is a wonderful publisher in so many ways, and we are so grateful to be able to work with them. Steve Piersanti from Berrett-Koehler was our conceptual editor and spiritual guide throughout the creation and writing. He was the perfect mix of criticism and encouragement. The entire BK team is important to us, including especially Edward Wade, Jeevan Sivasubramaniam, Michael Crowley, Valerie Caldwell, and David Marshall. Archie Ferguson was masterful in his creation of the cover, with Joseph's meticulous art direction. Thanks also to Dawn Hall for her excellent copyediting.

Our colleagues at the Institute for the Future were encouraging at every stage. Marina Gorbis, IFTF's executive director, is a groundbreaker on the future of work and the equitable enterprise.

Special thank you to Jean Hagan and the visual storytelling team, including Robin Bogott, Julie Ericsson, Trent Kuhn, and Robin Weiss.

We feel so fortunate to work with our colleagues and board at IFTF. They have created a culture and climate where books like *Office Shock* are possible. IFTF also has a long history of encouraging distributed work and flexibility.

Kathi Vian provided us with profound advice early in the project, and her wisdom guided us at each step. Kathi taught us that juxtaposition is a research methodology.

Both Toshi Hoo and Jeremy Kirshbaum contributed greatly to chapter 8 on the Spectrum of Augmentation. Toshi guided us as we tried to make sense out of the emerging metaverse, and Jeremy introduced us to GPT-3 and augmented writing. Rebecca Shamash was particularly helpful in reviewing chapter 5 on the Spectrum of Outcomes, and we thank her especially for recommending the work of Mariana Mazzucato.

Thanks to Simon Widmer for sharing his insights in chapter 6 on circular economies and on how companies can adopt policies to lessen their negative climate impacts.

Ibrahim Jackson was instrumental for us in thinking futureback about diversity, inclusion, and belonging. His detailed review of chapter 7 on the Spectrum of Belonging was very helpful through the many revisions to this chapter. Professor Lonny Brooks also reviewed this chapter and was extremely helpful as we figured out how to frame it and draw from Afrofuturism. And Hodari Davis provided useful guidance for us as we did the first drafts of chapter 7 on the Spectrum of Belonging. Noah Sindler shared his experiences as a native-digital gamer in chapter 10. Pete Blackshaw, CEO of Cintrifuse, an innovation hub in Cincinnati, gave helpful suggestions on chapter 14 for us on policy choices.

We had two group meetings, a workshop, and a symposium, in which all attendees were generous with their time and feedback and helped shape the final manuscript.

Meeting and Workshop Participants

Katharina Amann	Gill Parker
Laurent Crochet	Robert Price
Thomas Dienes	Sandra Schär
Katrin Eckert	Jon Thorson
Hiroshi Kawaguchi	Andrew Wittmayer

The task of curating and guiding the global group of artists who have contributed their evocative artwork for our part II chapters was impressively carried out by Anaelle Press, and we sincerely thank her for her efforts. See About the Artists for more details on their wonderful work.

Institute for the Future is on the cover of this book because we have drawn so much from our colleagues. While this isn't a consensus forecast and we as authors are responsible for any mistakes, these IFTF staffers have also influenced our understanding of emerging futures for work and living.

IFTF Staff

Eileen Alexander	Dylan Hendricks	Sean Ness
Cindy Baskin	Toshi Hoo	Carol Neuschul
Quinault Childs	Lyn Jeffery	Wayne Pan
John Clamme	Maureen Kirchner	Sara Skvirsky
Jake Dunagan	Bradley Kreit	Teff Teffera
Rod Falcon	Daria Lamb	Charles Tsai
Mark Frauenfelder	Ilana Lipsett	Lir Wang
Katie Fuller	Nathalie Lopez	Salley Westergaard
Georgia Gillan	Rachel Maguire	Lindy Willis
Ayca Guralp	Vanessa Mason	Jeff Yang
Ben Hamamoto	Jane McGonigal	

Institute for the Future is an independent nonprofit research organization with an all-volunteer board of trustees. We are so grateful to the board for all the guidance they provide.

IFTF Board

Berit Ashla	Jean Hagan	Steve Milovich
Karen Edwards	Marianne Jackson	David Thigpen
Marina Gorbis	Lyn Jeffery	Lawrence Wilkinson

After we had finished our first draft of the entire manuscript, we held a three-hour global symposium on *Office Shock* with about forty thought leaders, all of whom received our draft manuscript in advance. We conducted an online survey about the future of office shock during the workshop, organized around our Seven Spectrums of Choice for offices and officing. Then, we had small group conversations organized around the seven spectrums.

It was a great conversation and the participants sent us specific suggestions for the manuscript. The participants included:

Practitioners Who Are Managing Office Shock

Andy Billings, Electronic Arts

Maureen Cambridge, Target

Marius Dahler, La Prairie

Natasha da Silva, Hill's Pet Sciences

Laura Dulin, Target

Jonas Ebersold, BASF

Jen Gudgel, BorgWarner

Adam Hoy, GlaxoSmithKline

Marco Huber, JLL

Tswelo Kodisang, FirstRand

Catrin Krayer, KPMG

Emma Krippner, BSI Group

Maureen McGuire, Target

Greg Mottola, BCJ

Felecia Pryor, BorgWarner

Heli Rantavuo, Spotify

Edgard Soares, Colgate-Palmolive

John Stieger, Cintrifuse

Tony Strows, Philips

Milan Turk, Consultant/P&G Alum

Content Experts

Elena Antonacopoulou, Ivey
Business School

Pete Blackshaw, Cintrifuse

Lonny J. Avi Brooks, Afrofuturist
at Cal State Hayward

Cade Cowan, Executive
Development Consulting

Shermon Cruz, Association of
Professional Futurists

Dominic Deane, Oxford
University

Greg Demchak, Bentley

Franz Dill, PKL Knowledge
Partners

Mariel Ebrahimi, Built World

Cynthia Hansen, Innovation
Foundation/Adecco

Ibrahim Jackson, Diversity and
Belonging Consultant

Mark Johnson, Innosight

Jeanine Stewart, NeuroLeadership
Institute

David Vasquez-Levy, Pacific School
of Religion

Thanks to our families for their endless patience and support during the research and writing:

Christine: To my wonderful daughters—Valerie and Georgia—and their families, thank you for your support and ideas throughout the book writing process. I hope the concepts here will help Ava and Izzy experience a better future for working and living.

Joseph: To my wife Rachel and all our children, who teach and inspire us along the journey of life. I hope the concepts here will help you as they have helped me to imagine a better future for working and living.

Bob: To my wife Robin, our children (Cory and Lisa) and grandchildren (Nico, Everett, Robbie, and Nathaniel), who help me think futureback every day.

INDEX

Illustrations are denoted by page numbers in *italics*. The letter n indicates a note number.

abundance, 89, 231n37

"Action Office," 41

Afrofuturism, 49–50, 117–118

agility, 154, 202

    See also Spectrum of Agility

Agüera y Arcasn, Blaise, 127–128

AI (Artificial Intelligence). *See* Artificial
    Intelligence

AlphaGo, 26

Alston, Philip, 53

Amatullo, Mariana, 233n19

Amerika, Mark, 131

Anderson, Reynaldo, 117–118

"The Answers to Our Problems Aren't as
    Simple as Left or Right" (Friedman), 89

anthropomorphization, 127

Anticipations of the Reaction of Mechanical and
    Scientific Progress upon Human Life (Wells), 19

Anti-work, 18

anytime/anyplace (officeverse), 139

ARPANET, 35–38, 40–41

Artificial Intelligence (AI)

    AI coaches, 40

    for carbon goals, 55

    competition with humans, 26

    economic divide and, 128–129

    enchanted objects, 126

    ethics and common sense, lack of, 125

    graph, 123

    malicious use, 129, 235n13

    as poor terminology, 52

    practicality, 123–128

    risks, 128–130

    symbiotic work with humans, 123

    See also augmented intelligence

Augment (Tymshare), 37

augmentation

    augmented group intelligence, 39–40

    augmented knowledge work, growth from
        1970, 48

augmented reality, 139
augmented storytelling, 130–132
Augmented Workforce Initiative (World
    Economic Forum), 124
augmented intelligence, 177, 185, 194, 201
    See also Artificial Intelligence (AI)
avatar, 141–142, 178, 194

B Corp, 72
Baldwin, James, 28, 224n45
Barad, Karen, 171
Barron, Kayla, 156
Basquiat, Jean-Michel, 204
Beatles, 34
Beautiful Minecraft (Delaney), 144
Becker, Franklin, 44
Bedwell, Neil, 74
BedZED, 99
belonging, 112–115, 201
Belonging Organization, 114
Bennis, Warren, 20
Berners-Lee, Tim, 37–38
Berson, Josh, 169
"Better Life Index" (OCED), 231n29
Beyoncé, 66
Beyond GDP (European Union), 231n29
Beyond Net Zero (UK Design Council), 9,
    94–96, 183, 201
biomimicry, 102–103
Black Americans, 111–112
Black Lives Matter, 18
Blinkist, 153–154
blockchain, 83, 229n11
blockchain-based platforms, 237n7
Bobrow, Danny, 40
Bolzle, Aaron, 189
boundaries redrawn, 137–138, *138*, 178, 186
Boyer, Bryan, 233n19
Braided Agility (Iglesias), 148
Braided Organizations (Zarka), 153
Bratton, Benjamin, 127–128
Brave New Work (Dignan podcast), 82–83

"Break My Soul" (Beyoncé), 66
Brooks, David, 68
Brown, John Seely, 40–41
building construction and climate
    emergencies, 96
Bullen, Christine, 9, 168, 240n5
bureaucracy, 31
Burger, Joanna, 233n16
Bürolandschaft, 41, 225n16
Bush, Vannevar, 35
Butler, Octavia, 61, 161

Cabin, 82
"Can Companies Force Themselves to Do
    Good?" (Romeo; *New Yorker*), 83–84
Candy, Stuart, 157
Canon, Camille, 73
Capra, Fritjof, 102
carbon allotments, 93
Carryrou, John, 69
Carson, Rachel, 19
Cascading Outcomes (Iglesias), 78
Case, Amber, 122
Celebrating Uniqueness (Iglesias), 106
Centraal Beheer Office, 41–42, *42*, *43*
CERN and World Wide Web, 36
Cervantes, Gabe, 110, 189–190
Chen, Quifan, 123
Chikatai Toy Hospital, 99–100
Chile lithium mining, 101
China cultural revolution, 34
choices
    about futureback thinking, 28–29
    community choices, 188–196, 203
    consumption choices, 96–97, 192
    current actions for better futures, 200–202
    Spectrum of Agility, 160
    Spectrum of Augmentation, 132–133
    Spectrum of Belonging, 119
    Spectrum of Climate Impacts, 104–105
    Spectrum of Outcomes, 89–90
    Spectrum of Place and Time, 145–146

choices (*continued*)
  Spectrum of Purpose, 77
  See also Seven Spectrums of Choice
Chomsky, Noam, 235n10
Christensen, Clayton, 21
Churchill, Winston, 30–31, 44
circular design, 54–55, 93
circular economy, 97–99, 192, 232n11
circularity and regeneration, 175–176, 183
civil rights movement, 34
Climate Central, on flooding, 22, 223n23
Climate Disclosure Standards Board Value
  Reporting Foundation, 233n30
climate emergencies, 94–95, 108
climate impacts, 200–201
climate-negative supply chains, 95–96
Coach (nonhuman advisor), 40
code-switching behavior, 116–117
cognitive biases, 128
COLAB, 40
collaborative media. *See* social media
collaborative spaces, 74, 139
collective trauma, 111–112
"Combi office," 41
community identity, 191
Community Interest Company (CIC), 73
community value, 191
Comprehensive Wealth (Canada), 231n29
computer mouse, 36–37
computer tools development, 36–38
computers in the group, 125–126, 236n14
cone of uncertainty, 21–23, 24, 25
cooperatives, 84–85
COVID-19 pandemic (coronavirus)
  aftershocks of, 18
  freelance work growth in, 70
  "impossible offices" need, 44–47
  lockdown in, 137, 142, 224n1
  as social issues catalyst, 75–76
  2020 Threshold, 108
  unequal work experiences, 136
  vaccine development, 150

videoconferencing in, 30
Cozolino, Louis, 68
Crawford, Kate, 125
criminal use of augmented intelligence, 194
Critical Success Factors, 168, 240n5
cryptocurrencies, 237n7
current actions for better futures, 197–206
  choices, 200–202
  harmony vs. polarization, 204–205
  impossible futures, 198–199
  officing, 202–203
  work/life synchronization, 205–206
cybercrime, 129
cyberpunk, 49, 226n1
cyberterrorism, 129
cyberwarfare, 129
cyborg, 122
cyborg anthropologist, 122

DALL-E 2, 125, 235n8
Dan'Cares health coverage program, 73
Danone North America, 73
DAO (decentralized autonomous
  organization)
  as blockchain platform, 237n7
  defined and described, 82, 229n11
  LAOs as, 84
  Uber as, 230n20
Davis, Jerry, 82
DAWs (digital audio workstations), 227n12
decentralized autonomous organization
  (DAO). *See* DAO
decision augmentation, 127–128
deep work, 126
DeepMind, 235n8
Defense Advanced Research Projects Agency,
  36
DEGW office space types, 44, 225n26
Delaney, James, 144
diaspora studies, 110
different times/different places (home offices
  and regional hubs), 139

digital audio workstations (DAWs), 227n12
digital coordination economy, 83–84
digital diasporas, 110–111, 115–116
digital humans, 142, 238n13
digital natives, 141, 184
Digital Nomad Villages, 118
digital transformation, 82
digital twins, 126
Dignan, Aaron, 82–83, 230n20
dignity, role of, 115
distributed authority, 57, 149, 186
distributed value, 81–83
diversity
  Belonging Organization, 114
  for communities, 192–193
  diversity dilemma, 109–110
  in futureback thinking, 112–113
  on Spectrum of Belonging, 176–177, 184, 201
Dixon, Chris, 237n7
dopamine effects, 69–70
Dopamine Nation (Lembke), 69
Doughnut Economics (Raworth), 87
downtown living and commerce, 191, 194
drought, 94, 232n1
Drucker, Peter, 240n2
Duffy, Francis "Frank," 41, 43–44, 95–96, 136, 225n26
Dunagan, Jake, 125, 157
Dunne, Anthony, 127
durable disorder, 129

Earth Day, 34
Earth 2050 (website), 127
eco-capitalism, 231n37
ecological diplomacy, 104
Economics and the Public Purpose (Galbraith), 75
economies
  circular economy, 97–98
  digital coordination economy, 83–84
  economics of hope, 89
  equitable economies, 86–87
  of scale vs. organization, 87

Economy for the Common Good (ECG), 231n37
eco-socialism, 231n37
Ellen Macarthur Foundation Butterfly diagram, 99, 232n11
Ely, Peter, 225n26
Embodied Augmentation (Proxima Centauri B), 120
enchanted objects, 126–127
Engelbart, Douglas C., 36–37, 39, 41
English, Bill, 41
enterprises/equitable organizations, 87–88, 183
The Entrepreneurial State (Mazzucato), 205
entrepreneurship in Zebras Unite, 84–85
environmental, social, and corporate governance (ESG), 98–99, 104, 233n30
equitable economies, 86–87
"Equitable Enterprises" (IFTF), 87–88
equitable organizations/enterprises, 87–88, 183
equity, 113–114, 114
ESG (environmental, social, and corporate governance), 98–99, 104, 233n30
The Eternal Now, 24
Everything for Everyone (Schneider), 84
exoskeleton, 122
experiential value vs. exchange value, 81

facial mimicry, 142
Find Future Self, 165–166, 189
flat screen technology, 42
flexive intent
  for communities, 195–196
  defined and described, 24, 158–159
  direction and execution, 9
  as flexive command alternative, 239n21
  for individuals, 178
  "A Mission-Oriented Approach to Cleaning the Oceans" (Mazzucato), 240n22
  for organizations, 186–187
  in shape-shifting organizations, 152
flooding, climate change and, 22–23, 223n23, 223n25

foresight, 19–20, 28–29
  See also futureback thinking
freelance work as model, 85–86
[freespace] collaborative, 74
FridaysForFuture, 18
Friedman, Batya, 124
Friedman, Milton, 80–81
Friedman, Thomas L., 89
Fuller, R. Buckminster, 205
full-spectrum mindset, 16, 27–28
future, decisions about, 169–171
future, defining, 166–167
future, next, now, 23–25
future offices, 53–57
Future Self
  for communities, 189
  Find Future Self exercise, 165–166
  for organizations, 181
  for self, 13, 166, 172, 174
  in Seven Spectrums of Choice, 174
Future Shock (film), 17
Future Shock (Toffler), 17, 34–35, 204
Future State of the Office report, 188, 203
future work stories, 117–118
futureback stories, 25–27
futureback thinking, 17–29
  alternative futures and, 21
  augmenting intelligence, 125, 235n13
  change drivers for, 46–48
  choices for, 28–29
  clarity and, 24
  cone of uncertainty, 21–23
  as counterintuitive, 24
  diversity advantages, 109–110
  early futureback thinking, 19–21
  enchanted objects, 127
  equitable economies in, 88
  full-spectrum mindset, 27–28
  future, next, now, 23–25
  futureback stories, 25–27
  gaming as learning medium, 155–156
  imagining impossible offices, 12

product consumption and longevity, 97–99
  roots and routes in, 112
  shocks, continuation of, 18–19
  steward-ownership, 84
  storyline for, 13
  from ten years ahead, 9
  think futureback, 21–27
  as tool, 15
  values comparisons, 81
  as voluntary fear exposure, 157
future-ready officing, 150–155
future-ready organization, 151–154, 152
futures genres, 118
futures studies/futurology, 19

Galbraith, John Kenneth, 75
Galinsky, Ellen, 234n5
gaming
  agility for individuals, 179
  for communities, 195
  for the future, 158
  gameful readiness engagement, 155–156
  for organizations, 187
Gaye, Marvin, 35
Gehry, Frank, 74
genius loci, 144
Genuine Progress Indicator, 231n29
Ghosh, Amitav, 95
Gibson, William, 98
Giffone, Luigi, 225n26
gig workers, 82, 231n26
Glass, Philip, 204
global population ages, 108
Global Simulation Corps, 157
globalization vs. localization, 101
Go (board game), 26
Gochfeld, Michael, 233n16
Goldberg, Adele, 40
Gorbis, Marina, 83, 89, 150
Gordon, Mark, 84
Gorman, Amanda, 197
GPT-3 based technology, 125, 130–131

Great Derangement, 95
Great Opportunity, 1–14
  drivers of change, 46
  futureback thinking, 12, 13
  impossible futures, 7–8
  mixing board metaphor, 8–14, 11
  mules, 4–7
  office shock events, 1
  offices, officing, officeverse, 2–4, 3
  Seven Spectrums of choice, 11–12, 11
  social good in, 175
  synchronization, 12–14
Great Reset, x
Great Resignation, ix–x, 66
Green Future path, 104
Green New Deal, 231n37
Gross Domestic Product (GDP), 87, 231n29
"Groundswell" (World Bank), 232n2
groupware, 51
Groupware (Johansen), 39–40
grunge bands, 204
Guadagno, Rosanna, 237n9
"Guggenheim Effect," 74
Guggenheim Museum, Spain, 74
GUI (Graphical User Interface), 40
Guterres, António, 95

Habraken, N. John, 143
Hackl, Cathy, 230n20
Haley, Alex, 111
Haller, Fritz, 143
haptic suits, 142
Harari, Yuval Noah, 50
harmony vs. polarization, 204–205
The Healing Clinic, 73
Hebb, Donald, 68
Hepler, Lauren, 231n26
Herrera, Katia, 62, 65
Hersey, Tricia, 72
Hertzberger, Herman, 41–42
hierarchical organizations and offices, 31–33
hierarchy of needs, 67–68, 182

high-rise buildings, 33
Hillis, Jonathan, 82
hippocampus, 25
Holmes, Elizabeth, 69
Holmgren, David, 231n37
homeostasis, 28, 102
Huberman, Andrew, 76, 155, 228n7
hybrid offices
  adaption struggles, 18–19
  beyond hybrid offices, 139–141
  choices, 138–139
  from Networked Office, 44
  as temporary, 137–139
  work hours and scheduling across time
    zones, 137

IBM Selectric typewriter, 34
IDeaLs (Innovation and Design as Leadership)
  (Press), 169–170
IDeaLs' Transformation Scaffold, 170
IFRS (International Financial Reporting
  Standards) Foundation, 233n30
IFTF. See Institute for the Future (IFTF)
Iglesias, Analia, 62, 107
Iglesias, Yeti, 78, 149
The Iliad, 50
Imaginable (McGonigal), 23, 227n9
impossible futures, 49–59
  alien concepts in, 51
  for belonging, 115
  choices for, 213
  current actions for better futures, 198–199
  with gaming, 156–158, 187
  Great Opportunity, 7–8
  impossible offices, 53–57
  language of, 51–52
  mixing board, 57–58, 58
  navigation choices, 59
  possibility of, 49–51
  resilience in, 8
  rules of reality and, 50–51
  scenario convergences, 50

impossible futures *(continued)*
　smart cities and superminds, 193
　speed of, 50
　types, 198–199
　UN global goals, 52–53
　as unprecedented, 129
impossible offices, 44–48, 53–57
inclusion, 113, 114, 176–177, 184, 192–193, 201
Inclusive Wealth Index (UN Environment
　Programme), 231n29
Industrial Age, dehumanizing effects of, 17
"Inequality Kills" (Oxfam), 108
Ingels, Bjarke, 23
Institute for the Future (IFTF)
　funding sources, 36
　goals, 9
　long-term future focus, 21
　mission, 20
　60-year time periods, 30–31
integrated office system, 37
intentions, spectrum of purpose and, 66–67
interest/opportunity matching, 86
Intergovernmental Panel on Climate Change
　(IPCC), Sixth Assessment Report, 95
International Sustainability Standards Board
　(ISSB), 233n30
interpandemic (endemic) period, 18
Ivarsson, Melanie, 150

Jackson, Ibrahim, 113, 114
Jacobus, Dustin, 62, 93
Jain, Anab, 15
Jansen, Niklas, 153–154
Jeans Redesign initiative, 99
Jeter, K. W., 226n2
job as purpose, 70–72
Johansen, Bob
　at Crozer Theological Seminary, 112
　futureback, use of term, 21
　Groupware, 39–40
　at International Conference on Computer
　Communications, 36

The New Leadership Literacies, 154
　PARC presentation, 40–41
　as sociologist, 9
　worldbuilding of science fiction, 227n7
Johnson, Mark, 21
Jordan, Robert, 50
Joseph, Marc Bamuthi, 115, 169

Kaal, Wulf A., 230n20
Kariko, Katalin, 51
Kaufman, Scott Barry, 67, 76
Kay, Alan, 40
Kennedy, John F., 18
Kennedy, Robert F., 18
Ki-Moon, Ban, 53
King, Martin Luther, Jr., 18, 111–112
Kirshbaum, Jeremy, 130
Klein, Naomi, 18
knowledge worker
　as decision maker, 57
　in Spectrum of Agility, 152
　tracking technology for, 140
　work sharing via computers, 38, 40
　workplace freedom for, 45, 97
Kovel, J., 231n37
Koyaanisqatsi (film), 204
Kramer, Deirdre, 76–77

labels, 116–117
Ladder of Enchantment, 236n17
language models, 130
language translation, 142
Lanier, Jaron, 144–145
Larkin Administration Building (Wright),
　32, 33
Lee, Kai-Fu, 123
Lembke, Anna, 69
life/work navigation, 137, 140, 234n5
life/work synchronization, 205–206
Lim, Jenn, 68
Lipsett, Ilana, 74
localization vs. globalization, 101

lockdown in COVID-19 pandemic, 137, 142, 224n1
long-run investments, 231n32
looking back to look forward, 30–48
  business computer tools, 38–39
  computer tools development, 36–38
  hierarchical organizations and offices, 31–33
  impossible to mandatory offices, 44–48
  networked offices, 41–44
  remote work technologies, 35–36
  telecommuting development, 39–41
  turmoil on offices, 34–35
  unpleasant offices, 33–34
Lotus 1-2-3 software, 38
Lowy, M., 231n37
Luchetti, Robert, 43
Luisi, Pier Luigi, 102
Lying Flat (tang ping), 72

Macgadie, Colin, 42
Mad Men (TV show), 34
Madeira as Zoom Island, 118
Malone, Thomas W., 126, 236n14
Man of Steel (film), 50
mandatory offices, 44–48
Manzini, Ezio, 143
Martin, George R. R., 50
Maslow, Abraham, 67
May, Jennifer, 233n19
Mazzucato, Mariana
  on economic policy, 74–75
  The Entrepreneurial State, 205
  European Union missions, 159, 240n22
  Mission Economy, 75
  reforms proposed, 88, 231n32
  The Value of Everything, 81
McDowell, Alex, 50
McFate, Sean, 129
McGonigal, Jane, 23, 227n9
McLuhan, Marshall, 19, 141
Melithafa, Ayakha, 108
membership models, 85–86, 231n26

"Memex" (Bush), 35
MetaHuman Creator, 238n13
metaverse, 52, 56
#MeToo, 18
microprocessors/microcomputers, 37–39
Miller, George, 235n10
Miller, Herman, 41
mind as machine, 125, 235n10
Minority Report (film), 50
Minsky, Marvin, 235n10
Mission Economy (Mazzucato), 75
MIT Technology Review, on multiple selves, 26
mixing board metaphor, 221n6
  See also Spectrums Mixing Board
mobility of workplace, 18–19
moonwalk, 34
Morello, Tom, 204
Mori, Masahiro, 141–142
"The Mother of all Demos," 37
mouse (computer mouse), 36–37
mRNA vaccines, 51
Muigai, Makenna, 108
mules
  COVID-19 pandemic as, 47
  defined and described, 4–7
  Engelbart's inventions, 36–37
  as extreme surprises, 49
  internet as, 36, 47
  in officeverse, 56, 139–140
  as wild cards, 4

Nakabuye, Hilda Flavia, 108
Nakate, Vanessa, 108
Nanus, Burt, 20
Nap Ministry, 72
National Science Foundation, 36
National Welfare Index (Germany), 231n29
navigation choices, 59
navigational star, 166–167, 199, 207–209
Neruda, Pablo, 130–131
Net Zero/Beyond Net Zero, 9, 94–96, 183, 201
Network Information Center (NIC), 37

networked offices, 41–44, 136
neurological stimulation, 86
neuroplasticity, 68, 158, 187, 228n7
neuroscience of purpose, 68–70
neurotransmitters, 69, 228n7
The New Leadership Literacies (Johansen), 154
Newell, Allen, 235n10
Newport, Cal, 126
NIC (Network Information Center), 37
Nilles, Jack, 39
9 to 5 (film), 34
1960s stresses, 18
Nixon, Richard, 34
NLS (oNLine System), 37
"Nonhuman Participants" scenario, 40

"Ode to Augmented Intelligence" (GPT-3),
    130–131
The Odyssey, 50
Office and Organizational Waves, 46–47, 46–47
office shock events, 1
office supply chain issues, 95
offices
  defined and described, x
  new concepts of, 45
  office space types, 44
  as place and process, 21
  reconfigurations, 41–43
  unpleasant, 33–34
  See also hybrid offices; traditional offices
offices, future, 53–57
offices, officing, officeverse, 2–4, 3
officeverse
  challenges and risks, 142
  defined and described, 56–57
  emerging, 3
  genius loci, 144
  for individuals, 178
  innovation in organizations, 186
  participatory design, 143–144
  trust in, 140
Officeverse Emerging (Press), 134

officing, current actions for better futures,
    202–203
OpenLaw as LAO, 84
Operating Manual for Spaceship Earth (Fuller), 205
opportunity and interest matching, 86
organizational choices in Seven Spectrum of
    Choice, 180–187, 203
organizational models, 81–82
organizational roots, 111
outcomes, 200
ownership models, 83–85, 99–100, 183, 191
Oxfam, 108

paraplegic use of VR interface, 155
participatory design, 143–144
Parton, Dolly, 34
Patterson, Jacqui, 204
People Planet Prosperity (PPP), 93, 100
PeopleNotProfit, 18
permaculture, 231n37
perpetual-purpose trust, 84
persona and space, 141–145
personal choices in Seven Spectrums of
    Choice, 173–179, 202–203
Philips, David, 25–26
Piketty, Thomas, 75
place and time flexibility, 201–202
place as timeless, 144–145
platform cooperatives, 84
Playtime (film), 34
Polak, Fred L., 19
polarization vs. harmony, 204–205
polarized politics, 204–205
prefrontal cortex, 23, 25, 165
present-forward thinking, 21, 24
Press, Anaelle, 62
Press, Joseph, 9, 62, 135
The Principles of Scientific Management (Taylor), 31
product consumption and longevity, 99
prompts, 271
prosocial activity, 76
prosperity, 53, 102, 175, 214–215

See also People Planet Prosperity (PPP); Spectrum of Outcomes
Prosperity by Design (Gorbis), 83
Proxima Centauri B (artist), 121
psychohistory, 4
Public Benefit LLC, 72–73
purpose
  ambiguity of definition, 75–76
  purpose in place, 74–75
  purpose-driven organizations, 72–74
  spectrum of, 200
  See also Spectrum of Purpose
Purpose Foundation, 73, 84
purposely different, 115–116

Quick Start Guide, 163–172, 164
  for communities, 189
  flexive intent, 202
  future, 166–167, 169–171
  future self, finding, 165–166
  IDeaLs' Transformation Scaffold, 170
  for individuals, 174
  for organizations, 181
  Seven Spectrums of Choice, 171–172, 171
  Spectrums Mixing Board, 167, 168–169

Raby, Fiona, 127
Raworth, Kate, 87
readiness, leading with, 154–155
Ready Player One (film and book), 141, 156
Reed, Bill, 100
regeneration
  circularity and, 175–176, 183
  from Net Zero, 96
  regenerative communities, 100–102
  regenerative cultures, 103
  regenerative economy, 100–102, 192, 233n16, 233n19
  regenerative systems, 102–104
A Regenerative Office (Jacobus), 92
Reggio, Godfrey, 204
rejuvenation, 74, 145

remote work technologies, 35–36
resilience
  communal resilience, 159
  in impossible futures, 8
  in Permaculture, 232n37
  as priority, 57, 149
  resiliency vs. rigidity, 150–151
  in Spectrum of Agility, 160
  in supply webs, 151
resource competition, 94, 232n2
rest as spiritual practice, 72
results focus. *See* Spectrum of Outcomes
retirement planning, 22–23
RETRO (Google), 235n8
rigidity vs. resiliency, 150–151
risk tolerance, 23
Rockart, Jack, 168, 240n5
Rolodex, 33
Romeo, Nick, 83–84
roots and routes, 110–113
Rose, David, 126, 236n17

same place, different times (stores and factories), 138–139
same time, different place (virtual meetings), 138
same time, same place (office buildings), 138
Sanderson, Brandon, 50
scenario planning, 22–23
Schneider, Nathan, 84
science fiction, 49–50
scientific management, 31
Scientist Rebellion, 18
SDGs. *See* United Nations Sustainable Development Goals
search for belonging, 112–115
sensors
  for health oversight, 26
  prevalence in future, 21–22
sentience in computers, 127–128
Seven Spectrums of Choice, 11–12, 11, 57, 59, 171–172, 171

shape-shifting organizations, 150–152, 152
shared missions, 75–76
shared social value for organizations, 182–183
Sharing Navigational Stars (Herrera), 61
Shea, Andrew, 233n19
Shelley, Mary, 226n2
The Shock Doctrine (Klein), 18
shocks, continuation of, 18–19
signals
    avatars as, 141
    of equitable economies, 87
    of Futureback thinking, 21
    of governments making a difference, 203
    Great Resignation as, 66
    new social protocols as, 137
    of regenerative economy, 100
    of steward-ownership, 84
Simon, Herbert, 235n10
simulations, 157–158
"6 Young Activists in Africa Working to Save
    the World," (Global Citizen), 108
sliders. See mixing board metaphor
Sloan Sustainability Initiative (MIT), 103
smart cities, 193–194
smart contracts, 140, 237n7
"smart" objects, 126
Smith, Kenneth, 112
social cognition, 86
social injustice, 111, 175, 182, 191
social justice
    awareness of, 75
    equity in, 114
    examples, 18
    King's activism, 112
    in Nap Ministry, 72
    Patterson on, 204
    in Spectrum of Belonging, 184
    in Spectrum of Purpose, 182, 191
social media, 37, 140
social synapse, 68
social technology, organizations as, 150
social value, 191

Sodel, Lee, 26
Solarpunk, 49–50, 226n5
space pollution, 94
Spectrum of Agility, 149–160, 150
    choices, 160
    for communities, 195–196
    flexive intent, 158–159
    future-ready officing and organization,
        150–155, 152
    gameful readiness engagement, 155–156
    gaming for the future, 158
    for individuals, 178–179
    leading with readiness, 154–155
    for organizations, 186–187
    voluntary fear engagement, 156–157
Spectrum of Augmentation, 121–133, 122
    Artificial Intelligence, 123–130
    augmented storytelling, 130–132
    choices, 132–133
    for communities, 193–194
    decision augmentation, 127–128
    enchanted objects, 126–127
    for individuals, 177
    for organizations, 185
    superminds, 124–126
Spectrum of Belonging, 107–119, 109
    choices, 119
    collective trauma, 111–112
    for communities, 192–193
    diversity dilemma, 109–110
    future work stories, 117–118
    for individuals, 176–177
    labels and beyond, 116–117
    for organizations, 184
    purposely different, 115–116
    roots and routes, 110–113
    search for belonging, 112–115
Spectrum of Climate Impacts, 93–105, 94
    choices, 104–105
    circular economy, 97–99
    climate emergencies, 94–95
    climate-negative supply chains, 95–96

for communities, 192
consumption choices, 96–97
for individuals, 175–176
for organizations, 183–184
ownership models, 99–100
regenerative communities, 100–102
regenerative systems, 102–104
sustainability, 103–104
systems view of offices and officing, 102–103
Spectrum of Outcomes, 79–90, 80
choices, 89–90
for communities, 191
distributed value, 81–83
economics of hope, 89
equitable economies, 86–87
equitable enterprises, 87–88
for individuals, 175
membership models, 85–86
for organizations, 182–183
ownership models, 83–85
values comparisons, 80–81
Spectrum of Place and Time, 135–146, 136
beyond hybrid offices, 139–141
boundaries redrawn, 137–138, 138
choices, 145–146
for communities, 194–195
hybrid office choices, 137–139
for individuals, 177–178
for organizations, 185–186
persona and space, 141–145
place as timeless, 144–145
uncanny valley, 141–143
workspace design, 143–144
Spectrum of Purpose, 65–78, 66
choices, 77
for communities, 190–191
hierarchy of needs, 66, 67–68
for individuals, 174–175
job as purpose, 70–72
neuroscience of purpose, 68–70
for organizations, 182
purpose in place, 74–75

purpose-driven organizations, 72–74
right vs. wrong and, 69
shared missions, 75–76
wisdom of purpose, 76–77
Spectrums Mixing Board, 8–14, 11, 57–58, 58,
167, 168–169, 197, 200, 227nn12–13
Spectrums of Choice
defined and described, 9–13, 11
harmony vs. polarization, 171
polarities in, 168
in traditional officing, 61, 197, 200
UN global goals and, 207
See also mixing board metaphor; specific
spectrums
Sponge Cities (Yu), 103
Stahel, Walter R., 232n11
stakeholder capitalism, 80, 83
Steampunk, 49, 226n2
Steel, Fritz, 44
Stefik, Mark, 40
Stephenson, Neal, 18
Sterman, Jon, 103
steward-ownership, 84
Stone, Philip, 43
Stonewall riots, 34
Storr, Will, 26
storytelling, 25–27
strategic foresight, 20, 28
Striding Out training center, 73
superminds, 124–126, 177, 185
supply webs/supply chains, 151
surveillance capitalism, 129
sustainability, 103–104, 184, 192, 233n26
Suzman, James, 70
Swisher, Kara, 237n7
symbiosis, 93
synchronization
for communities, 194
individual, organizational, and community
choices, 12–14
between storyteller and listener, 27, 224n40
synchronizing future selves, 198

synchronization *(continued)*
  of three elements of music, 240ch12n1
  through stories, 177, 185
The Systems View of Life (Capra and Luisi), 102
systems view of offices and officing, 102–103

tang ping (Lying Flat), 72
Tati, Jacques, 34
Taylor, Frederick Winslow, 31, 81
Taylorism, 31, 33, 82, 96
telecommuting, 39–41
ten years ahead, 9
Termination Shock (Stephenson), 18
terminology correctness and effectiveness,
  51–52, 227n9
The Theory of Social and Economic Organizations
  (Weber), 31
Theory Z (Maslow), 67
think futureback, 21–27
  See also futureback thinking
Thunberg, Greta, 112–115, 234n1
thymotic desires, 69
tipping point
  COVID-19 pandemic as, 45, 47
  futureback thinking and, 48
  social injustice and economic inequality
    as, 175
Toffler, Alvin, 17, 204
Tolkien, J. R. R., 50
Tottenville plan, 101
traditional offices
  advantages and constraints, 138
  death of, 19
  impossible offices to mandatory offices,
    44–48
  networked offices, 41–44
  as rigid, 150–151
  turmoil on, 34–35
  unpleasant offices, 33–34
tragedy of the commons, 233n16
Transcend (Kaufman), 67
transcendence, 67

transformation, 82, 124, 169–170, 170
trigger movements, 75–76
Tulsa Remote, 189–190
Turkle, Sherry, 142
turmoil on offices, 34–35
2010 and 2020 Threshold, 108

Uber DAO, 230n20
ubiquitous computing, 40
UN Climate Change conference, 233n30
UN global goals. *See* United Nations
  Sustainable Development Goals
uncanny valley, 141–143, 237n12, 238n13
United Nations Sustainable Development
  Goals (SDGs)
  as direction to future, 52–53, 167, 240n4
  on diversity and inclusion, 118
  Genuine Progress Indicator, 231n29
  inclusive and equitable education, 129–130
  navigational stars, 207–209
  officeverse contributions, 145
  for organizations, 187
  significance of purpose as motivator, 76
  stakeholder capitalism and, 80
  worldwide cooperation for, 55

Vallee, Jacques, 37, 39, 227n7
The Value of Everything (Mazzucato), 81
values comparisons, 80–81
The Vanishing American Corporation (Davis), 82
Varoufakis, Yanis, 81
Verne, Jules, 226n2
Vian, Kathi, 227n7
video games, 140–141, 156, 237n9
  See also gaming
videoconferencing, 30
virtual meetings, advantages and constraints,
  30, 138
virtual reality (VR) learning, 143–145, 155,
  238n21, 238n23
virtual simulations, 157–158
VisiCalc software, 38

voluntary fear engagement, 156–157
von Neumann, John, 235n10
VR (virtual reality). *See* virtual reality learning
VUCA (Volatile, Uncertain, Complex, and
    Ambiguous) world
  collaborate with competitors, 150
  defined and described, 20
  disorder in, 129
  flexibility in, 159, 207, 216
  flux in, 119
  futureback thinking in, 24
  human life and, 28
  public purpose and, 75
  self-awareness in, 165

Wahl, Daniel Christian, 103
Wang Laboratories, 38
Web3, 82–83, 84, 140, 237n7
Weber, Max, 31
WEF (World Economic Forum), 80, 87, 97
Weiser, Mark, 40
Welles, Orson, 17
Wells, H. G., 19, 226n2
"What's Going On?" (song), 35
wisdom game, 182
wisdom of purpose, 76–77
Woodstock, 34
word processor development, 38
Work: A Deep History (Suzman), 70
work environment, 182

work hours and scheduling, 137
work sharing and distribution, 38
worker-owned cooperatives, 83
working and living choices, 61–62
workplace architecture design, 31–33, 35, 195
workspace design, 143–144
World Economic Forum (WEF), 80, 87, 97
World Wide Web, 36–38, 74
worldbuilding, 50, 227n7
Worthington, John, 225n26
Wright, Frank Lloyd, 32
WYSIWIG (What You See Is What You Get),
    40

Xerox PARC, 40–41
XR-Natives, 141

Yeti Iglesias, 62
"You Are the Object of a Secret Extraction
    Operation" (Zuboff), 129
young people's activism, 108–109
"Your Office Is Where You Are," 43
Yu, Kongjian, 103

Zac, Jason, 227n12, 240n1
Zebras Unite, 84
Zoom calls and meetings, 30
Zoom Island, Madeira as, 118
Zuboff, Shoshana, 129
Zuckerman, Mike, 74

ABOUT THE RESEARCH

At the height of the first COVID-19 wave, the Institute for the Future (IFTF) received a call from Colin Macgadie, creative director of the architectural firm BDG. One of BDG's clients, the Swiss-based furniture company USM, was looking for a partner to forecast the future of the workplace.

A few weeks later, Bob and Joseph spoke with USM's CEO Alex Schärer. Alex was indeed interested in increasing his clarity about the future of the workplace. More importantly though, he wanted to start a new conversation about the workplace and its role in society.

The IFTF team mobilized a diverse research team and enlisted Christine as coauthor to explore the future of the workplace. Just as the research began, African American George Floyd Jr. was murdered by a white police officer in Minneapolis. Sixteen months later, world leaders fell short of agreement on climate change at COP26 in Glasgow. These events, and the ongoing pandemic, expanded our research beyond the workplace. Our work revealed what IFTF forecasted after the pandemic, what our colleagues call the *deeper diseases* (iftf .org/whathappensnext/).

With Alex's objective of triggering an in-depth conversation, Bob and Joseph shared the research at a meeting of global CEOs in Switzerland. Office shock did indeed trigger a deeper conversation, and in the C-suite no less. A few months later a group of architects, futurists, and leadership experts came together for a virtual symposium to stress test the research. Once again, office shock was a catalyst for opening constructive conversations. With this group's feedback, and additional feedback from our conceptual editor Steve Piersanti, we wrote *Office Shock*.

Our purpose is to provide provocative stories from the future that provoke your thought. We are not experts in the present. We are not here to predict the future (nobody can do that), but we are writing this book to provoke creative thought about the future of distributed work. We have all been thinking futureback for decades but in very different ways. Bob's career has focused on the intersection of technology, organizations, and humans. Joseph designed offices early in his architecture and consulting career and then focused on digital transformation. Christine has viewed the future through information technology and communications. Together we have a broad, colorful, and varied experience with the future of working and living.

Our goal is to create a framework for choice-making about offices and officing. We are writing for individuals, organizations, and policy makers. We are not here to tell you what to do, but we do include our assessments and recommendations—particularly in part III on making smart choices—given the external future forces of the next decade.

To amplify and expand conversations about the future of the office, we invited a group of diverse artists from across the globe to illustrate our future scenarios. We hope the illustrations help our readers to imagine the future and prepare for the futures they choose. We don't predict the future. Our goal in this book is to empower people, organizations, and society to create better ways of working and living.

Throughout the writing our conversations have been incredibly rich. We have learned immensely from each other, even agreeing to disagree on occasion. We have learned from the plethora of experts writing about these topics. This book is built on their shoulders as well as ours. We've done our best to increase the clarity amid the complexity but acknowledge that surely we have missed much along the way.

Our hope is that with this book we have achieved Alex's vision of triggering a deeper and diverse conversation about creating better futures for working and living. We invite you to share your stories and join our ongoing conversation exploring office shock at www.officeshock.org.

ABOUT THE AUTHORS

Bob Johansen, Joseph Press, and Christine Bullen

We are three futurists, focusing ten years ahead and thinking futureback. Bob Johansen is a futurist focused on top leadership in shape-shifting organizations. Joseph Press is an architect, experienced digital transformation advisor, and design futurist. Christine Bullen is an information systems practitioner and researcher who has worked closely with CIOs and other senior executives.

Each of us was disrupted by office shock, which was a significant catalyst for writing this book. In the summer of 2020, Bob moved from Silicon Valley, where he and his family had lived for thirty-five years, to Bainbridge Island, Washington, to be closer to his kids. He went from being a road warrior, on the road several times each month, to working almost all virtual.

Joseph spent a week on the floor in early 2021 not knowing if he would survive COVID-19, which hit him before vaccines were available. The experience and the aftershocks inspired him to envision a better future for industries that had historically contributed to social, economic, and climate injustice. Working in his officeverse with over a dozen global colleagues with similar expertise and aspirations, MakeOurFuture was launched. Dedicated to helping companies transition to more sustainable business practices, MakeOurFuture is a mission-driven consulting cooperative. It offers members opportunities to advise companies in an equitable and transparent business model. For more information, please visit www.makeourfuture.coop.

When the pandemic required lockdowns at home, Christine had been suddenly widowed from her husband of almost fifty years. Her family was 600 miles away and the loss plus the lockdown compounded her sense of isolation. Having researched and taught in the field of information technology, Christine was well acquainted with the tools needed to support distance relationships, so she quickly transitioned to using these for both work and family. The family part was straightforward: she set up a schedule of visits, and that was a great support. But the work, which required interacting with several government offices that were now empty of people and were not equipped for distance working, was frustrating.

Bob is a milkman's son from the small town of Geneva, Illinois. His father inspired him to get there early for everything—a discipline he still practices that fits well with his role as a futurist. His mother taught him to bloom where he is planted. He was the first in his family to graduate from college, attending the University of Illinois on a basketball scholarship. Bob went to divinity school (Crozer Theological Seminary, where Martin Luther King Jr. had attended) on a fellowship for students who were exploring religion but not committed to the ministry. He was at Crozer when Dr. King was killed, and this experience provoked his interest in social justice and the future. He continues to be fascinated by the effects of religion and spirituality, but he is not an advocate of any brand of religion. Bob received his PhD at Northwestern University, where he was based in the Sociology Department and was focused on sociology of religion, the emerging areas of networked computing, and future studies. Bob was one of the first social scientists to study the human, social, and organizational effects of the ARPANET, which was the predecessor to the internet. *Office Shock* is the thirteenth book that Bob has authored or coauthored. In 2023, Bob will have been a professional futurist for fifty years. He now lives on Bainbridge Island, Washington.

Joseph was inspired by his mother, an art educator and children's story writer, to follow in his immigrant grandfather's footsteps to become an architect. After finishing his BS in Economics at Carnegie Mellon, he went to MIT to start a master's in architectural studies, eventually completing his PhD in Design Technology, a workplace research group in the MIT School of Architecture. Joseph capped his ten-year architectural career by designing the headquarters of AOL Time Warner in Paris. Soon after the headquarters' completion, he brought this insight into management consulting with Deloitte. After working in the trenches of digital transformation for eleven years, he founded and led Deloitte Digital Switzerland—an interdisciplinary team of strategic consultants and designers who built digital platforms for global, cross-industry clients and supported their transformation to more sustainable business models. Joseph went on to learn about the missing link of most transformation initiatives, leadership, at the Center for Creative Leadership. To deepen his understanding, he cofounded IDeaLs at the Politecnico di Milano. This action-research community of over ten global corporate partners investigates how to engage people with innovation and design to make transformation happen. The first book from the research was IDeaLs (Innovation and Design as Leadership): Transformation in the Digital Era (Emerald Publishing, August 2021). As the lead author, Joseph researched personal and organizational change through the lenses of innovation, design, and leadership. The second book, Storymaking: How the Co-Creation of Narratives Engages People for Innovation and Transformation, examines the processes and outcomes of storymaking. Joseph is currently a visiting professor of Innovation, Design, and Leadership at the Politecnico di Milano. He is also adjunct faculty at the Parsons School of Design / The New School, where he coauthored with fellow faculty A Design-Driven Guide for Entrepreneurs: Strategies for Starting Up in a Multiverse. Joseph currently lives in Zurich, Switzerland, with his wife and their daughter and often travels to see his family in the United States and his older children in Tel Aviv.

Christine's father came to the United States from Italy and managed to master electronics and woodworking to instill a powerful work ethic in his children. Christine was the first in her family to graduate from college, thanks to an academic scholarship to Barnard College. She worked early in her career at the elite consultancy Arthur D. Little, then received her master's degree at MIT Sloan School of Management. Her mentors at MIT founded the Center for Information Systems Research, and she was the assistant director there for seventeen years. Christine's research at CISR covered a wide range of topics with the focus always on the practical question of how information technology can support and improve management. CISR research delved into the future of office work, the future of microcomputers (i.e., laptops and eventually smart everything), the future of telecommunications, and the Critical Success Factor method. More recently she has been a professor of information systems at Fordham University and Stevens Institute of Technology, where she completed her PhD. Christine has authored or coauthored ten books and twenty-six journal articles. She now lives in New York.

ABOUT THE ARTISTS AND ARTWORK

ANAELLE PRESS (Curator)

Anaelle Press is a French multidisciplinary artist and curator living in Israel. Her work ranges from observational painting and drawing, and graphic design, to leading creative community-based projects. She is committed to using art and creativity as a means to connect with people on an intimate level. As a curator, she has worked with artists all around the globe both physically and digitally. You can find her work on Instagram@anaelle_press.

KATIA HERRERA (chapter 4: *Sharing Navigational Stars*)

Katia Herrera is an Afro-Latina artist from the Dominican Republic. Growing up in an artistic family, Herrera began exploring her vision by using existing photographs to create scrapbook collages. Nowadays, her collages have migrated to the digital space, where she creates digital photo manipulations and illustrations. Herrera's works celebrate her African roots with a touch of surrealism and Afro-futurism. You can find her work at creativepowerr.art.

YETI IGLESIAS (chapter 5: *Cascading Outcomes*, and chapter 10: *Braided Agility*)

Yeti Iglesias is a Mexican illustrator and 2D animator from Mexico City. She gravitates to bold and bright colors, with wild and dynamic designs. Besides cats and coffee, she loves collaborating with brands and creating colorful and powerful messages through illustration. You can find her on Instagram@ yetiglesias.

PROXIMA CENTAURI B (chapter 8: *Embodied Augmentation*)

Proxima Centauri B is a Visayan artist living in Germany. They have been working with AI since stumbling on generative adversarial networks (GANs) in 2018. By using digital painting tools and a variety of ever-evolving open-source code, each artwork is a collaboration between human and machine intelligence. They draw inspiration from the intersection of technology and nature, sci-fi literature, biophilic design, and solarpunk futurism. You can find their work on proximacentaurib.xyz.

DUSTIN JACOBUS (chapter 6: *A Regenerative Office*)

Dustin Jacobus is a Belgian artist and industrial design engineer with interests in biomimicry, sustainable design, and futurism. He started his career as an illustrator for the textile industry and worked several years as a freelance designer. In 2020 he finished his project "Universitas," in which he explores a futuristic world where creativity meets science and ecology. In his latest artwork he explores what a SolarPunk future might look like. You can find his work on dustinjacobus.com.

ANALIA IGLESIAS (chapter 7: *Celebrating Uniqueness*)
Analia Iglesias is an Afro-Indigenous artist from Argentina. She began her exploration as a visual artist and designer through collage, illustration, animation, and street art. She uses digital art as a means to tell stories about her African and indigenous ancestry, and as a way to express social commentary. In a world where capitalism and colonialism have tried to erase her cultures, her work is revolutionary and committed to making a change. Her work is informed by Afrofuturism as well as her own research and understanding of her African and indigenous roots, of which she is very proud. You can find her work on Instagram@afroana_.

MIDJOURNEY (chapter 9: *Officeverse Emerging*)
Midjourney is an AI Art Generator that creates artwork from text prompts in a neural network architecture published through OpenAI. Midjourney is an independent research lab, exploring new mediums of artistic expression to expand the imaginative powers of the human species. You can augment your imagination with Midjourney by applying to the beta at https://discord.com/invite/midjourney or follow others on twitter https://twitter.com/midjourney.

MUSIC ADVISOR (Mixing Board Metaphor)
Jason Zac runs the Nathaniel School of Music, an online music school providing access to world-class music education by identifying, nurturing, and promoting talent. Based in Bangalore, India, Jason is the grandson of Walter Satyaraj Nathaniel, the first Indian to take over the baton of Western music from the British, after 1947. Walter's vision of music was a source of vitality not just for the individual but also for society at large. He transformed the British Musical Association into the Bangalore Musical Association, a musical institution that has shaped many of today's stalwarts. As one of the earliest flag bearers of music's universality and potential for social transformation in independent India, Jason continues his grandfather's vision by nurturing musicians across the globe. To engage with Jason and the school, visit https://www.nathanielschool.com/.

ABOUT INSTITUTE FOR THE FUTURE

Institute for the Future (IFTF) is the longest-running futures organization in the world. A spinoff of the Rand Corporation and Stanford Research Institute (SRI International), IFTF started in 1968 with a founding grant from the Ford Foundation to help society's decision makers acquire capabilities to identify and cope with large socioeconomic questions before they become critical public problems. *Future Shock* author Alvin Toffler was on IFTF's founding advisory committee. Paul Baran, one of the inventors of packet switching, the core technology of the internet, was a founder along with Olaf Helmer, the Swedish mathematician who invented the Delphi Technique. Marina Gorbis, the current executive director, is a regional economist who researches transformations in the world of work and new forms of value creation.

IFTF brings people together to learn the tools of foresight in order to prepare for any future—today. Using innovative research methodologies, IFTF draws on its worldwide network of thought leaders and professional researchers to produce leading-edge foresight. From intimate workshops to global online games, IFTF applies frameworks, processes, and platforms to tap the best insights of groups to imagine—and create—the futures they want for their organizations, their communities, and the world. Since 1970, IFTF has curated this foresight into ten-year forecasts, maps of the emerging landscape, and artifacts of the transformative possibilities across all sectors that together support a more sustainable future.

IFTF researches cutting-edge technologies and practices to help address the pressing issues facing tech, society, and democracy. IFTF's Emerging Media Lab focuses on the future of virtual and augmented reality. IFTF's Governance Futures Lab is helping governments prepare for the unintended consequences of new technology. IFTF Vantage works with organizations to become climate positive and future-ready for the coming decades. In collaboration with academics, researchers, activists, and futurists, the IFTF Equitable Enterprise Initiative will map diverse pathways for a broad national transition to a more equitable and worker friendly economy.

IFTF prepares the world to be ready for any future by infusing the present with transformative possibilities. For over fifty years, businesses, governments, and social impact organizations have depended on IFTF global forecasts, custom research, foresight education, and training to navigate complex change and develop world-ready strategies.

Institute for the Future is a registered 501(c)(3) nonprofit organization based in Palo Alto, California.

Dear reader,

Thank you for picking up this book and welcome to the worldwide BK community! You're joining a special group of people who have come together to create positive change in their lives, organizations, and communities.

What's BK all about?

Our mission is to connect people and ideas to create a world that works for all.

Why? Our communities, organizations, and lives get bogged down by old paradigms of self-interest, exclusion, hierarchy, and privilege. But we believe that can change. That's why we seek the leading experts on these challenges—and share their actionable ideas with you.

A welcome gift

To help you get started, we'd like to offer you a **free copy** of one of our bestselling ebooks:

www.bkconnection.com/welcome

When you claim your **free ebook**, you'll also be subscribed to our blog.

Our freshest insights

Access the best new tools and ideas for leaders at all levels on our blog at ideas.bkconnection.com.

Sincerely,

Your friends at Berrett-Koehler